C. Rajagopalachari

C. Rajagopalachari

Series Editor
Dr. M.H. Syed

Editor
Imran Ahmed **N.P. Sharma**

Himalaya Books Pvt. Ltd.

'Ramdoot', Dr. Bhalerao Marg, Girgaon, Mumbai - 400 004
Tel : (022) 23863863, Fax . (022) 23877178
Email : himpub@vsnl.com

First Edition : 2010

Published by : **H.B.P.L.**
"Pooja Apartments", 4-B, Murari Lal Street, Ansari Road,
Darya Ganj, New Delhi-110 002
Phones : 23270392, 23278631 Reliance : 30180392 to 396
Fax : 011-23256286 Email : hphdel@vsnl.com

Sole Distributers : HIMALAYA PUBLISHING HOUSE PVT. LTD.

Branch Offices

Mumbai : "Ramdoot", Dr. Bhalerao Marg, Girgaon, Mumbai-400 004.
Phones : 23860170/23863863 Fax : 022-23877178
Email : himpub@vsnl.com
Website : www.himpub.com

Nagpur : Kundanlal Chandak Industrial Estate, Ghat Road, **Nagpur 440-018.**
Phone: 2738731, 3296733 Telefax : 0712-2721215

Bengaluru : No. 16/1 (Old 12/1), 1st Floor, Next to Hotel Highlands,
Madhava Nagar, Race Course Road, **Bengaluru - 560 001.**
Phone : 22281541, 22385461, Telefax: 080-22286611

Hyderabad : No. 3-4-184, Lingampally, Besides Raghavendra Swamy Matham,
Kachiguda, **Hyderabad - 500 027.** Phone: 040-27560041,
27550139, Mobile:- 09848130433 Telefax: 040-27560041

Chennai : No. 85/50, Bazullah Road, T. Nagar, **Chennai - 600 017.**
Phone: 044-28344020, 32463737, 42124860

Pune : No. 527, "Laksha" Apartment, First Floor, Mehunpura,
Shaniwarpeth, (Near Prabhat Theatre), **Pune - 411 030.**
Phone: 020-24496323/24496333/32326733

Lucknow : Jai Baba Bhawan, Near Dr. Sanjiv Awasthi, Church Road,
Kurshi Road, Aliganj, **Lucknow - 226 024.**
Phone: 9305302158, 9415349385

Ahmedabad : No. 114, "SHAIL", 1st Floor, Opp. Madhu Sudan House, C.G.Road,
Navrang Pura, **Ahmedabad – 380 009.**
Phone: 079-26560126, Mobiles: 09327324149,09314679413

Ernakulam : No. 39/104 A, Lakshmi Apartment, Karikkamuri Cross Rd.,
Ernakulam, **Cochin – 682011**, Kerala.
Phone: 0484-2378012, 2378016, Mob.: 09344199799

Bhubaneswar : 5 Station Square, **Bhubaneswar (Orissa) - 751 001.**
Mobile: 9861046007, E-mail:-orissa@himpub.com

Indore : Kesardeep Avenue Extension, 73, Narayan Bagh, Flat No. 302,
IIIrd Floor, Near Humpty Dumpty School, Narayan Bagh,
Indore (M.P.) 452 007 Mobile: 09301386468

Kolkata : 108/4, Beliaghata, Main Road, Near ID Hospital, Opp. SBI Bank
Kolkata - 700 010. Mobile: 09910440956

Printed at : H.S. Offset Printers, Daryaganj, New Delhi-110 002

Preface

Biography, is now a form of literature, very much in vogue. In fact, biography is a description or account of someone's life and the times, which is usually published in the form of a book. A biography is more than a mention of personal facts (life, education, work, relationships and death), it also portrays the subject's experience of events. Technically speaking, a work is biographical, if it covers, all of a person's life. Biography writing has a long history. A biography is real. Ancient Greeks developed the biographical tradition, which we have inherited, although until the 5th century AD, when the word 'biographia' first appeared, in Damascius' "Life of Isodorus," biographical pieces were called simply "lives". It is quite likely that the Greeks were drawing on a pre-existing eastern tradition. Certainly Herodotus' "Histories" contains more detailed biographical information on Persian kings and subjects. The earliest surviving pieces, which we would identify as biographical are Isocrates' "Life of Evagoras" and Xenophon's "Life of Agesilaos," both from the fifth century BC. "Parallel Lives" by Plutarch, a Greek writing under the Roman empire, is a series of short biographies of eminent men.

The Golden Age of English biography emerged in late eighteenth century, the century in which the terms "biography" and "autobiography" entered English lexicon. The classic works of the period were Samuel Johnson's "Critical Lives of the Poets" and James Boswell's "Massive Life of Johnson". Generally American biography followed English model. By World War I, cheap hardcover reprints had become popular. The decade of the 1920s witnessed a biographical 'boom'. Later, biographical writings developed a lot and today biographies are written and compiled in the finest form of the genre. In India too, biography, as a form of literature has been evolved, cultivated and polished over the years. Here is an effort to promote this tradition further.

This series of biographies of great men, great women and celebrities in all walks of life is an adventurous academic endeavour, in its own right. A team of researchers and compilers has worked for a good period of time to accomplish the project. For this purpose, hundreds of books by eminent authors and editors have been consulted and referred to. We have benefited from various works, liberally, in order to illustrate and enrich this effort of ours. Present book is devoted to the great personality of Chakravarthi Rajagopalachari.

Great statesman and thinker, Chakravarthi Rajagopalachari, more popular as Rajaji, was a well known lawyer, writer and politician. He was elected the second governor-general of India after independence and following this, Rajaji was made the chief minister of the Indian state of Madras. His interest in politics started at the inception of 1900s. After Mahatma Gandhi returned from South Africa in 1919, Rajaji made up his mind to follow him. He was appointed the general-secretary of the Congress in 1921 and thus, got opportunity to gain acquaintance with other leaders like Jawaharlal Nehru, Vallabhbhai Patel, Maulana Azad, Rajendra Prasad et al. Rajaji steadily rose in rank and even came to be regarded as Gandhiji's successor. He shared close kinship with both Jawaharlal Nehru and Sardar Patel, despite difference in their viewpoints. Being among the five most important leaders in Indian National Congress, C. Rajagopalachari played a pivotal role in the life history of this party. He was always known to be a staunch protector of his political principles and never hesitated to disagree with his closest allies, even in front of public. He also founded a new political outfit, Swatantra Party.

This is a compact and comprehensive account of the above mentioned great life, which is bound to attract the attention of scholars, researchers, students and the general readers alike. Let's hope this humble effort would receive a warm welcome and due applause.

— ***Editors***

Contents

An Illustrious Life

Great statesman and thinker, Rajagopalachari was born in Thorapalli in the then Salem district and was educated in Central College, Bangalore and Presidency College, Madras. Chakravarthi Rajagopalachari (10 December 1878 - 25 December 1972), informally called Rajaji or C.R., was an eminent lawyer, independence activist, politician, writer, statesman and leader of the Indian National Congress who served as the last Governor General of India. He served as the Chief Minister or Premier of the Madras Presidency, Governor of West Bengal, Minister for Home Affairs of the Indian Union and Chief Minister of Madras state. He was the founder of the Swatantra Party and the first recipient of India's highest civilian award, the Bharat Ratna. Rajaji vehemently opposed the usage of nuclear weapons and was a proponent of world peace and disarmament. He was also nicknamed the Mango of Salem.

In 1900 he started a prosperous legal practise. He entered politics and was a member and later President of Salem municipality. He joined the Indian National Congress and participated in the agitations against the Rowlatt Act, the Non-cooperation Movement, the Vaikom Satyagraha and the Civil Disobedience Movement. In 1930, he led the Vedaranyam Salt Satyagraha in response to the Dandi March and courted imprisonment. In 1937, Rajaji was elected Chief Minister or Premier of Madras Presidency and served till 1940, when he resigned due to Britain's declaration of war against Germany. He advocated cooperation over Britain's war effort and opposed the Quit India Movement. He favoured talks with Jinnah and the Muslim League and proposed what later came to be known as the "C. R. Formula". In 1946, he was appointed Minister of Industry, Supply, Education and Finance in the interim government.

He served as the Governor of West Bengal from 1947 to 1948, Governor General of India from 1948 to 1950, Union Home Minister from 1951 to 1952 and the Chief Minister of Madras state from 1952 to 1954. He resigned from the Indian National Congress and founded the Swatantra Party, which fought against the Congress in the 1962, 1967 and 1972 elections. Rajaji was instrumental in setting up a united anti-Congress front in Madras state. This front under C. N. Annadurai captured power in the 1967 elections.

Rajaji was an accomplished writer and made lasting contributions to Indian English literature. He is also credited with composition of the song *Kurai Onrum Illai* set in Carnatic music. He pioneered temperance and temple entry movements in India and advocated Dalit upliftment. Rajaji has been criticised for introducing the compulsory study of Hindi and the Hereditary Education Policy in Tamil Nadu. Critics have often attributed his pre-eminence in politics to his being a favourite of Mahatma Gandhi and Jawaharlal Nehru. Rajaji was described by Gandhi as the "keeper of my conscience".

Family Background

Rajaji married Alamelu Mangamma in 1897. The couple had four children — two sons and two daughters. Mangamma died in 1916 and Rajaji took the sole responsibility of taking care of his children. Rajaji's son C. R. Narasimhan was elected to the Lok Sabha from Krishnagiri in the 1952 and 1957 elections and served as a Member of Parliament for Krishnagiri from 1952 to 1962. He later wrote a biography of Rajaji. Rajaji's daughter Lakshmi was married to Devdas Gandhi, son of Mahatma Gandhi. His grandsons include biographer Rajmohan Gandhi, philosopher Ramchandra Gandhi and former governor of West Bengal Gopalkrishna Gandhi.

Early Life

Rajagopalachari was born to Chakravarti Venkatarya Iyengar and Singaramma on 10 December 1878 in a devout Iyengar family of Thorapalli in the Madras Presidency. Chakravarti Iyengar was the *munsiff* of Thorapalli. According to popular folklore, while Rajaji was a child, an astrologer told his parents that their child would have the "fortunes of a King, a guru, an exile and an outcaste. The people will worship him; they will also reject him. He will sit on an Emperor's throne; he will live in a poor man's hut."

Rajaji attended school in Hosur and college in Madras and Bangalore. He graduated in arts from Central College, Bangalore in 1897, and in law from the Presidency College, Madras in 1897. He started practising as a lawyer in 1900. When in Salem, Rajaji showed keen interest in social and political affairs.

Early Career

Rajagopalachari was born on 10 December 1878 at Torrapalli in Hasur Taluk of Salem district of the Madras Presidency. The family traced its origin from the Srivaishnava community of Brahmins. His father, Chakravarthi Iyengar was the Munsiff of Torrapalli. He was very keen to impart the best possible education to his son. Rajaji had his early education in Hosur. Later on, he joined the Central College, Bangalore. He took his B.A. degree in 1897 and was sent to Madras to study law. He was awarded the Bachelor Degree in Law in 1899, at the age of twenty-one and commenced his legal practice at Salem.

He was married when he was a student in the Law College. As a lawyer, he it did not take him much time to be a prominent lawyer in his region. His income increased day by day. He, now, began to take part in the socio-political activities of his region by addressing several meetings attended by both educated and uneducated people. He was also in touch with the national leaders like Mahatma Gandhi, C. R. Das and others. At this point of time, he began to attend the annual sessions of the Indian National Congress where he represented as a prominent delegate from the Madras Presidency.

He was very humble in his statements. He did not make a show of his capabilities. Once he opined thus: 'I have no experience in governing a country. I have some experience in conducting cases in courts. That experience is of no use in governing the country. The habit of speaking for a party is of no use in administration. My twenty years' experience as a lawyer at the war is of no use to me'.

He also did the editing work of *Young India*. He also launched the programme of prohibition in 1928. Indeed his *Ashram* at Pudupalayam became a place of pilgrimage for several people of the region. The Khaddar depot was a useful feeder for the masses.

At the call of Mahatma Gandhi for Non-cooperation Movement, he at first swore not to enter the courts. He also pulled out his two sons in college, according to the boycott of schools and colleges programme, with the help of Mahatma Gandhi, he organised the All India Spinners Association, Allied to it was the Khadi Board. He also established an Ashram to propagate the Gandhian ideology. He asked the people around him to spin Khadi.

He was one of the signatories to the famous manifesto of October 4, 1921, declaring that it was the duty of every Indian soldier and civilian to sever his connection with the British Government and find some other means of livelihood.

At Salem he made himself busy in public and literary work. He was one of the founders of the Salem Literary Society and very often attended its meetings and participated in the deliberations. Thus, he developed a new social and political ideology which had deep linkage with the life of a common Indian. He did not believe in the caste barriers. He even recommended scholarships to the promising untouchable students.

He was a modest person and lived a simple life, He was a staunch believer in the *karma* theory. He has been called a true *karma yogin,* doing his duty as was assigned to him. He indeed was a practical man and firmly believed in action — an action mostly for the welfare of the masses of our country.

He was a very fine writer. He wrote Tamil books on Socrates and Marcus Aucrlins, and in English the Mahabharata, the Mayana and upanishad and fables and short stories. His commentaries on the Bhagavad Gita are regarded as outstanding on the subject.

In the following years, when the Swaraj Party became the dominant wing of the Congress. Rajaji devoted himself to the constructive work such as Hindu-Muslim unity, eradication of untouchabilitity, the Swadeshi movement and prohibition.

He was also instrumental in evolving the Yervada Pact between the representatives of the Hindu conference and those of the depressed classes.

Indian Independence Movement

Rajaji's interest in public affairs and politics began when he was elected to the Salem municipal government. In the early-1900s, he was inspired by Indian radical Bal Gangadhar Tilak. In 1917, Rajaji was elected Chairman of the Salem municipality. As Chairman of the Salem municipality, he was responsible for the election of the first Dalit member of the Salem municipality. During this time, Rajaji joined the Indian National Congress and entered the Indian independence movement. In 1908, he defended Indian freedom fighter P. Varadarajulu Naidu from the charges of sedition levelled against him. He participated in the agitations against the Rowlatt Act in 1919. Rajaji was a close friend of V. O. Chidambaram Pillai. He was also highly admired by Indian independence activists Annie Besant and C. Vijayaraghavachariar.

When Mahatma Gandhi entered the Indian independence movement in 1919, Rajaji followed him. He participated in the Non-cooperation Movement and gave up his profession as a lawyer. In 1921, he was elected to the Congress Working Committee and served as the General Secretary of the party.

When the Indian National Congress split in 1923, Rajaji was a member of the Civil Disobedience Enquiry Committee. He supported the old guard and opposed the council entry programme of the Swarajists.

Rajaji was one of Gandhi's chief lieutenants during the Vaikom Satyagraha. It was during this time, that E. V. Ramaswamy functioned as a Congress member under Rajaji's leadership. The two later became close friends and remained so till the end despite their political rivalry.

In the early-1930s, Rajaji emerged as one of the foremost leaders of the Tamil Nadu Congress. When Mahatma Gandhi organised the Dandi march in 1930, Rajaji broke the salt laws at Vedaranyam near Nagapattinam along with Sardar Vedaratnam and suffered imprisonment. Rajaji was subsequently elected President of the Tamil Nadu Congress Committee. When the Government of India Act was enacted in 1935, Rajaji was instrumental in getting the Indian National Congress to participate in the general elections.

Madras Presidency

The Indian National Congress was elected to power in 1937 election for the first time in Madras Presidency (also called Madras Province), a province of British India; with the exception of the six years when Madras was in a state of Emergency, ruled the Presidency until India became independent on 15 August 1947. Rajagopalachari was the first Chief Minister of Madras Presidency from the Congress party.

Council of Ministers in Rajagopalachari's Cabinet (15 July 1937 - 29 October 1939):

Minister	*Portfolio*
C. Rajagopalachari	Chief Minister, Public and Finance
T. Prakasam	Revenue
P. Subbarayan	Law and Education
V. V. Giri	Labour and Industries
Bezawada Gopala Reddy	Local Administration
T. S. S. Rajan	Public Health and Religious Endowments
Maulana Yakub Hasan Sait	Public Works
V. I. Munuswamy Pillai	Agriculture and Rural Development
S. Ramanathan Pillai	Public Information and Administration Reports
Kongattil Raman Menon	Courts and Prisons

On 7 January 1939, Raman Menon died and C. J. Varkey, Chunkath was inducted into the Cabinet. Education portfolio was transferred from Subbarayan to Varkey and instead Subbarayan was given additional charge of Courts and Prisons.

Rajagopalachari issued the Temple Entry Authorisation and Indemnity Act 1939 by which restrictions were removed on Dalits and Shanars entering Hindu temples. In the same year, the Meenakshi temple at Madurai was also opened to the Dalits and Shanars. Rajaji also issued the Agricultural Debt Relief Act in March 1938 to ease the burden of debt on the peasants of the province.

Rajaji also introduced prohibition, and also a sales tax to compensate for the loss of government revenue that resulted from prohibition. Because of the revenue decline resulting from prohibition the Provincial Government shut down hundreds of government-run primary schools. Rajaji's political opponents alleged that this decision deprived many low-caste and Dalit students of their education. Rajaji's opponents also assigned casteist motives to his government's implementation of Gandhi's Wardha scheme into the education system.

Rajagopalachari's rule is largely remembered however for compulsory introduction of Hindi in educational institutions, which made him highly unpopular. This measure sparked off widespread anti-Hindi protests, which led to violence in some places. Over 1,200 men, women and children were jailed for participating in these protests. Two protesters, Thalamuthu Nadar and Natarasan, were killed. In 1940, Congress ministers resigned protesting the declaration of war on Germany without their consent, and the Governor took over the reins of the administration. The unpopular law was eventually repealed by the Governor of Madras on 21 February 1940. Despite the numerous shortcomings, Madras under Rajagopalachari was still regarded as the best administered province in British India.

Second World War

As soon as the Second World War broke out Rajaji resigned as Premier along with other members of his Cabinet to protest the declaration of war by the Viceroy of India. Rajaji was arrested in

December 1940 in accordance with the Defence of India rules and sentenced to one-year in prison. However, subsequently Rajaji differed in opinion over opposition to British war effort. He opposed the Quit India Movement that Gandhi had initiated in 1942 to pressure the British government to grant independence, and instead advocated dialogue with the British. He reasoned that passivity and neutrality would be harmful to India's interests when the country was threatened with invasion. He also advocated dialogue with the Muslim League, which was demanding the partition of India. He resigned from the party and the assembly following differences over resolutions passed by the Madras Congress legislative party and with the leader of the Madras provincial Congress K. Kamaraj.

With the end of the war came in 1945, elections were held in the Madras Presidency in 1946. Kamaraj, the President of the Tamil Nadu Congress Committee backed Tanguturi Prakasam as the Chief Ministerial candidate to prevent Rajaji from coming to power. Rajaji, however, did not contest the elections and Prakasam was elected.

In the last years of the war, Rajaji was instrumental in negotiations between Gandhi and Jinnah. In 1944, he proposed a solution to the Indian Constitutional tangle. In the same year, Rajaji proposed that 55 per cent be the "absolute majority" threshold for deciding whether a district should be a part of India or Pakistan, triggering a huge controversy among nationalists.

From 1946 to 1947, Rajaji served as the Minister for Industry, Supply, Education and Finance in the Interim Government headed by Jawaharlal Nehru.

Governor of West Bengal

When India attained independence on 15 August 1947, the British province of Bengal was divided into West Bengal and East Bengal, with West Bengal becoming part of India and East Bengal part of Pakistan. With the support of Jawaharlal Nehru, Rajaji was appointed the first Governor of West Bengal.

Rajaji was disliked by Bengalis for his criticism of Subhash Chandra Bose during the 1938 Tripuri Congress session. His appointment was unsuccessfully opposed by Subhash's brother Sarat Chandra Bose. During his tenure as Governor, Rajaji's priorities were dealing with refugees and bringing peace and stability in the aftermath of the Calcutta riots. He declared his commitment to neutrality and justice at a meeting of Muslim businessmen: "Whatever may be my defects or lapses, let me assure you that I shall never disfigure my life with any deliberate acts of injustice to any community whatsoever." Rajaji was also strongly opposed to proposals to include areas from Bihar and Orissa in the province of West Bengal.

To one such proposal by the editor of an important newspaper, he replied: "I see that you are not able to restrain the policy of agitation over inter-provincial boundaries. It is easy to yield to current pressure of opinion and it is difficult to impose on enthusiastic people any policy of restraint. But I earnestly plead that we should do all we can to prevent ill-will from hardening into a chronic disorder. We have enough ill-will and prejudice to cope with. Must we hasten to create further fissiparous forces?" Rajaji was highly regarded and respected by Chief Minister Prafulla Chandra Ghosh and the state Cabinet.

Governor General of India

From 10 November 1947 to 24 November 1947, Rajaji served as Acting Governor General of India in the absence of Lord Mountbatten of Burma, who was on leave in England to attend the marriage of Princess Elizabeth to Mountbatten's nephew Prince Philip. Rajaji led a very simple life in the viceregal palace, washing his clothes and polishing his own shoes. Mountbatten was so impressed with Rajaji's abilities that when he was to leave India in June 1948 Rajaji was his second choice to succeed him after Vallabhbhai Patel. Rajaji was eventually chosen as the Governor General when Nehru disagreed with Mountbatten's first choice, as did Patel himself. Rajaji was initially hesitant but accepted when Nehru wrote to him, "I hope you will not disappoint us. We want you to help us in many ways. The burden on some of us is more than we can carry." Rajaji served as Governor General of India from June 1948 to 26 January 1950 and was not only the last Governor General of India but the only Indian Governor General of India.

By the end of the year 1949, it was assumed that Rajaji, already Governor General, would continue as President. Backed by Nehru, Rajaji wanted to stand for the presidential election but later withdrew, due to the opposition of a section of the Indian National Congress mostly made up of North Indians who were concerned about Rajaji's non-participation during the Quit India Movement.

Union Home Minister

In 1950 Rajaji joined the Union Cabinet as Minister without Portfolio, at Nehru's invitation. In the Union Cabinet, Rajaji served as a buffer between Nehru and Home Minister Patel and occasionally, offered to mediate between the two. Finally, with Patel's death on December 15, 1950, Rajaji was put in charge of Home Affairs, serving as the country's Home Minister for nearly 10 months. He warned Nehru about the expansionist designs of China and expressed regret over the Tibet problem, his views being shared with his predecessor Sardar Patel. He also expressed concern over demands made to establish new linguistically-based states, arguing that they would generate differences amongst the people.

By the end of 1951, the differences between Nehru and Rajaji came to the fore. While Nehru perceived the Hindu Mahasabha to be the greatest threat to the nascent republic, Rajaji held the opinion that the Communists posed the greatest danger to the nation. Rajaji also strongly opposed Nehru's decision to commute the death sentences awarded to those involved in the Telengana uprising and his strong pro-Soviet leanings. Tired of being persistently overruled by Nehru in making critical decisions, Rajaji submitted his resignation on "grounds of ill-health" and returned to Madras.

Madras State

In the 1952 elections, the Indian National Congress was reduced to a minority in the Madras state assembly, and a coalition led by the Communist Party of India won most of the seats in the state. Though Rajaji had not participated in the elections, the governor Sri Prakasa appointed him as the Chief Minister after nominating him to the Madras Legislative Council without consulting either the Indian Prime Minister Nehru or the ministers in the Madras state Cabinet. Rajaji was able to prove his majority by luring MLAs from opposition parties to join the Indian National Congress. Nehru was furious and wrote to Rajaji that "the one thing we must avoid giving is the impression that we stick to office and we want to keep others out at all costs." Rajaji, however, refused to contest a by-election and remained an unelected member.

Council of Ministers in Rajagopalachari's Cabinet (10 April 1952 - 13 April 1954):

Minister	*Portfolio*
C. Rajagopalachari	Chief Minister, Public and Police Affairs
A. B. Shetty	Health
C. Subramaniam	Finance, Food and Elections
K. Venkataswamy Naidu	Religious Endowments and Registration
N. Ranga Reddi	Public Works
M. V. Krishna Rao	Education, Harijan Uplift and Information
V. C. Palanisami Gounder	Prohibition
U. Krishna Rao	Industries, Labour, Motor Transport, Railways, Posts, Telegraphs and Civil Aviation
R. Nagana Gowda	Agriculture, Forests, veterinary, Animal Husbandry, Fisheries and Cinchona
N. Sankara Reddi	Local Administration
M. A. Manickavelu Naicker	Land Revenue
K. P. Kuttikrishnan Nair	Courts, Prisons and Legal Department
Raja Sri Shanmuga Rajeswara Sethupathi	House Rent Control
S. B. B. Pattabirama Rao	Rural Welfare, Commercial Taxes and Scheduled areas
D. Sanjeevayya	Cooperation and Housing

The Changes

Ministers belonging to Bellary and Andhra constituencies (Naganna Gowda, Sankara Reddi, Pattabirama Rao, Sanjeevayya and Ranga Reddi) stepped down on 30 September 1953, a day before Andhra split to form a separate state. The portfolios of Agriculture, Forests, Fisheries, Cinchona, Rural Welfare, Community Projects and National Extension Schemes were handed over to M. Bhaktavatsalam on October 9, 1953. Jothi Venkatachalam was made minister for Prohibition and Women's Welfare. K. Rajaram Naidu became the Minister for Local Administration. C. Subramaniam was given the additional portfolios of education, information and publicity. V. C. Palaniswamy Gounder was put in charge of Veterinary, Animal Husbandry and Harijan welfare.

During Rajaji's tenure as Chief Minister, a powerful movement for a separate Andhra State comprising the Telugu-speaking districts of the Madras State, gained foothold. On October 19, 1952, an Indian independence activist and social worker from Madras named Potti Sriramulu embarked on a fast unto death demanding a separate Andhra state for Telugu-speaking people and the inclusion of Madras city in it. Rajaji remained unmoved by Sriramulu's fast and refused to intervene. Sriramulu eventually died on December 15, 1952 after fasting for days triggering riots in Madras city and the Telugu-speaking districts of the state. Initially, both Rajaji and Prime Minister Nehru were against the creation of linguistic states but when the law and order situation in the state grew worse, both were forced to accept the demands. Andhra State was created on October 1, 1953 out of the Telugu-speaking districts of Madras, with Kurnool as its capital. However, the boundaries of the new state were determined by a commission which decided against the inclusion of Madras city in it. Though the commission's report suggested the option of having Madras as the temporary capital of Andhra State for the smooth partitioning of the assets and the secretariat, Rajaji refused to allow Andhra State to have Madras even for a day.

On May 31, 1952, Rajaji put an end to the rationing of sugar. He followed it by abolishing control over food supplies on June 5, 1952. He also introduced measures to regulate the functioning of universities in the state. In 1953, Rajaji introduced a new education scheme known as the Modified System of Elementary Education according to which, schooling hours for elementary school students were reduced to three per day. The students were expected to learn the family vocation at home during the remainder of the day. This scheme was sharply criticised and evoked strong protests from Dravidian parties. The Dravida Munnetra Kazhagam dubbed the scheme as *Kula Kalvi Thittam* or Hereditary Education Policy and attempted to organise massive demonstrations outside Rajaji's house on 13th and 14th July 1953. The rising unpopularity of the Rajaji government forced K. Kamaraj to withdraw his support to Rajaji. On March 26, 1954, Rajaji resigned as President of the Madras Legislature Congress Party thereby precipitating new elections. During the elections held on March 31, 1954, Rajaji fielded C. Subramaniam against Kamaraj. But Subramaniam could garner only 41 votes to Kamaraj's 93 and lost the elections. Rajaji eventually resigned as Chief Minister on April 13, 1954, explaining that his decision was caused by poor health.

Formation of Swatantra Party

Rajaji left the Indian National Congress and along with a few other dissidents, organised the Congress Reform Committee (CRC) in January 1957. K. S. Venkatakrishna Reddiar was elected President. The party fielded candidates in 55 constituencies in the 1957 state assembly elections and emerged as the second largest party winning 13 seats. The Congress Reform Committee also contested 12 Lok Sabha seats during the 1957 Indian elections. It was converted into a full-fledged political party and renamed as the Indian National Democratic Congress at a state conference held in Madurai on September 28-29, 1957.

On June 4, 1959, at a meeting held in Madras, Rajaji, along with Vaidya and Minoo Masani, announced the founding of the Swatantra Party.

In 1956, Rajaji resigned from the Indian National Congress and formed the Congress Reform Committee along with some of his followers. He came to an understanding with his former adversary, Forward Bloc leader U. Muthuramalingam Thevar, in forming an anti-Congress front. The two parties contested the elections jointly. In September 1956, the Congress Reform Committee was renamed the Indian National Democratic Congress. In July 1957, Rajaji created the Swatantra Party. He attacked the license-permit Raj, the complex post-World War Two bureaucracy introduced by Nehru's government that regulated business activity, fearing its potential for corruption and stagnation notwithstanding public support for Nehru's government. He wrote in his newspaper Swarajya.

Encouraging competition in industry and giving incentives for higher production are good for the public as well as for the private interests. I want an India where talent and energy can find scope for play without having to cringe and obtain special individual permission from officials and ministers, and where their efforts will be judged by the open market in India and abroad.... I want the inefficiency of public management to go where the competitive economy of private management can look after affairs.... I want the corruptions of the permit-license-raj to go.... I want the officials appointed to administer laws and policies to be free from pressures of the bosses of the ruling party, and gradually restored back to the standards of fearless honesty which they once maintained.... I want real equal opportunities for all and no private monopolies created by the permit-license raj.... I want the money power of big business to be isolated from politics.... I want an India where dharma once again rules the hearts of men and not greed.

Prominent individuals affiliated with the Swatantra Party included K. M. Munshi, Prof. N.G. Ranga, Minoo Masani, H. M. Patel, V. P. Menon and Maharani Gayatri Devi, Queen of Jaipur.

Beginning in the early-1960s the Congress base in Madras state began to erode. The decline was partly due to the entry of the Dravida Munnetra Kazhagam into the political arena, and partly due to increasing corruption in the Congress. Rajaji capitalised on the weakness of his adversary and strengthened the Swatantra Party.

Rajaji criticised India's use of military force against Goa. Referring to India's acts of international diplomacy, he said that India "has totally lost the moral power to raise her voice against the use of military power."

Anti-Hindi Agitations in Tamil Nadu

After independence the Indian government had declared in its Constitution that Hindi was to be the official language of the country, along with English, but because of objections in non-Hindi areas had allowed for a fifteen-year period for the requirement to be phased in. From 26 January 1965 onwards, Hindi was to be made the sole official language of the Indian Union and people in non-Hindi speaking regions were compelled to learn Hindi. This was vehemently opposed and just before Republic Day, severe anti-Hindi revolts broke out in Madras State. Rajaji reversed his earlier position in support of Hindi and took a strongly anti-Hindi stand in support of the protests. On 17 January 1965, he convened the Madras state anti-Hindi conference in Tiruchirapalli. He angrily declared that the Part XVII of the Constitution of India which declared that Hindi was the official language should "be heaved and thrown into the Arabian Sea."

1967 Elections

In 1967 the fourth general elections were held in Madras state. At the age of 89, Rajaji worked to forge a united opposition to the Indian National Congress by forming an alliance between the Dravida Munnetra Kazhagam, Swatantra Party and the Forward Bloc. The Congress party was defeated in its first defeat in Madras in 30 years as the coalition led by Dravida Munnetra Kazhagam was elected to power. C. N. Annadurai became Chief Minister of Madras state, serving from 1967 to 1969. During this period he changed the name of the state to Tamil Nadu and introduced reforms in the administration. Annadurai died in 1969 and was succeeded by M. Karunanidhi.

The Swatantra party also did well in elections in other states and to the Lok Sabha, the directly elected lower house of the Parliament of India. It won 45 Lok Sabha members in the 1967 general elections and emerged as the single largest opposition party. It was the principal opposition party in the states of Rajasthan and Gujarat. It formed a coalition government in Orissa. It also had a significant presence in Andhra Pradesh, Tamil Nadu and Bihar. In the mid-1960s it won nearly 207 legislative assembly seats all over India, compared to 153 for the Communists, 149 for the socialists and 115 for the Jan Sangh. But the Party started to disintegrate after the death of Rajaji. It finally merged with Charan Singh's Bharatiya Lok Dal in 1974.

Later Years and Demise

In the 1971 Lok Sabha elections, Rajaji organised a united right-wing opposition to Indira Gandhi. The opposition once again created a major impact as it had during the 1967 elections. However, the Indian National Congress government was left unscathed and its majority had considerably increased compared to the 1967 elections, in large part because of the impact of Gandhi's *Garibi Hatao* anti-poverty programme. In his later years, Rajaji was opposed to the repeal of prohibition in Tamil Nadu by the Karunanidhi government. As a result, the Swatantra Party withdrew its support for the Dravida Munnetra Kazhagam during the 1972 state elections and Rajaji strongly opposed some of the government's policies.

By November 1972, Rajaji's health began to decline. On 17 December 1972, a week after celebrating his 94th birthday, Rajaji was admitted to General Hospital with uraemia, dehydration and urinary infection. At hospital, he was visited by Chief Minister M. Karunanidhi, V. R. Nedunchezhiyan, V. V. Giri, Periyar and other state and national leaders. Rajaji's condition deteriorated in the following days as he frequently lost consciousness. Rajaji died at 5:44 p.m. on 25 December 1972 at the age of 94. His son C. R. Narasimhan was beside him at the time of his death reading to him verses from a Hindu holy book.

Contributions to Literature and Music

Rajaji was an accomplished writer both in his mother tongue Tamil as well as English. He was the founder of the Salem Literary Society and regularly participated in its meetings. In 1922, he published a book *Siraiyil Tavam* (Meditation in jail) which was a day-to-day diary about his first imprisonment from 21 December 1921 to 20 March 1922.

In 1916, Rajaji started the Tamil Scientific Terms Society. This society coined new words in Tamil for terms connected to botany, chemistry, physics, astronomy and mathematics. At about the same time, he called for Tamil to be introduced as the medium of instruction in schools.

In 1951, Rajaji wrote an abridged retelling of the Mahabharata in English, followed by one of the Ramayana in 1957. Earlier, in 1955, he had translated Kambar's Tamil Ramayana into English. In 1965, he translated the Thirukkural into English. He also wrote books on the Bhagavad Gita, the Upanishads, Socrates, and Marcus Aurelius in English. Rajaji often regarded his literary works as the best service he had rendered to the people. In 1958, he was awarded the Sahitya Akademi Award for Tamil for his retelling of the Ramayana - *Chakravarti Thirumagan*.. Rajaji was one of the founders of the Bharatiya Vidya Bhavan, an organisation dedicated to the promotion of education and Indian culture.

Apart from his literary works, Rajaji also composed a devotional song *Kurai Onrum Illai* devoted to Lord Krishna. This song was set to music and is a regular in most Carnatic concerts. Rajaji composed a benediction hymn which was sung by M. S. Subbulakshmi at the United Nations General Assembly in 1967.

Legacy

In 1954 while Richard Nixon, then Vice-President of the United States, was undertaking a nineteen-country Asian trip he was lectured by Rajaji on the consuming emotional quality of nuclear weapons. They discussed spiritual life, particularly reincarantion and predestination. Nixon filled three pages of notes recording what Rajaji told him, claiming in his memoirs thirty-six years later that the afternoon "had such a dramatic effect on me that I used many of his thoughts in my speeches over the next several years."

While on a tour to the United States of America as a member of the Gandhi Peace Foundation delegation, Rajaji called upon American President John F. Kennedy in the White House in September 1962. Rajaji explained to Kennedy the dangers of embarking on an arms race, even one which the US could win. At the end of the meeting President Kennedy remarked "This meeting had the most civilizing influence on me. Seldom have I heard a case presented with such precision, clarity and elegance of language".

E. M. S. Namboodiripad, a prominent Communist Party leader, once remarked that Rajaji was the Congress leader he respected the most despite the fact he was also someone with whom he differed the most. Periyar, one of Rajaji's foremost political rivals remarked that Rajaji was "a leader unique and unequalled, who lived and worked for high ideals". On his death, condolences poured in from all corners of the country. Indira Gandhi, the then Prime Minister of India remarked:

> Mr. Rajagopalachari was one of the makers of new India, a sincere patriot, a man whose penetrating intellect and moral sense added depth to national affairs. His analysis, his anticipation, his administrative acumen and his courage to steer an unpopular course if he felt the need, marked him as a statesman and made an impact on the national history at several crucial junctures. He had held the highest positions and lent distinction to every office.
>
> – *Swarajya, 27 January 1973*

Rajaji was regarded as a pioneer of social reform. He issued temple entry proclamations in the Madras Presidency and worked towards the upliftment of Dalits. He played a pivotal role in the conclusion of the Poona Pact between B. R. Ambedkar and the Indian National Congress and spearheaded the Mahabal Temple Entry in 1938. He was a staunch advocate of prohibition and was elected Secretary of the Prohibition League of India in 1930.

When elected as Premier of Madras Presidency, he introduced prohibition all over the province. Prohibition was in vogue all over the province until its removal by M. Karunanidhi over thirty years later. Rajaji was also an active member of the All India Spinners Association.

Rajaji is also remembered for his literary contributions, some of which are considered modern-day classics. He also frequently wrote articles for Kalki and his own journal Swarajya.

Richard Casey, the Governor of Bengal from 1944 to 1946, regarded Rajaji as the wisest man in India. The best possible tribute to Rajaji was from Mahatma Gandhi who referred to him as the "keeper of my conscience".

Criticism

Despite the fact that Rajaji was considered to be one of the most able statesmen in the national arena, his provincial and then, state administrations are believed to have fared badly. Critics opine that he completely failed to gauge the thoughts and feelings of the masses. His introduction of Hindi and the Hereditary Education Policy have been the target of extensive criticism. His anti-reactionary stance during the Quit Indian Movement and his "C. R. Formula" angered most of his colleagues in the Indian National Congress. Alluding to Rajaji, Sarojini Naidu, who was never on good terms with him, once remarked that 'the Madras fox was a dry logical Adi Shankaracharya while Nehru was the noble, compassionate Buddha'.

Although Rajaji's popularity at the regional level fluctuated greatly, it is believed that he was able to exercise his stranglehold over provincial politics mainly because he was favoured by national leaders as Mahatma Gandhi, Sardar Vallabhbhai Patel and Jawaharlal Nehru. Critics feel that when the President of the Tamil Nadu Congress Committee K. Kamaraj and a majority of the provincial leaders turned against him in the 1940s, Rajaji clung on to a position of influence in regional politics through support from his colleagues at the Centre.

Rajaji has always been the archetype of the Tamil Brahmin nemesis of the Dravidian movement. Deeply religious and a pious Hindu and follower of the Vedas and Upanishads, he was accused of being pro-Sanskrit and pro-Hindi, a stigma which Rajaji found difficult to erase despite his vehement protests against the imposition of Hindi during the Madras anti-Hindi agitations of 1965. He was also accused of attempting to heavily Sanskritise Tamil vocabulary through the inclusion of a large number of Sanskrit words in his writings. His Hereditary Education Policy was seen as an attempt to reinforce Varnashrama dharma. His Indian nationalist and anti-secessionist leanings formed the inspiration for Periyar's coining of the term "Brahmin-Bania combine".

Political Ideology

Rajaji found in Gandhi a leader who could lead the millions of his nation towards Swaraj. He himself joined the first Non-cooperation Movement and the Civil Disobedience Movement. Besides he spelt out his political ideology through his speeches and writings. He gave up his legal practice when Gandhi gave a call for the Non-cooperation Movement. He also showed his resentment at the promulgation of the Rowlatt Legislation which had greatly demoralised the people of the Punjab. C. Rajagopalachari was in his mid-30s when he came under the influence of Mahatma Gandhi who came back to India during the second year of the first global war. In 1915, Gandhi happened to tour all the regions of India in order to understand the socio-economic condition of the masses of India.

Rowlatt Legislation

The Government Explanations Answered

C. Rajagopalachari issued the following noteworthy reply to Government resolution dated 14th April 1919 regarding the Rowlatt Legislation:

> "The Government of India complain that the character of the Rowlatt Legislation has been much

misrepresented in the present agitation, and that the intensity of the popular feeling against the legislation it due to such misrepresentations. Government has taken action to meet the agitation by issuing its own literature "to explain the very great value of this legislation to all peaceable and law abiding persons in this country"!

Whatever the merits of this agitation against the Rowlatt Law may be, one just victory has been already achieved, in that the Government has realised its duty to appeal to the people at large to obtain their consent to an enactment, though after the event it may be. This is a success of no mean constitutional importance; for it may well be claimed that the Government has in this for the first time acted as if it were constitutionally responsible to the people. All that we yet want is that the appeal to the people should be before the legislation and not after.

The point most strongly urged in the Government explanation is that the law can have operation nowhere except where there is anarchical crime prevalent. We answer that this would have been a really protective clause, if any legislative council or other body responsible to the people bad the power to decide this. Under the Rowlatt Law the provisions come into force as soon as the declaration is made by the Executive Government that in their opinion there exist such crimes or movements tending to such crimes. The declaration is not subject to any test or appeal or veto of the legislature. On what insufficient grounds such operative formulate can be uttered would be apparent on an unbiassed consideration of the circumstances, under which a stale of open rebellion has been recently declared in order to bring martial law into operation, though all the riots were practically completely quelled even before such declaration. The manner in which the Press law has been worked throughout India, and the case with which the deportation regulations have been utilised, do not create any confidence in the unfettered discretion of the Executive in matters relating to political crime.

It is said that the first part of the Act merely provides for the speedy trial of certain grave offences. No one objects to speedy trials, provided they are not hasty: but every one objects to the

Executive Government, who is the prosecutor in the case, to have power by its own unappealable order to bring any case within the jurisdiction of a Special Bench which can exclude the public and try without jurors or assessors.

It is said that in the second and third parts provision is made "for preventive action against persons suspected of revolutionary or anarchical crime." "Preventive action" is to put suspected men in prison or under other restraints, without trial according to law. Whatever language Government may employ, it means imprisonment without trial: and the people cannot be very misguided in objecting to such legislation. The Local Government's executive order arresting and confining persons suspected by it is final, and there is no appeal to law. The Government explanation lays stress on the point that such orders are to be made only in the case of persons suspected of anarchical or revolutionary crime, and assures us that the provision need cause no fear or apprehension to any person other than the revolutionary or anarchist. Government in effect tells people that in such cases courts are not necessary, and that they may depend on the Executive Government's decisions without enquiry as to whether men are innocent or not. It assumes that innocent men can never be suspected or misunderstood by the Executive Government. As long as Government does not suspect you, you are safe; but when it suspects you, or rather when it declares it suspects you, you are no longer free, and the protection of the courts is taken away. Whether a man is innocent or not can only be decided by trial. How then can the executive declaration be a protection.

The statement that the terms of the Act definitely exclude its use in any case not falling within the definition of anarchical or revolutionary conspiracy is delusive; for there is no remedy open to any man or woman who is proceeded against under the Act and who is not guilty of such crimes. The word of the Executive is final, and there is no appeal to any court on the ground that the case is not one of anarchical or revolutionary crime.

The provision as to the investigating authority which is to examine and report on the cases in which action is taken under the Act is of no consequence. This investigation is done in secrecy, without the man charged hearing the evidence, cross-examing the witnesses, or defending himself by counsel Further the report is not binding on the Government. It is no wonder that such a safeguard is considered a sham and a delusion.

It is claimed that no, unusual or extended powers have been given to the police. When men can be interned deported and imprisoned without appeal to courts, on the mere executive order of Government, it is vain to contend that there is no increase of the powers of police officers, on whose *ex parte* reports such orders are necessarily based. To what extent the Executive Government gets within its sole jurisdiction powers which according to the Constitution should vest in judicial tribunals to that extent the police undoubtedly get increased powers.

The Government desire it to be understood that they will protect all well behaved citizens. In the vernaculars of the country Sirkar means the Government as well as the Courts established by law. But here the protecting Government is only the Executive Government, and not the courts of law. May not the people claim that just and independent tribunals should protect them against the assaults of an irresponsible Executive? Even if the Executive Government were responsible to the people as in democratic countries, that responsibility alone is not deemed in those countries to be adequate protection, and courts are constituted as the supreme authority in matters affecting the freedom of person and property. How much more necessary then, it such protection, in a country where the Executive Government consists of an irresponsible bureau of salaried officer?

Let it be clearly understood that we would oppose such legislation vesting in the Executive Government the absolute right to suspect and imprison without trial, even if the Government be democratic and purely Indian, and not bureaucratic and foreign.

We invite the Government to answer these difficulties truly and fairly, and enlighten the people on the merits of the agitation.

Some Objections to Satyagraha

(By C. Rajagopalachari)

Some people imagine that the practice of civil disobedience is likely to lead men into a general habit of disobedience of law endangering peace and good order in the state. This apprehension can be felt only by those who have no practical experience or mental realisation of Satyagraha, and who make calculations and portend consequences ignoring certain of the essential elements of the movement. If the movement of civil disobedience is accompanied by violence or hatred, it may be taken for granted that it cannot for one moment succeed and that any government be it the present bureaucratic form or any future administration commanding the resources of the State, can easily and at once put it down with a strong hand.

One need, therefore, have no anxiety in respect of the evil consequences of spurious passive resistance movements. For a Civil Disobedience Movement to succeed or command respect and attention it hat necessarily to be conducted strictly on the lines emphasised repeatedly by Mr. Gandhi.

There can be no violence or hatred or untruth. Every person actively taking part in the movement will, have to develop an extent of purity of thought, word and deed and self-restraint, which guarantees for the society and the state of which he is a member, that he will not be a danger to its peace or order, but on the contrary will be a source of strength and elevation of general morals. Those who are incapable of that self-restraint which is demanded by Satyagraha will, far from being led to disobedience of the law by the example of Satyagrahis, be deterred from it by a contemplation of the suffering and difficulties undergone by those in the movement. Thus, neither by themselves nor through others will those who adopt Satyagraha endanger peace and order in Society.

Another apprehension felt by some people who wish to see representative institutions developed in this country and real administrative functions transferred to them, is that the spirit of passive resistance, encouraged by success against certain obnoxious laws made by the present government will not stop there, but will rise to manifest itself on every occasion, when any body of perons can combine for trifling or selfish ends to get rid of any rule or law whatsoever passed in the general interest of the community; and this, too, more easily when the functions of government are transferred to the people of this country and their representatives; that, thus, the inculcation of the theory and practice of Satyagraha is opposed to the success and progress of self-government in this land.

This again is an objection arising out of ignorance of the essential features of Satyagraha. The first lesson of the experience of Satyagraha is a realisation of how difficult it is for those swayed by selfish motives, successfully to practise Satyagraha even for one day. Satyagraha is not mere disobedience. It demands courage and the spirit of sacrifice of the highest order. A just cause is in the nature of the thing an essential requisite. Those who have undergone the actual experience of Satyagraha and its difficulties will be the last persons to advise or undertake it on slight and insufficient grounds, or hastily and without trying all other methods of remedying any great and serious wrong. In fact it is in this very feature that the superiority of Satyagraha lies. Protests and demonstrations can be organised by interested or prejudiced classes against every measure even though it may be just and for the good of other classes.

But Satyagraha can be undertaken with any degree of success only for just causes. No one would sacrifice and go to person while many may go to a meeting and pass resolutions for unjust or slight causes; even if some one did it out of ignorance no one would be moved by it. Satyagraha is a weapon in the hands of both parties in a struggle. It is the one mechanism for the remedy of social wrongs which contains within itself its own checks and adjustments. Just as, or perhaps more truly than, in physical warfare the more powerful party ultimately wins, in spite of temporary results to the contrary, in the warfare of Satyagraha the forces which may for sometime gather round the unjust cause drop off by the very nature of the warfare and the just cause always issues triumphant.

There are the chief arguments of those who raise their hands in horror at the proposal of civil disobedience. What course of action do they themselves suggest? If they deprecate Satyagraha, they must stand for one or other of three things, continuing a lifeless agitation in which they themselves have no more belief, total resignation to evil, or violence. Stated thus, every one would reject all the alternatives; and then, in truth, only Satyagraha remains.

Civil Disobedience and Disturbances

(By C. Rajgopalachari)

Sufficient time has now elapsed to take a dispassionate view of the disorders in the Punjab and other places and to apportion the blame therefore. How far outside causes such us Afghan, German and Bolshevik intrigues had anything to do with them we shall not now discuss. We shall simply state that we are not prepared to believe such theories without any proof whatever worth the name. In any event we shall confine our remarks to day to the undoubted internal causes of the outbreak.

It is commonly stated that Mr. Gandhi admitted that clever revolutionaries conspired secretly and took advantage of the Satyagraha Movement and organised the disorders. Stated in this general way, it is absolutely unwarranted by what Mr. Gandhi said. He has long ago made it clear that his remark about clever men inclined to violence was only about Ahmedabad disorders, and had no reference either to revolutionaries or to the Punjab. It is unfortunate that what Mr. Gandhi said has been twisted and misapprehended and made the basis of statements of such responsible authorities as even the Secretary of State.

It is right to connect the Satyagraha Movement with the disturbances? This question is answered in the affirmative by some who, therefore, deprecate resumption of the movement in any shape. To us this imputation seems wholly unjust. It arises out of a fallacy to common in political and historic discussions conducted in a party spirit, viz.. *post hoc proctor hoc.* The men who attribute the disturbances to Satyagraha ignore altogether the general political situation in the country and look with a narrow event only the new factor, and believe that anything is attributable to it. The best way of examining the matter would be, for a moment, to divest ourselves of all in as connected with Satyagraha, and to imagine for ourselves the state of the country if Mr. Gandhi had not even thought about the passive resistance movement.

No one can maintain for one moment that there would have been no discontent in the country but for the Civil Disobedience Movement. The Rowlatt Legislation, the Muslim question, the economic distress, the feeling of bitterness in consequence of the material disappointment of hopes of a great measure of political emancipation after the close of the war and other important causes of acute discontent would all be there even if Mr. Gandhi had not started any movement. To crown all, the deportations in the Punjab would have taken place none the less, at the instance of the strong Lieutenant-Governor. A point is reached in the psychology of all nations, when if constitutional agitation is widely felt to have been worked to its fullest limit, and yet fails to bring about remedy, an outburst becomes imminent. It is only a question what shape this explosion must take. Such a bursting point was reached when the Rowlatt Legislation was passed amidst the surrounding circumstances indicated above.

Now if civil disobedience had not been thought of at all, what would have been the programme of politicians and leaders? There would have been certainly strong protests, huge mass meetings and great popular excitement all the same. The acuteness of feeling together with a sense of despair would still be there, and we venture to think that upon the deportations the outbursts would have taken place just as they did now in spite of Satyagraha. In fact, we may be at liberty to state that the effect of Satyagraha throughout the country was rather to moderate the resentment by giving definite hope through peaceful work, where otherwise it was blank despair. It gave a self-reliant and dignified line of action, where otherwise the only alternatives were an impossible submission, or violence.

We wish to emphasise one more point. It is a poor understanding of Satyagraha to mistake the events and the programme of the 6th April or the 13th March with Satyagraha proper. The meetings and fasts observed on that day though prescribed and undertaken by the Satyagraha leaders, were not by themselves either Satyagraha, or passive resistance. In the Punjab, where the outburst took place, passive resistance had not been begun at all, and it is idle therefore to talk of Satyagraha as having been in any way directly or indirectly connected with the disturbances in the Punjab.

The tiller of the soil ought not to be neglected. The best intellects arose from the tillers of the soil — Tiruvalluvar Kamban, Ottakuthan, and Auvai. The greatest men were born of the humblest class of people, not of the upper classes. The upper classes are living on other's labour and do not look upon labourers as their benefactors. There is awakening among the people. According to Varnasrama Dharma one at the top must always be there and one at the bottom must always be at the bottom, and he must have his thin gruel, scanty clothing and must work day and night and cannot have a share in the profits of the field or other concerns. That has been the deception practised by the people. A certain class of people are untouchables but their productions are touchables. False interpretation put upon Varnashrma Dharma has been the bane of the country. The lower classes have not had the courage to question the correctness of Varnashrma Dharma. Owing to contact between the East and the West there has been a change.

We are today assembled representing all classes of people, demanding their right to be treated as human beings. This is an achievement of which we are glad. This is only a beginning and we have a long vista before us. Labour should be represented in the Legislative Council. Their representatives should be either appointed or elected. The big trader, manufacturer and landlord would look at the question from a different point of view. I am sure that the Government of Lord Willingdon would be solicitious about the condition of labourers. His Excellency has indicated his sympathy by the appointment of Mr. Paddison as Labour Commissioner. Mr. Paddison is a tactful and sympathetic gentlemen and knows Tamil and Telugu and studies labour questions and would be intermediary between the employer and the employee. I am sure Lord Willingdon's Government will do more to give a status to labour in this country. Labour has been long despised in this country. Government should lay down rules in recognition of Labour Unions.

Most of the capitalists are objecting to outsiders taking part in much Unions. For some time more, outsiders who are educated men should be allowed to be the guides of these illiterate men who are pressed by hunger. I don't think outsiders who have some in the Country would give the labourers any bad advice that would land them in difficulties. We find strikes all over the country. Strikes are less frequent in Madras on account of these Labour Unions. If there were no Labour Unions and if there were no educated people at their helm, strikes would have been more frequent. Labourers in Bengal and Bombay are going to have some representation in Legislative Councils. Why should not the labourers in Madras have the some privilege and why should they not be content with their position? The labourer in Madras is more liberal in his views and more loyal. These people deserve to be treated with greater consideration by the employer, European or Indian. I know what *mirasdars* and *zamindars* are. The village labour is in a fur better condition than the labourer in town. I do not know much of Tanjore but I may say generally that village labourers get more wages then labourers in Ceylon or anywhere else. They get 8 annas a day and get also something to cat in the villages, whereas in Ceylon and other plantations they get only 5 annas. Their prayer is that it may be raised to 8 annas. A women labourer in plantations gets only 3 annas. Labour demand is that women should be treated as human beings.

At this stage the European visitors rose to leave the hall. Before doing so Mr. Robertson, on behalf of the Europeans present at the meeting thanked Mr. Kesava Pillai having expressed his views in English for the benefit of persons like them who knew English alone, and said they were all glad of the message given by Mr. Kesava Pillai to the workmen. If they kept to that message, he added there would be no trouble between European employers and the workmen.

Dewan Bahadur Kesava Pillai said "Let us be humble partners in the art of making money, and thanked them for their presence."

Resolutions Passed

Mr. C. Rajagopalachari moved the following resolution in the all India Labour conference in 1920.

1. (a) This Labour Conference while welcoming the recommendations of the Joint Committee to extend the franchise to include a proper proportion of the urban wage earning classes, expresses its grave surprise and dissatisfaction at the official statement recently made implying that the benefit of the recommendation is not to be extended to the City or Presidency of Madras.

(b) This Conference considers that a minimum qualification for franchise of Rs. 15 income per month by wages may be fixed for the urban wage-earners.

(c) This Conference recommends that all factories coming under the purview of the factory law should be required to furnish to the electoral officers lists of persons employed who have earned for six months continuously Rs. 15 or more, to facilitate the proper registry of such wage-earners in the electoral rolls and that other employers may be supplied forms for sending similar lists.

He said that there was no use of one or two members of the Council taking up the cause of labourers, but every member sent to the Council should have the deepest interest of the labourers at heart. They would think of the labourers only when the latter had the privilege of voting. If Bolshevism was not to enter this land, law should be so framed as to adequately represent the interests of labour.

Mr. Kumaraswamy Naicker seconded the resolution and Mr. Subramania Sastri of Arni supported it.

The resolution was unanimously carried.

From his Solitary Cell

Here is a titbit from C. Rajgopalachari from Vellore Jail:

> "I guess you have not started for Bardoli and Anand yet. I am allowed to write one letter a month and to receive similarly one letter a month, and am completely shut out from all politics, news and newspapers. What an ideal condition which I know you are envying!"
>
> "The greatest common measure between thoughts, words and what the jail authorities would allow and what I need write to you at all, it but little."
>
> "It took me till now to get rid of the boils. I am now quite free from the trouble. It must horrify you to learn that I willingly underwent five injections of vaccine for these boils."

"My asthma persists, though by keeping my stomach light I hold the upper hand over the enemy. I have gone down from 104 to 98 lbs. but that does not matter."

"Your eyes would flow with delight if you saw me here in my solitary cell spinning not as a task imposed by a tyrant faddist, but with pleasure. Between spinning and beautiful Ramayana I have been spending practically the whole of the time left me by the agony of eating, washing of dishes, etc. The spinning wheel I have is a real beauty. It is a live companion and younger brother in my cell."

"This Ashram is very much less congested than yours at Sabarmati and I wish more people understood the real advantaged of this retirement and discipline."

Great Disappointment

Judge Broomfield said to Mahatmaji when he stood before him as prisoner: "It will be impossible to ignore the fact that you are in a different category from any person I have ever tried or am likely to have to try. It would be impossible to ignore the fact that in the eyes of millions of your countrymen, you are a great patriot and a great leader. Even those who differ from you in politics look upon you as a man of high ideals and of noble and of even saintly life."

These beautiful words falling from the lips of an apparent enemy led India to rest in the belief that despite the exigencies of warfare, the soul in man had triumphed over the brute and that the officers to whom Mahatmaji's body was to be entrusted according to the sentence would realise their privilege. We believed that the Superintendent and the Jailor of the prison that was to hold Mahatmaji within its walls would feel proud of this great charge and carry out the punishment not in a spirit of revenge or pettiness, but in a noble spirit.

We had reason to hope that the punishment that was voluntarily sought and accepted by Mahatmaji in double atonement of the sins of our rulers as well as all the crimes of the people who had misused the strength to which he had opened their eyes, would be carried out in a spirit of worship and not that of the Jail Manual.

But our hopes have received a rude shock. Devadas, Mahatmaji's youngest son, and I, who were at our respective posts of duty and, therefore, had not the privilege of being present during the great trial, went to Poona on the 1st of April and applied to see Mahatmaji in accordance with the rules as to interviews of prisoners. In a few minutes as we were at the gate looking through the bars, my heart leaps as I saw the old and familiar source of inspiration and joy. The frail form clad in a single loin-cloth jumped into the Gate Passage from inside through the wicket door. He was immediately led up the stairs into the Superintendent's Office Room and we were called in. As was right and proper according to the code of official dignities and prestige, the Prison King, the Superintendent, was in his throne; and the prisoner was kept standing all the time during our talk, which on account of the Superintendent's justification and explanations and the Jailor's interruptions, took longer than we had expected.

We had a peep into the truth, and it was disappointing in the extreme. The curse of vulgarity and ignorance rendered ugly what otherwise would have been the most beautiful thing in the world. We saw at once that the Superintendent and the Jailor of Yervada had failed to realise their great opportunity. They bad not the eyes to see what the cultured Judge of Ahmedabad had seen. They did not see that they were honoured with the privilege of being custodians of a man greater than the Kaisar, greater than Napoleon of St. Helena, greater than the biggest prisoners of war, a man of world-value, one whose fellows in history and companions in Heaven will be Buddha, Socrates and Jesus and others of that class. Mahatmaji's jailors cannot claim the ignorance which had blinded the persecutors of Jesus or Socrates, for times have so far changed that even during the lifetime of the great Indian seer, his worst enemies have understood and explained to the world his purity of purpose and his greatness.

The crime of the people to whose charge an indifferent government has entrusted him is all the greater. Food Mahatma has. The little bread goat's milk his body wants is no doubt given to him. They give him also two oranges a day as it was notoriens, be lived mainly or bait. They may even improve the quantity and quality when they learn by and by what he was all these years used to. They have not given him his own bed, but make him sleep on regulation jail blankets without a pillow. We will presume they will now give him even a pillow. His solitary cell has ventilators. He can use the verandah during day time, though at nights he has to sleep is the little space locked in with a commode.

The food, air and water that the animal functions of his body require, he no doubt has, or they will soon be supplemented adequately. Even otherwise, the body will adjust itself after perhaps some trouble to the conditions laid down. But what grieves us is that we saw indifference and blindness where we had believed there would be full recognition of their great duty. The human soul is not recognised by the jail code. But we had expected Government would not leave it in this case to the poor jail officials to find out their duties towards their great prisoner from the articles in the Jail Manual.

We know that Jail single-cells are constructed for condemned murderers and recalcitrant and dangerous felons. But if necessary, it is not too much for a great and powerful Government to build afresh to find suitable prison accommodation for one whose life and self-inflicted punishment are things standing in a category apart altogether from the Jail Manual.

All prisoners should be locked in at night: but surely, Government ought to be able to find a verandah for Mahatmaji to sleep in as he has been all through doing after his pleurisy, barred and locked if they think it necessary to prevent his escape! He is asked to petition and obtain orders from Government to have even his own religious books. He is not given such human companionship as even ordinary prisoners have. Such simple imprisonment is indeed worse than hard labour.

The whole story is sad and disappointing But what is the thing to be remembered? Our great leader's indomitable spirit cannot be broken by such or even worse treatment. About that all may be certain. But it is a severe test of our strength and our faith. Anger would be a fatal outlet for the resentment which the nation must feel at Government's indifference and pettiness. Best of all cost must be our watchword now. Otherwise, the great Sacrifice would indeed be fruitless.

A grin determination to clothe India in white Khadi and silently organise the nation into a disciplined army of non-violence is the only worthy form which our great resentment should take.

(*C. Rajagopalachari*)

Government Contradicts

I have just been shown the following note issued by the Director of Information, Bombay:

> Misleading and a certain respects entirely untrue statements regarding the treatment of Mr. Gandhi in Yervada Jail have appeared in certain newspapers. The following note gives the facts:
>
> "Mr. Gandhi is given precisely the same diet to which he was accustomed when he was free, namely, goat's milk, bread, oranges, lemons, sugar, tea and raisins. He brought his own raisins to prison with him which he used until they were finished and a fresh supply was provided for him by the jail authorities. It is untrue to say that he is locked in at night. He has separate quarters of his own, one cell to sleep in and the other to work in during the day. The sleeping cell he is allowed to keep open at night. Half the yard is reserved for him to exercise and the space is ample for the purpose, as Mr. Gandhi has stated to the authorities or several occasions. Mr. Gandhi has not asked for any newspapers and but regret in the allowed to retain some of his private books was granted at soon at it was made. A pillow, in addition to the usual bedding, was supplied when it was asked for. A commode for use at night was placed in the cell on medical grounds for the benefit of the prisoner.
>
> It should be added that Mr. Gandhi has been seen by the Inspector-General of prisons on several occasions

and has each time made no complaints, but on the contrary, expressed himself as completely satisfied with the treatment he is receiving. Moreover, on the occasion of the interview which some of Mr. Gandhi's friends had with him and of which distorted accounts have appeared in the press, Mr. Gandhi distinctly stated that he did not want his prison life discussed in the papers, but only that it should be stated that he was quite well."

The article 'My Great Disappointment' was in type before the above was received in the *Young India* Office. It is a satisfactory feature that the Government have paid attention to the matter so speedily. But to speak the truth, I did not expect that the Director of Information would stoop to such evasion as I see in this Note. I assume the reference is to the facts elicited from me by the *Bombay Chronicle* representative and published on the 3rd inst. I am charged with having made misleading and untrue statements. Let me take the facts one by one.

"Mr. Gandhi is given precisely the name diet to which he was accustomed when he was free, viz. goat's milk, bread oranges, lemons, supper, tea and raisins."

It was stated distinctly by me that goat's milk and bread were given. I stated also that he had two oranges a day (which is insufficient in quantity but I avoided this aspect of the matter) Mr. Gandhi does not take tea. There must be some mistake here, which is, however, immaterial now. As for the raisins, I repeat what I have already stated that the Superintendent noted the request only at the interview and said he would give them.

"It is untrue to say that he is locked in at night .... the sleeping cell he is allowed to keep open at night."

I assure the public that Mr. Gandhi was locked in at night and that the cell in which he slept was not allowed to be kept open at night till the time of my Interview.

The Superintendent and Jailor discussed this matter with me at some length and so, there can be no mistake about it. I shall be glad if Government since then have allowed Mr. Gandhiji to sleep in the Verandah as he has been accustomed for so long, and which I believe is necessary for his health. But the Director of Information, if he gave dates, would have to admit that this was done only after ray interview. The evasion is perfect. "It is untrue to say that he is locked in at night" perhaps now; but it was quite true up to the 1st of April when I saw him.

"He has separate quarters of his own."

Here also it is a clever evasion to make the privation of human intercourse look like a privilege. Is Mr. Shankerlal Banker who was sentenced with Mr. Gandhi allowed to see or live and sleep with him, or any other prisoner for that matter? Let the Government make it clear that Mr. Gandhi is not compelled to suffer absolute seclusion.

"Half the yard is reserved for him to exercise." "Here too it is a reservation, not a limitation." "Mr. Gandhi has not asked for any newspapers."

This is truly a wonderful statement to make. The Superintendent and Jailor were both particularly persistent in refusing all private books, even though they may be purely religious and as for newspapers, none was allowed. Here too the Director evades dates.

"A pillow in addition to the usual bedding was supplied when it was asked for."

Note the double evasion here. When was the pillow given? Had he one during the ten days he was in Yervada Jail till I saw him? Did not the Superintendent raise objections even during my interview, when I expressed painful surprise at their having allowed no pillows? Again, what is "usual bedding"? It is Mr. Gandhi's own bedding which a prisoner undergoing simple imprisonment is according to my understanding of even Jail code entitled to? The Director evades this question.

"A commode for use at night, etc."

When? After my interview, but the Director's note is silent. The Director's note is silent again as to interviews and letters. It is desirable that this matter as well as that of the enforced seclusion from all fellow prisoners, are all made clear without evasion or equivocation. We have all no doubt that Mr. Gandhi will express himself 'completely satisfied' with any treatment; but this does not in his case absolve a civilized Government from its duties. It is true that Mr. Gandhi told me that he did not want his prison-life to be discussed in the papers. But I told him he should trust my judgement in the matter. I consider it my duty to state the truth in a matter of such public importance and could not find my way to suppress or evade. It may not be easy hereafter to obtain interviews or correct information and we may have to rely only on such evasions as I see the Director of Information of Bombay has been guilty of (and be adds insult to injury by charging me with having made misleading and untrue statements).

Treatment such as I found after thorough cross-examination of Mr. Gandhi as well as of the Superintendent and the Jailor, has given us an insight into the spirit of the whole thing. Details do not matter. Subsequent mending in this or that trifle is not what we are concerned about. The evasive note issued in reply to my statements and the bold charge of untruth on the top of it do not improve the position.

(*C. Rajagopalachari*)

Our Work during the Halt

Mahatmaji has ordered a halt and has asked his non-violent army to utilise the time gained to increase its fighting efficiency, by solid work of organisation. In a war of violence, the capture of a general by the enemy would be a fatal blow. Many among us being new to the science of Mahatmaji's non-violent war, and familiar only with the principles of wars of destruction and gunpowder, are grieved over the arrest and imprisonment of our beloved leader and consider it a fatal blow to our movement. On the contrary, what in a war of violence would rightly be deemed a reverse, in a war of non-violence has just the opposite effect. It is clear that the principles of a war of non-violence must be in vital respect the exact opposite of the principles of a war of violence. Consequently, the Government being guided by a totally inapplicable body of rules would take action which, instead of hurting or hindering us, morally speaking would on the contrary be more likely to help us in developing our moral powers of resistance, through a greater capacity for loving sacrifice and suffering. The loss of a general in a campaign of gunpowder and steel would be the severest blow that an army could sustain. In our campaign of non-violence, it is the opposite. It strengthens and spreads more extensively the determination to suffer, which is our ammunition; it creates self-reliance, which is our simple drill; it increases the power of love, which is the basis of all non-violent discipline. Above all, the indomitable spirit of the imprisoned saint climbs over the prison walls and is still with us to guide and help. Therefore, the halt that has been ordered should be quickly utilised to the fullest advantage.

The immediate duty of Congress workers is:

1. To create throughout the country a network of non-violent organisations, enrolling as large a number of members as possible and as quickly as possible.
2. To collect donations for the Tilak Swaraj Fund on which all Congress activities of the year will be a charge.
3. More than all, to make the use of Khaddar universal.

At Bardoli and Delhi, mass civil disobedience was suspended; and individual civil disobedience also has been practically suspended, if not by resolution, by the weighty advice of Mahatmaji. The reason for the suspension was insufficient discipline and strength of organisation. Whether it may become necessary to resume civil disobedience of either type will depend on the future; for the campaign in favour of Non-violence and Khaddar in the opinion of our great leader, if prosecuted throughout with unabated zeal is bound to lead to victory — the goal of Swaraj. But it is clear that if it becomes necessary at all, we shall not be able to undertake it unless we lay: the necessary foundations of non-violent discipline and organisation. It is a noteworthy feature that the common people have understood and realised the importance of following Mahatmaji's advice that before we proceed further, we must consolidate our organisations. It is, therefore, expected that if leaders and workers throughout the country harness them selves to this work, there will be no want of response on the part of the people to carry out the parting wish of Mahatmaji in regard to Congress work.

There should be an enrolment of members in each unit who by their quality and numbers will be able to control and direct the activities in that area in the channels laid down by the Congress without error or deviation, and prevent not only apathy, but also undiscipline and violence in any shape.

A specially and carefully selected body of volunteers must be brought into existence in every area who will carry out in letter and spirit all the pledges which they have to sign under the resolution passed by the National Congress which is worth repeating here in extenso:

With God as witness I solemnly declare that:

1. I wish to be a member of the National Volunteer Corps.
2. So long as I remain a member of the Corps, I shall remain non-violent in word and deed and shall earnestly endeavour to be non-violent in instant, since I believe that as India is circumstanced, non-violence alone can help the Khilafat and the Punjab and result in the attainment of Swaraj and consolidation of unity among all the races and communities of India whether Hindu, Muslim, Sikh, Parsee or Jew.
3. I believe in and shall endeavour to promote such unity.
4. I believe in Swadeshi as essential for India's economic, political and moral salvation, and shall use hand-spun and hand-woven Khaddar to the exclusion of every other cloth.
5. As a Hindu, I believe in the justice and necessity of removing the evil of untouchability and shall, on all possible occasions, seek personal contact with, and endeavour to render service to the submerged classes.
6. I shall carry out the instructions of my superior officers, and all the regulations not inconsistent with the spirit of this pledge prescribed by the Volunteer Board or the Working Committee or any other agency established by the Congress.
7. I am prepared to suffer imprisonment, assault or even death, for the sake of my religion and my country without resentment.
8. In the event of my imprisonment, I shall not claim from the Congress any support for my family or dependence.

In the enrolment of members, it must be clearly understood that every one who accepts the Congress creed is entitled to be enrolled, and neither civil disobedience nor non-cooperation is a necessary part of the creed, but only the attainment of Swaraj by all legitimate and peaceful means.

The enrolment of members for this year is not only necessary for carrying on normal Congress activities, but it also will be in its numbers the nation's answer to the arrest and imprisonment of Mahatmaji and to the threat of 'hard fibre'

The collection for the Tilak Swaraj Fund must be vigorously proceeded with in order to successfully carry on the Congress programme. Unless the nation taxes itself, it cannot achieve the great object it has set before itself. A study of the resolutions already passed by the Working Committee and the AICC from time to time would show how every local purpose can be served through this fund and at the same time how the central fund has been used for giving relief to local Congress finances.

In order to encourage the principle of provincial autonomy and to induce efforts to make each province self-supporting, the Working Committee has recommended that only 5 p.c. of the provincial collections should go to the central fund instead of the 25 p.c. as in the past. While the T.S.F. Collections will go on throughout the year, the Working Committee has passed a resolution that the 18th of every month should be observed as a day of sacrifice and prayer so long as Mahatmaji is kept away from us and that every person should offer hit actual income on that day as his contribution towards the Tilak Swaraj Fund.

While we have made much progress in developing the Khaddar programme, it must be admitted that we have not yet fulfilled our great leader's expectations. Even as he went away from us the one word on his lips was Khaddar. His faith in the spinning wheel as the one invincible weapon of non-violence which will purge us of our sins of untouchability, idleness and apathy towords national affairs and will bring us prosperity, peace, unity and freedom, was at its maximum, when he cheerfully retired into prison, leaving all the national affairs in our hands. Let us be true to his faith and see that every man and every women who have faith in the nation and affection for the saint who guided us and whose indomitable spirit continues to guide us, shall pin his or her faith on Khaddar alone as a symbol of the nation's determination to be innocent and free.

(*C. Rajagopalachari*)

The Key-stone

By far the most important part of the Nagpur Subcommittee's Report is where they make general observations on matters of principles. The difference between our school of thought and the other is not in mere detail. In our opinion, it serves no good purpose, if vital differences be ignored and a patched up agreement is arrived at over details. After two years of joint labour and most cordial effort at agreement on both sides, the two schools of thought remain as far apart as ever. Dr. Moonje and men of his school of thought hold, as we hold, that Swaraj is the only panacca for all our wrongs and grievances. But they do not believe in emphasising on non-violence or self-suffering or on any other moral principle as a means to that end. The aim of the Congress is worldly. So, they say, let there be no religion or morals introduced in our programme. Our policies and programmes, they hold, should be governed only by considerations of expediency and practicability. To expediency in the best sense of the term there is no objection; and to practicability there can never be any objection. But the object is by these formulae to exclude religion and morality. Here lies the main issue.

Religion and morality have, we believe, a place in everything, in commerce, in art, even in science, certainly in all human activities, including politics. The success, so far achieved by us under Mahatmaji's guidance, is entirely due to the introduction of religion and morality into politics which had hitherto been thought to be solely governed by the principle of expediency. Mahatmaji's priceless contribution to politics in India and in the world is the introduction of the moral principle of non-violence. Non-violence is the key-stone of the structure we have raised. To take it down is to pull the whole structure down. The Nagpur Subcommittee sees the importance of a firm and cordial unity between the different religions and races inhabiting and owning India as their "motherland." Yet it fails to grasp the key to the whole situation.

If we put non-violence in the background of national life and policy, there can be no trust, no safety and no unity among the different religions and races.

The suggestion of the Nagpur Subcommittee that we should have all the Congress programme, except the creed of self-suffering, would be like a man approving the whole of Islam, but asking to be relieved of its inconvenient system of prayer; or, like one accepting marriage without the inconvenience of its restraints; or like one accepting military life, but pleading to be relieved of the liability to serve in the front. Even as prayer it the essence of Islam, as restraint is the essence of matrimony, and as readiness to give up life is the essence of military service, so is non-violence and self-suffering the essence of the Congress programme. It is only by accepting the essential restraint and privation that the other active parts of our programme get strength and effectiveness.

The Subcommittee appears to understand by non-violence mere abstention from violence. In this, it is greatly mistaken. Non-violence is a great deal more than a mere negative. It is the method of love and peace as opposed to hatred and anger. It is this important and active principle which the nation accepted, when it accepted Mahatmaji's leadership. Is the policy impracticable? Certainly not, not more impracticable than the policy of honesty or of trust or of fidelity, which we still teach our boys and girls to follow as good practical principles of conduct, though we know that universal honesty, universal trust and universal fidelity are unattainable except in the millenium.

The fact of the matter is that Dr. Moonje and some others are where they had stood before, not changed. They believe in hilling back, in diplomacy, in demonstration, in fighting in the law-courts and in fighting in the councils. They have not yet realised that in love there is a stronger weapon than hatred, that in diplomacy, they are more than matched by their adversary, that agitation has proved futile, that law-courts are but instruments of the Executive and that obstruction in the councils is cooperation of the finest sort.

The last point deserves fuller notice. The question of entering the Councils is at the bottom of many a difference. We entirely agree that no fetish should be made of any item of the Congress programme, and that the national movement should be allowed to take shape in varied channels. If people desire to enter the Councils, in order to oppose bad measures and support good ones, help the making of precedents and conventions and try to achieve liberal amendments of the Government of India Act, in fact, to work the Reform Scheme, if not exactly like moderates with full faith in it, but making the best use of it though thoroughly discontented, we have no quarrel with such men.

But they would no longer be non-cooperators. They would frankly be cooperators, and we never want to prevent any one cooperating who sincerely hopes to help India that way. What, however, is proposed in some quarters, or at least what is commonly understood when entry in the Councils is suggested from non-cooperation quarters, is that the legislative Councils should be used for obstruction, i.e. obstruction of all work, good or bad, as Mrs. Das put it. A careful study of the Government of India Act would show that it is so framed that serious obstruction of this sort is not really possible. When we enter the Councils, we go there to exercise either our legal powers or our moral influence. The legal powers are strictly limited and, if exercised merely for obstructing the administration, will be much further reduced. Moral influence cannot be acquired or retained by people who set themselves to obstruction, pure and simple.

Much help by cooperation, either direct or indirect, is a necessary preliminary for any moral influence or power outside the legal Constitution. If obstruction is immoderately persisted in, there would be absolutely no moral influence whatever, and nothing to prevent the legal powers against obstructive tactics being fully utilised by government. So sooner or later, obstructionist nationalists must face the dilemma, i.e. either to save their own moral influence become cooperators and moderates, or indulge in obstruction, but become impotent and entirely harmless. We need hardly refer to the divisions that will split our ranks as soon as such a dilemma presents itself. So long as we are pledged to non-cooperation, we should recognise that non-violence is the key-stone of the principles on which our movement rests, and abstention from Councils is the key-stone of the super-structure.

(*C. Rajagopalachari*)

Why Khadi for Civil Disobedience?

A question was raised by the Secretary of the Bengal Khilafat Committee on the right of the provinces to declare Civil Disobedience, irrespective of progress in Khaddar. Where an intolerable situation is created by interference with the elementary rights of association and free speech, and the magistracy issues orders making normal Congress work impossible, the Provincial Congress Committees have the power under the Delhi Resolution to organise Civil Disobedience to meet such a situation. In as much as this would be a purely denfensive measure to protect the elementary rights of citizens, why, it is asked, should it be necessary to satisfy any preliminary self-imposed condition such as the universal use of Khaddar. We do not need to wear Khaddar in order that we may claim the right to eat food, drink water, sleep or offer prayers to God.

It is argued, therefore, that Provincial Committee should not be limited by the Khaddar condition, when they are satisfied that Civil Disobedience is necessary to protect such elementary rights. The answer lies in the meaning of Khaddar. It is admitted that non-violence is an essential condition for organising Civil Disobedience, even in such urgent and purely defensive cases. However, justifiable the cause, however fundamental the rights infringed, without non-violence, no disobedience could be organised within the Congress programme. The Khaddar condition is really a part of the non-violence clause. We are firmly of opinion that so long as the Congress leaders in any area are not able to universalise the use of Khaddar, in that area they have failed to obtain that control over the people, which is a necessary condition for the maintenance of true non-violence in that area. Non-violence is not mere present abstention from violence.

It is a positive state of mind, in most cases implying a change of heart and life, truly and conclusively proved by the wearing of Khadi and the turning of the Charkha. It is not assured by mere oral statement. When the leaders of any place assure the Working Committee that they have perfect control over the people, and that they expect the latter to carry out all their orders from time to time, it is an assurance which carries no conviction, if they have not so far succeeded is inducing the people to wear Khadi or spin.

It is not unreasonable that a certain standard of concrete proof should be demanded before taking a very grave step.

(*C. Rajagopalachari*)

A Grave Warning

In spite of much protestation and equivocation, it is increasingly clear every day that a section of the Press both in England and in India are feeling intensely anxious over the Hindu-Muslim unity. Their disappointment at the steadiness of the Hindu support of the Khilafat claim, and the Muslim support of the agitation for immediate Swaraj, and their eager desire to see disunion and division among the two great communities of India are but thinly wired. In Government policy, there is a frankly avowed reversion to the old policy of favouring the Muslim element, but it is so obviously a camouflage, unaccompanied by any sincere attempt on the part of England to bring about a Turkish settlement such as the Indian Muslims want, that no one can be deceived by it. Indian Muslims are asked to be satisfied with the excellent intentions of the Government of India. The very hurry in publication of these intentions is too obvious a race with the determination of the British Cabinet not to carry them out. Meanwhile, those Muslim leaders who are believed to be responsible for the extreme demands of the agitation in India are to be removed from the scene, dividing them into two classes, one for prosecution and imprisonment, and the other for invitation to England for a prolonged education in diplomacy.

We cannot be too careful in guarding the sacred bond between the two great communities. The two things of the greatest importance in our movement are non-violence and Hindu-Muslim Unity. During Mahatmaji's stewardship, we bad an ever-watchful and long-visioned master, guiding, guarding warning, chastising, and helping us as occasion demanded. We have now to help and watch over ourselves. Too much caution cannot, therefore, be exercised by us. We should preserve inviolate the principle of non-violence in thought, word and deed. During Mahatmaji's separation from us, purity of thought and word has to be more carefully guarded than ever before, so that we may not lead ourselves and others into the path of error. Hindu-Muslim Unity also — which is a short phrase to indicate the unity among all the communities that claim India as Motherland — should be preserved in thought, word and deed and when we are sheep without our shephard, if we should not make sad mistakes, we should be more watchful over thought and word than ever before.

It has sometimes been asked, what should the Hindus do if the British give all that the Muslims want in respect of the Khilafat. If such a thing should happen, Hindus should hail it as the happy consummation of their desires and as their greatest victory. It is impossible to imagine that the Muslims after victory in the greater struggle would give up the lesser struggle for Swaraj. For the Swaraj objective is comparatively a small thing by the side of the Khilafat demand, which though unimpeachably just and proper, is in effect as Sir Valentine Chirol put it the other day, a claim not merely for managing our own affairs be to shape the policy of the Imperial Government on a great question of international policy which concerns the whole Empire. Success in the Khilafat agitation is success in attaining for India a status really higher than Dominion status. If the Muslims after restoring the Khilafat with Hindu aid agree to live in an India not fully free, and give up the Swaraj agitation, i.e. if the impossible should happen, surely even then, Hindus can fight their battle alone, and with a moral strength inconceivably greater than before.

Let us not forget the firm basis of the creed of non-cooperation and non-violence, viz. faith in the essential goodness of human nature; and let us serve without looking for a return. Hindus should place themselves in the position of the Muslims and ask themselves whether under the circumstances, they would leave their brethren to fight their own battle. They should not imagine that Muslims would be less patriotic or be less responsive to be promptings of human nature.

(C. *Rajagopalachari*)

Much the Better for Happiness

The demand for individual civil disobedience is becoming irresistible. Before this is read, the All India Congress Committee will have met at Lucknow and decided on this question. The operations of the Government against the Non-cooperation

Movement are taking intolerable forms of interference with the fundamental rights of citizenship. There are increasing signs everyday that the restraints against courting imprisonment laid down at Delhi and the injunctions issued by Mahatmaji as hit own considered opinion are straining the loyalty of Congressmen to the utmost. There is a point beyond which, in times of revived national life, the strain of interference by the Government with natural and elementary rights cannot be borne. Apart from any constructive plans for the attainment of freedom, the sheer force of repulsion will operate to drive men into the prisons.

The secession of the Plebeians is a very early historical example of organised non-cooperation. The services and the cooperation of the Plebeians were necessary to the Patriciana of Rome, in peace as well as in war. In such a state of things it was seen that a bloodless revolution could be effected by the swift and sharp method of withdrawal in a body. In a small state like what Rome was at the time, secession in a body to the neighbouring sacred mount with a determination to live apart till satisfactory terms were offered, was the natural form which the principle of peaceful non-cooperation took. The *Hijrat* recommended by Islamic tradition is also based on the same universal principle. If any Muslim is not at liberty in any state or country to follow his religion, he it recommended to withdrew himself from that state to some other country where he can enjoy the liberty of his faith without interference. As industrious and honest citizens are a strength to all societies and states, such withdrawal acts as an effective deterrent on interferences with their liberties.

Withdrawal to a different country as an answer to tyranny or injustice is a difficult remedy in the state of society in which we are living in India. It is impossible to find suitable places for emigration in the present conditions of the world, and the hardships involved in movements of large bodies of citizens are well-high insurmountable. It is true that under compulsion, even in the present day, such movements of large bodies sometimes take place, as the happenings in Eastern Europe and Asia Minor show. But to people in India, such a remedy is practically impossible. There is, however, a substitute to which the actions of the Government are naturally driving the people. The movement to fill the jails is often misunderstood to be a trick to embarrass the administration. Rightly understood, however, it is based on the same principle of secession. If in modern times, it is difficult to find a suitable country to emigrate to, there are places set apart by the Law within the hostile State itself, into which those who feel that they cannot honourably remain as limbs of the State or Society can withdraw themselves. The prisons are places into which oppressed people may, without having the country, retire in order to free themselves from voluntary surrender to wrong, and to withdraw their sciences from the state or society which oppresses them. No civilized state can function for long with a large number of its honest citizens thus acceding from it and retiring into its prisons. Enforced work in the prisons cannot be a substitute for the free cooperation of honest citizens, which is the very life of a state.

Individual Civil Disobedience is an act of the highest moral significance. In proportion to the purity and intensity of the motive that drives one to it, is its efficacy. In its purest form, it is an act, the spiritual value of which is strong enough to dissolve the corruption of a whole state or civilization. It is essentially a religious act. It is not a thing to be done in a spirit of bravado or of mechanical party discipline, when it is almost worthless. "Swaraj for my country is what I want, but between remaining out without Swaraj and prison-life, much the better for my happiness is the latter." Every one who feels, thus, is fit for individual civil disobedience; and if feeling thus, our best man and women surrender themselves to arrest, their fetters will be the trophies of true Swaraj.

(C. *Rajagopalachari*)

Dangerous Doctrine

The practice of good and sincere men is often better than their theory. Mr. Bapat's appeal to the people of Maharashtra on the Mulshi Valley struggle contains many statements about Satyagraha, which would have surprised the inventor of the term, if he had been free to read them. India teems with examples of the perversion of good ideas, which should be warnings enough. In the new and all-amending definition of Satyagraha which Mr. Bapat gives in all receipt Mulshipets pamphlet be includes the very opposite of Satyagraha. "When group is opposed to group and all possible Satyagraha efforts by the party of justice to work a psychological change in the opposing party fail miserably, then arises a case where the restriction of non-violence may be justifiably removed and what is called pure of *shuddha* Satyagraha may be tried." Removing the restrictions of non-violence, that is to say, adopting the methods of violence, there would be nothing left of Satyagraha, which after that would be a pure misnomer.

The basis of Satyagraha is self-suffering, which again it bated on the force of Truth. Physical force is rigorously excluded; for when once such force is called in, the party that has the larger force on his side wins and not necessarily Truth. It is quite a different question whether it is justifiable to use physical force in a just cause. Many systems of Dharma allow it; but Satyagraha has no place for it. The Satyagrahi knows that love and not retaliation, nor the hatred born of the use of brute-force, can ever end a quarrel. According to him, the right to use physical force cannot accrue so long as human judgement is not final.

Physical force can achieve a temporary victory in unjust as well as just causes. Even where one is conscientiously convinced that one's cause is right and uses brute-force in support of it, inflicting injury on others, it often turns out that one's judgement was wrong and the injury inflicted was undeserved. The beauty of Satyagraha is that it can never go wrong. Self-suffering is bound to win when the cause in just. Where it is unjust, it automatically fails by its own inherent weakness, but it will have caused no harm to any one but oneself. There may be some incidental and unavoidable injury to others involved in the methods of Satyagraha; but the real objective is not this, and it should be always avoided or reduced to the minimum.

The psychological change in the party doing wrong is not sought to be attained by any loss or injury inflicted on him, but rather by the inherent force of one's own suffering. The Satyagrahi believes that human nature is essentially good and must respond to suffering, and his persistent appeal to the natural force is based on this faith. It is a great mistake to believe that the success of Satyagraha is to follow from the injury or loss caused to the wrong-doer. It is this misapprehension that leads to many an erroneous plan in the name of Satyagraha. Injury may be unavoidable, but to the extent that it is caused, it is a source of weakness and retards the effect of Satyagraha. In proportion to the elimination of injury to the opposing party, the suffering undertaken by oneself avoids hatred and anger, and the effect of Satyagraha is accelerated.

The struggle which the Mavlas are engaged in is from all accounts a just one. But it is one demanding the exercise of all the moral strength of which the registers are capable. Unless the methods employed are kept absolutely free from all taint and impurity, the results will be disastrous. It is necessary, therefore, that those who guide and advise the registers should strictly guard the fundamental principles of Satyagraha against all misinterpretation and misunderstanding.

Mr. Bapat's extension of Satyagraha may be nothing more than an attempt at philosophical synthesis. But we cannot be too careful in the conduct of great and severe struggles in keeping within the strict limits of non-violence, the fundamental condition of success in Satyagraha. When Satyagraha was started at Mulshi in April last year, Gandhiji wrote:

> "The duty of the Satyagrahis is written in letters of gold. There can be no Satyagraha in an unjust cause. Satyagraha in a just cause is vain, if the men responsing it are not determined and capable of fighting and suffering to the end; and the slightest use of violence often defeats a just sense. Satyagraha excluders the use of violence in any shape or farm, whether in thought, speech or deed. Given a just cause, capacity for endless suffering and avoidance of violence, victory is a certainty." (C. *Rajagopalachari*)

A Fundamental Error

Judging from what is often spoken and written, one might think that the difference between Mahatma Gandhi's plan of action and the bomb-throwers is that while the latter believed we could be saved by killing Englishmen in India, the former believes that we will achieve our salvation by injuring them in their trade or by making their lives uncomfortable without directly, causing physical injuries on their persons. This conception of Mahatma Gandhi's doctrine is, it should be needless to say, radically wrong Again, it is believed by many that the only difference between Mahatmaji's method and the old constitutional method is that while the latter consisted in begging and protesting and raising a big noise, the former is based on hitting and embarrassing — only no physical weapons should be used. This, too, is a vitally erroneous conception of Satyagraha. The fundamental basis of Mahatmaji's doctrines, as well as of his plans, is that the law of life is love. Human nature, be holds, must respond to love. Hatred, ill-will, tyranny and cruelty are all deviations from the natural law. To put things in the right path, we have only to apply the force of love. If another does you wrong, bear the injury yourself and return good-will. The suffering should be all yours; then, the opponent's heart will melt. The only embarrassment intended by Mahatma Gandhi is the pain arising out of the Constitution of human nature on the sight of a fellow bring's suffering which is called sympathy, or *Hamdardi.* This is the energy on which Satyagraha is based, no energy as true and as potent as electric energy generated in a power station.

If any person does not accept this basic doctrine that every human being is essentially good and must respond it you only know how to reach his heart and undertake suffering, returning good for evil, then there is no common ground between that person and Mahatma Gandhi. There is no use believing that we follow Mahatma Gandhi simply because we go to the prison or strike work, or close shops, or wear Khaddar or withdraw from practice or boycott schools or disobey laws, as and when be directs. All these acts have two effects. In so far as they injure the other party they are unavoidable incidents and to that extent cause anger or ill-will and retard the attainment of our goal. In so far as they bring suffering on ourselves and bring home to the mind of the wrong doer that we undertake that suffering on account of his wrong, they are Satyagrahi processes leading to the purification of the wrong-doer. Our aim and object should be to reduce the evil arising out of the former incidents by special efforts, and increase the letter to the maximum degree attainable.

The best way to attain this is by developing good-will in our hearts while we offer non-cooperation or civil disobedience.

The erroneous conception of Mahatma Gandhi's programme pointed out above is at the basis of many of the suggestions for improvements and modifications of his plans which have, therefore, been rejected. It is also at the root of much of the hostile criticism of his work, from friends as well as enemies. It is enough if a flagrant instance or two are pointed out. Mr. Bapat suggested in a pamphlet that Satyagraha should include the use of physical force and she causing of injury to persons and property, because, he said and perhaps truly believed, that Mahatmaji's non-cooperation is a media-causing injury to the Government and Englishmen. Again, one often bears at Khaddar meetings descriptions of the prospect of hungry and dying families in Lancashire as if that would give joy to our hearts. If Mahatmaji heard such propaganda used in the cause of his Khaddar, he would shudder in pain and anguish of heart. Again, counter-offensives and retaliations by way of mass civil disobedience are all talked of, as if the secret of civil disobedience were the tactical blow or a modified form of violence; forgetting that the essence of civil disobedience is the suffering undertaken and not embarrassment and that the latter should in fact be reduced to the minimum and the former to the maximum in order to produce quickest effect.

(C. *Rajagopalachari*)

Construction but not Cooperation

The *Indian Social Reformer* advises Congressmen to go into the Councils and "work there as well as outside to advance the Bardoli programme which is the only programme before them."

It may be true that the Bardoli Programme is the only programme before non-cooperations, but a programme should not be confounded with, or be carried out at the sacrifice of, principle which is of far more vital importance. How does the *Reformer* propose that we should work in the Councils to advance the Bardoli Programmes? Are we to attempt to get laws passed to further Swadeshi, e.g. by protective measures and subsidies?

Are we to get the Government to recognise national schools? Shall we get laws to compel the admission of the depressed classes to public schools, wells, etc. and attempt to abolish untouchability by legislation? Are we to work in the Councils for the absorption of panchayats in the judicial system? To attempt to state how the other items in the Bardoli programme could possibly be advanced by entering the Councils would amount to burlesque.

Except in the one matter of temperance, attempt to advance the Bardoli Programme by the influence or the power we can acquire by entering the Council's would be a self-contradiction. The constructive programme has its value in the effort and in the self-reliance it involves, and should not become an end in itself, to be attained anyhow. We could not, for instance, agree to the removal of untouchability or to effect the boycott at foreign cloth or to carry out any of the other items of the Bardoli programme by the use of force or by intimidation; no less can we agree to attain these objects by giving up non-cooperation.

Non-cooperation is not to us a "Dead Caronse" nor do we think it is on its "funeral pyre." It is yet the living principle of our politics and will continue to be so as long as it is true that our own cooperation is the measure of our degradation, and that rigorous self-reliance is the only antidote to the process of emasculation that has been going on. For causes known to all and needless to repeat, Mahatmaji suspended the aggressive activities of our movement but it would be a grave error for any one to suppose that non-cooperation has been given up and social reform has replaced it in the non-cooperator's programme.

There is a whole world of difference between social reform on the non-cooperative plan and carried out for the non-cooperator's ends, and social reform carried and effected, with the aid and by the compulsion, of a system with which we should abstain from cooperating. If one believes, honestly, as non-cooperators do, that cooperation in the councils will prolong the question of the present system and therefore add to the degeneration of the nation, then, it is his duty to carry on the Bardoli Programme unaided by the powers attainable through the councils.

(*C. Rajagopalachari*)

Swaraj

The question mixed has been many times answered by Mahatmaji and I can add nothing to what he has written and said on the subject. The Congress creed is perfectly clear. It contemplates a breaking of the British connection if for full national development it becomes necessary. It desires to retain that connection if we can rise to our full height with it. I admit that there are two great impediments for Swaraj within the Empire. The equality which we claim for Indian citizens in the Commonwealth appears to be a fatal impediment, if we judge from the obstinate conduct of the white Colonies of the Empire, and the constitutional impossibility of Imperial interference in such matters. If this spirit of inequality continues, it means separation. The other great impediment arises out of the peculiar situation of India. While Canada, Australia, New Zealand and South Africa may have no foreign politics different from Britain, India cannot but claim that the Commonwealth should not drag her into wars with Turkey or the Muslim-states of Asia or use her resources to humble them.

This claim may or may not be capable of being granted to India as a member of the Commonwealth, but on it depends the possibility of her remaining in it. The idea, that India can never have real freedom within the Empire for the sole reason that the people of India have not the same customs, manners, traditions, religion and language as the other components of the Empire, is as erroneous as the common notion imparted to us in Government schools and through English books that because the people of India are divided into a number of communities with different customs, religions, languages, etc. they can never become one nation or hope to be a free people. If South Africa and its Boer people could accept the domination of the Empire and attain to quality and full freedom in spite of differences in language and nationality, it should be also not impossible, though of course harder, for India to enjoy similar freedom and equality within the Empire.

So long as there are wars in the world, alliances and *enientes* are necessary, and no single nation can stand by itself. Why should free India reject the readymade bond of friendship in which she finds herself if it means nothing dishonourable or detrimental? With the two impediments pointed out above solved, membership in the Commonwealth will mean nothing more than an honourable alliance.

(*C. Rajagopalachari*)

Mahatmaji's Bold and Clear Path

The following is the text of Mr. Rajagopalachari's speech delivered at Nagpur:

> It is really a wonderful thing that a man, in the southern corner of this country should be heard by you with patience as such a late hour — that this vast audience should wait to listen to me knowing that I am compelled to speak in a tongue which they cannot understand. All this wonderful magic has been wrought by one man who is now in prison. He united together all the languages and religions of India. In other countries they have only one language and one religion: but here we have many languages and many religions, but let us hope, one heart. I have heard the legend attributing particular characters to different provinces but I have found in my travels that at bottom all is one. The whole country from the Himalayas to the Cape Comorin is as strong as ever in its affection for and loyalty to Mahatmaji. The people may have fallen in their standard of action but certainly there is no change in their sympathy for his movement. The great population of our country is like an ocean. Just as the ocean retains the same normal level in spite of its waves our people retain their affection towards Mahatmaji.

Government's Challenge

Yet I have to remind you today that Mahatmaji has been imprisoned twelve months ago. You have read the history of India. I too have read it and let me tell you that the last three years are the most glorious in that history for the last thousand years Mahatmaji started this glorious career in our history and it is now in your power to being it to an inglorious end or to continue it.

When Mahatmaji went to prison he went in the full confidence that the 300 millions of his countrymen will act as one man and there will be no differences. He wrote at that time that be hailed his imprisonment with pleasure because the world would have an opportunity to see that the people of India stood on their own legs. He was glad for the opportunity to disprove the charge that it was the mere influence of his personality that was guiding them. Mahatmaji declared, when he went to prison, that the people would carry on the work. The Government imprisoned Mahatma Gandhi and said "we will now easily subdue the people." Which will you prove to be the truth? If we do not perform our duties, if we hear speeches and forget them the next day, if we do not put on Khadi the Government's word will be true.

There is no use in our being tall and strong men and women if at the first attack we give in. If you told any man coming from some remote part of the world that the country holds within its boundaries 300 millions of men and women and that it has been possible for an alien Government to imprison a man loved by all these, he would not trust his eyes and ears. He would be bewildered to know that for twelve months we have been eating, drinking and making marry. If you only cost yourselves forward to the time where we shall have finished our brief periods of life, and our children would look behind to our own achievements, you would realise that they would be ashamed of their forefathers. I know that many a brave boy and girl, when they come across a passage in our history telling us how our forefathers fled from a battlefield hang their heads in shame and wish they could draw over the passage a black line and deface the passage so that nobody may read it. In our sloth and neglect we are writing indelible records of shame and degradation which our own children will have to draw a black line across.

(Here the speaker dwelt briefly on the forthcoming anniversary of Mahatmaji's incarceration).

Still Time

We have lost much time but we have plenty of it yet if we only use it. Government has locked Mahatmaji in prison but we have the keys in our own hands. It rests with us to use them. If the Government opens the prison gates and lets him out what would be the reason? If it were certain that we were as weak and powerless as we appear to be; that we were worthless and that Mahatmaji would be of no use to us; if it felt that the movement is dead beyond recovery. Government would let him out tomorrow. But the Government is under no such delusion. We are glad that Government still thinks that we will be a great source of danger if Mahatmaji is let out. We must open the prison gates ourselves.

Become Mad after Freedom

This movement that has been started by Mahatmaji can never die until we reach the goal. If we take any backward steps the people may stand it for 2 or 3 months, but we are bound to have soon to revert to the bold and clear path of Mahatmaji. Because it is the only way to revive the health of the nation. So long as the people remain clever and not mad, to long will they be governed as they are row. We must change the manner of our thought and action. When Sita was lost, Rama did not rest patient, but went mad and thought of nothing but her recovery. Damayanti too became mad when she lost Nala. Is not our freedom dear to us as Sita and Nala to Rama and Damayanti? But I forget that by year of slavery we have lost the very use of freedom. As a blind man does not know what light is and as a deaf man does not know what music is; we do not know what freedom is. Like birds born inside a cage, we do not know what is to fly in the air and greet the Sun. A man came to give us back that lost sense of freedom. We have neglected that man. People who have forgotten how to pray to the unseen God make an idol and offer their prayers through it. We are unable to understand freedom but there is Mahatmaji through whom by our sacrifice we realise and worship Freedom.

What is the examination to which the country will be subjected during the next two months? We have to proclaim to the world that we all stand for the Congress. Just think for a moment, if after this speech of mine, tomorrow you all enrol yourselves as members this year what will be the effect throughout the country and on the Government? Yet this is so easy that you can perform it with the short space of an hour. If only the necessary forms had been here and volunteers could go out among you; you would gladly sign your names and pay the four annas. I hope tomorrow you will flood the Congress office and enlist in large numbers.

"Do Your Duty"

Let us forget the country, for a moment; let us forget for a moment that we are citizens of a nation fighting for freedom. Would you not have signed a monster petition praying for the release of Mahatmaji if it could secure our purpose? I am sure you would have. But such a step today would be a disgrace. I want you to express your passion to free Mahatmaji in a brave and noble manner. I want you to formulate a petition of a very different kind — a petition of brave and solid action. If all the adult population had realised this duty, Mahatmaji would have been set at liberty long ago. I want each one of you not to think of what others think or do not think, or do or do not do, but individually you do your duly. Do not continue in the habit of saying "This country is doomed. It will never rise to do its duty", but look to yourself each individual. It is your religious duty. As you go to a temple and each one individually among a multitude of worshippers, offer prayers and speak to your God, you are required to offer prayers in the form of sacrifice at the altar of freedom.

The Congress is also in need of funds and it cannot be expected to keep the movement alive without funds. It is the only body that is fighting for Swaraj. Within these two months we have to give twenty-five lakhs. This is the minimum required for the work to be done. Do you know how much the Government have budgeted for their expenditure this year? The amount is in so many crores that I may well leave out a few. They want 200 crores of this year and we are to pay it. The Congress asks not for a hundred crores, not ten crores, not even one crore but just a quarter of a crore. If you divide the amount among the various provinces and districts, you will find that Nagpur has a very small share which even one honest merchant here can pay.

But it is neither good nor proper that one person should pay. All of you must contribute your share to it. It will show your undaunted loyalty to the Congress and trust in it. Unless we help the Congress how can you expect it to bring Swaraj. Before the 18th of March I beg that each of you should pay your mite and induce your friends to do like-wise. Your very waste-money for a month would be enough to fulfil your quota. What for instance, you would pay for tobacco to injure your health in one month would be more than the sum required of Nagpur.

The Crore well Spent

So many ask, What has happened to the one crore subscribed the year before last? Even if you yourself do not believe the charge contained in the question, I want you to be able to answer it. It was spent to give political education in the course of one year to a country which had lost, the sense of freedom. With this one crore Mahatmaji was able to make his country, 2,000 miles long and 2,000 miles broad, reverberate with the cry of Swaraj. If you only would look to the Government records you would see how many crores were spent to give you a worthless education — an education which taught a few of you to read and write and that too not well but which killed your spirit of independence. What it failed to achieve during the course of so many years and with many crores of rupees Mahatmaji achieved with this one crore in one year. Any other nation would have given many times the amount for the object achieved. Friends, tell those who talk about this crore that it was spent thus. But there are other things also which the crore has achieved. Put your hands on your khaddar shirts and coats and you will see what I mean. It is due to the crore that we are all wearing Khaddar today. If you had not worn Khaddar, crores of rupees would not have been lost to Lancashire and saved for India. Two thousand million yards cloth went out of Lancashire's Indian trade last year. We are told that 500 millions per year have been lost permanently. Even if it had not been due entirely to Khaddar. I say the crore was well spent. If Lancashire could spend a crore and get back the trade it would readily do it. I want you to tell me whether in view of this, in your opinion, the crore was well spent or wasted.

I want you to endorse this assurance by paying twenty-five lakhs again to keep up the institution which is responsible for carrying on the movement. You will have to do it in any case before the close of two months. But I ask you to do it before the 18th so that you may have something to offer at the altar of Mahatmaji's memory on the anniversary of his imprisonment. If any volunteers come to you, I ask you to receive them well. Take them to your relations and friends and make their task easy and pleasant. Do not argue over differences of opinion. There is no time for that. The Congress has accepted the challenge which the

Government has thrown. If it fails before the 18th it has time up to the 30th April. If we fail to fulfil this quota, the Government may well deride us and look upon us with contempt.

One thing more before I sit down. Great sacrifices are demanded only of a very few. From all others I crave active sympathy and help. I am sure you will not reject this demand of mine for I know that as long as an obscure man like myself can come in the name of the Congress and convene such a great meeting there is hope for the country.

Worse than Jallianwala

We wonder if the people can find time out of their daily worries — arising out of the general atmosphere of inertia in most parts of the country, and out of the divided counsels and the nauseating sectarian squabbles that poison the national life of today, we wonder if this worried public can find time to follow other happenings in the country. If they did, would they sit still stricken with inertia? Do not the Sikhs and the Muslims and the Hindus in the Punjab, if not in other parts of India know anything of the little tragedies enacted in the Punjab, if not in broad daylight as in the Jallianwalla or *Guru-ka-Bag* days, at least within sufficient knowledge of the ever-vigilant Shiromani Gurudwara Committee? The chroncile published daily and hourly by this Committee reveals a reign of unbridled lawlessness which no amount of council controversies or *Shudhi* activities can overshadow. We reproduce here some out of the numerous crimes perpetrated in that unfortunate province.

Press communique No. 432 says: "On 20th February another 500 Akalis are reported to have been transferred from Attock Jail. Mr. Saint G. A. Beaty of the Guru-ka-Bag fame was specially requisitioned from Rawalpindi and placed in charge of the operation. On the arrival of the first Jatha of 100 Akalis at the gate of the Attock fort jail, 2 Akalis who happened to be there greeted them with 'Sat Sri Akal'. This evidently was too much for the nerves of the gallant police officer. He first treated the erratic couple of Akalis to a generous shower of hunter cuts with his own saintly hand and then ordered his equally gallant subordinates to throw the Akalis into the Indus. No sooner was the chivalrous order given than obeyed. Propelling them by sheer first-pushes the policemen took the submissively non-violent Akalis to the edge of the river bank and there hesitated for a minute. A *Namak halal* Subinspector at once reminded them of their promise to unquestioningly obey orders and commanded them to carry out the saint's bidding. The unresisting Akalis were dumped into the river and got their clothes drenched. As they swam back to the river bank, they were ordered to be shut up in the fort and the order was obeyed then and there.

We have reproduced the note verbatim, which if we take out one or two needless adjectives seems to be free from exaggeration.

There is communique No. 433 which is full of tales of draggings and pullings by *keshas*, and kicks with boots by the Superintendent of Police. Milltan. "Prayer books and extracts from the scriptures were forcibly taken away from the Akalis by the Superintendent of the jail and trampled upon by the constables. All this was serenely watched by half a dozen officers present on the spot." And still more from the same communique; "There is hardly any watertap that is in working order and yet steps are not taken to repair them. Cries of "water" continue proceeding from the grinding mill celts even during night."

Here are a few samples of lawful lawlessness indulged in the course of realisation of fines. A zaildar, and some policemen went to the house of Bhai Santosh Singh, who was sentenced to 9 months' imprisonment and a fine of Rs. 150. His mother was not in the house. "They broke open the locks and took away thing they found." (Comm. No. 437)

Bhai Tehl Singh son of Mian Singh was sentenced to 3 months' simple imprisonment without fine. "Yet a sum of Rs. 100 has been realised from the property of Bhai Hazara Singh who has nothing to do with Bhai Tehl Singh. Bhai Hazara Singh has got land on contract from Bhai Surain Singh, nephew of Bhai Tehl Singh."

Bhai Kartar Singh *alias* Ajit Singh of village Kasail was sentenced to 2 years' imprisonment and a fine of Rs. 100 by Lala Amarnath magistrate. "He was released on consideration of age. Recently a line of Rs. 200 has been realised from him on the basis of a warrant issued against another man of the village named Bhai Ajit Singh who was sentenced to 9 months' imprisonment and a fine of Rs. 200".

"What surpasses all", says Communique No. 438, in this tragedy of fines is the case of Bhai Hazara Singh, son of Bhai Jhand Singh of Narli, District Lahore. He was arrested under section 108 in the early days of Guru-ka-Bag affair and was sentenced at Kasur to one year's imprisonment. It is strange that on 3rd February a warrant was issued from the court of Mr. Banwarilal, Magistrate Amritsar for the realisation of a fine of Rs. 150 from Bhai Attar Singh. All the *lambardars* and watchmen of the village testified to the effect that he had never been sentenced at Amritsar, and yet a second warrant was issued on 25th February. Not satisfied with this a third warrant bearing the same name is said to have been issued from the court of Nawab Aslam Hayat Khan, Magistrate Amritsar to realise a fine of Rs. 200."

Here is the harrowing account of the indignities and cruelties perpetrated on Bhai Randhir Singh in Nagpur Jail. Having refused to hold out his hands, he was deprived of the privilege of cooking his own food, of his clothes, turban and shoes.

Bhai Randhir Singh resolved to go without food. "For about 8 or 9 days", the chronicle records, "Bhai Randhir Singh was without food and then an English officer began to apply all sorts of cruel methods to force the Bhai saheb to take food. This Englishman after trying to thrust the food into the south of the prisoner with the help of filthy abuse came to apply fisticuffs and kicks. The helpless prisoner cried out to a policemen who was looking on, but he did not help. Bhai Randhir Singh complained to the Superintendent but it was of no avail. Then the Jailor and his assistant came with a few others and tried to apply anema simply to disgrace and trouble him. He protested saying that he had no complaint about digestion, that he had nothing inside him. But without listening to him the thing was done after knocking him down against a wall, which made him insensible. Next day they threatened to insult his religion if he did not submit. They threw him on the ground and securing him with handcuffs attempted to feed him with milk with a rubber tube. His mouth was forcibly opened, and it was not until a few teeth were broken that some milk could be forced in." This was thrown out with the result that his *keshas* and beard were pulled and after "being kicked and beaten he was left half-dead." And so on and so forth until a member of the jail committee is on a visit, and things change for the better.

It should be observed that all these communiques are only signed by the General Secretary Gurudwara Committee, Amritsar. No successful attempt has yet been made to contradict them. It is useless to say anything more on happenings which may be said to be of daily occurrence. The people may be dead enough to put up with this. But surely Nature is not so dead.

Behar the province which had produced Babu Rajendra Prashad, was beautiful to see. We may well judge a tree by its fruits. The unfaltering faith and the consequent strength mark this province out. Some of the districts have such a number of strong and brave workers that it is no wonder that in village organisation this province stood first.

We were somewhere near Mokammah Ghat. The train stopped at a station and as usual there was a crowd round our compartment. An old woman, dressed in clothes that showed that her daily lot was hunger and hard work, made her way to our compartment and got in. She went straight to Devadas, "Is this Mahatmaji's boy?" she asked, and with a mother's bands she stroked his head and caressed his face after placing her gift for the cause at his feet. Even the rustic crowd was moved at the scene. "Is Mahatmaji kept in jail by the Government?" she asked of the son, and burst into an imprecation. Of course she knew about the imprisonment already. But she wanted the actual provocation to find outlet for the word of anger. She left the carriage having given Rs. 106 for the fund; it was all her savings probably for many a weary day.

(C. *Rajagopalachari*)

Speech at Patna

Below is the speech that Mr. Rajagopalachari delivered at Patna:

> "Till yesterday we spoke at various places looking forward to the celebration of the great anniversary.

Now we have come to the other side of the hemisphere, leaving behind the light that has led us so far. But we all know that the sun will continue to give light whether it is in front of us or behind us. Whether we look forward to fulfilment of duties or look backward to the promises and pledges we have made, our action must be guided by our resolve. Till yesterday we all looked forward to the anniversary to remind us of our duties. Today I want you to remember the pledges you have given, to help you in the work you have undertaken. I do not think that a race noted for keeping its pledges and promises as the Hindu race will not fulfil them. We are a nation known in the times of the Greek travellers as a nation that did not want any document or agreement to keep its pledges. We never needed any witness for our promises. We are a nation which called the sun and the moon as our witnesses. I, therefore, feel that till the goal is reached we should keep fast to our pledges. The anniversary was not an ordinary demonstration. It was a proof of the grim determination of the people to carry on the struggle. Never before in the history of any country, had any nation expressed its grim determination in the manner you did on the anniversary day. There were eyes keenly watching whether the movement was really dead or whether there was still fire burning in the ashes. The statesmen and military commanders that governed India are keenly watching us. For they are able to perceive the strength of the struggle more than Indians themselves. A movement inaugurated by a great military commander like Mahatmaji can only be understood by other great military commanders like him. Government knows that they must keep Mahatmaji in jail though everybody swears that the movement is dead and that it is perfectly safe to release him. The Government knows very well that it is not dead and that it needs only to be strengthened. Even a child knows that if the movement is dead there can be absolutely no harm in releasing

Mahatmaji. But Mahatmaji is still in jail and that is sufficient proof that the movement is not dead or weak. Even in your own province of Behar and Orissa there is a partial confession of this truth by the Government. One of the members of the Government said that the Government was not dead but was simply disorganised. So long as the patient is not dead it is in your hands not only to cure him but to make him strong. The duly of a doctor is greater when he is told that the patient is alive and can very well be saved. Therefore, it is our first duty to look to the patient. There can be no better news than that a member of the local Legislative Council asked the Government to release all political prisoners, and that the Government refused to do so. The request of the councillors to release all the political prisoners, however, pleasant to the weak minded, was a confession that the movement was weakening. For apparently, they thought, the Government would be safe if these prisoners were released. But when the Government refused to concede their request it showed that it was not safe to release the prisoners.

I remind you of your duties and their fulfilment. I ask you, first, to look to your organisations and put them on a strong basis. Every Congress Committee, whether in a village, in a district, or a subdivision, must stand as strongly as the Government organisations. Our duty is to see that even as a Thana or any other Government office is strong in its place so our Congress Committee should be. All the talk of the weakness of the movement is due to one and only one reason as we could see everywhere in our tour in the country. There is no faltering in the loyalty of the people. There is no want of affection on the part of the masses towards the Congress. Wherever we went we found the same absolute faith in the Congress amongst the masses as existed before. There was no feeling of disappointment or despondency amongst the thousands of people whom we met, wherever we went. Some of the workers were disappointed and not the people. On examination, it will be found, that the chief cause of the despondency among the workers is due to their having come to the end of their material resources on which they were depending no long. You know what a siege means. When an army surrounds a fort, it does not fight with the men inside the fort. It simply stops food and water being taken inside the fort and thus compels those inside the fort to surrender. Likewise poverty has besieged our workers and we are disappointed and despondent. Government knows its battle and is simply waiting for poverty to break workers' patience. But all know that if the people resolve to be generous, the movement will be up again and Government will have to fight a grim battle. If your brothers were imprisoned in a fort and if they were about to surrender to the enemy, I ask, will you not take food and water to them? The majority of the workers hail from classes which do not know what poverty means. They are now feeling the pinch of it and are ashamed of begging. Their silent patience is now coming to an end. And unless you come to their succour, the Movement may break down. If you want your organisations to be strengthened you must realise your duty and come forward with money. Your brethren the thousands of workers are ashamed to beg. But we stand here shamelessly to beg, because our country is so poor. It is not begging, ray friends, it is taxation, if only we had Swaraj. But because we have no power to govern ourselves taxation becomes begging. You must know how Government is begging for two hundred crores from the country. They are begging this sum today of the members of the Legislative Assembly. Of this 200 crores that they are begging, more than 60 crores is for spending over the army which is kept to govern this country. They are not only begging, but are preparing to raise a loan because begging will not suffice. When Government is prepared so shamelessly to beg and to raise a loan why should we not beg? It is not the workers that are begging of you. It is the Congress that begs this sum of you. It is in your hands to look upon your workers as beggars or as tax-collectors. If we bad liberty, if we were a free people, these beggars should have gone to you as tax-collectors.

In any free country every tax is a voluntary donation. It is only in a slave country that taxation becomes involuntary payment. The day you learn to tax yourselves voluntarily that day you will be near the gate of freedom. I have sufficiently explained to you, I think, the necessity, the urgent necessity, of collecting money; and I hope all will cooperate with us to make this Congress organisation go on.

I know that there is a strong temptation to know the accounts of the income and expenditure of last year. I know that every time, the Congress wants money some mysterious person comes out with the condemnation of past years' expenditure and immediately we find leading articles in some newspapers about the danger of any further payment. But I hope you will not sit down as auditors and spend your times in bookkeeping while you are fighting an enemy. If you have spent one crore you have achieved an amount of work which could not have been achieved by spending even hundred crores I would ask of any businessman how many crores he would spend in advertisements to hit Lancashire to the extent our movement has done. I would ask of proprietors of any tea estate whether they have spent more or not to push on their sales in this country. If I had to give a contract of advertisement for Khaddar, I think, I shall have to spend more than one crore to achieve what we have achieved within one year Khaddar means 60 crores and to spend 1 crore for the spreading of the knowledge of Khaddar which will save us 60 crores is too little even from the business point of view. Any military ruler will say how much he will have to spend for gaining the affection of thirty crores of people. And to spend one crore to spread disaffection among them is nothing. Leaving alone the merchant's and commander's points of view, I ask if 1 crore of rupees is much from the point of view of a social reformer, for what has been achieved in the matter of removal of untouchability and cementing of brotherly and cordial relations between the different communities? I ask further if 1 crore is too much for giving political education to the people who have been sleeping so long? Government is engaged in giving literary and political education to the people and how many crores has it spent? But with what result?

Has it been able to achieve the result which the 1 crore of rupees has achieved? With 1 crore Mahatmaji gave political education from which Swaraj will spring like a plant from the seed. This crore, therefore, has done so much work within such a short time. As to the accounts, I would ask you, to look at them and audit them after we have achieved Swaraj. You may bring all your leaders to book and confiscate all their property. But in the meantime I want you to act up to the solemn promise you have made. Your first duty, therefore, is to unite your pursestrings and bring life to the disponet. That alone will be enough to make the heart of the Government beat quicker. I hope, before we disperse, you will have given whatever you have with you, as a symbol of your love, affection and loyalty to the Congress and the resolve to make good the solemn promises made by you. I do not think that you have all assembled here to listen to me and then go home and think later. I know that you have not brought much with you.

But I want only a symbol of your affection. As for national resolve you have had sufficient sign and proof of it. Men and women have come forward each with a rupee at least which perhaps is more valuable to him than thousands to others. If we want Swaraj our organisation must be strong. We want men loyal to the Congress. The Congress has not been enrolling members this year in such numbers as it did last year or the year before last. It is necessary to enrol more members if you want to show that your affection for Mahatmaji continues to be the same as before and if you want to show that the Congress is a living organisation. I know it was thought once that it was not necessary to enrol members. It was considered that every adult, male or female, was a member of the Congress whether he paid four annas or not. Although I also thought like that I consider that the present rule to enrol members should continue for some time more. And it is necessary to have such members in large numbers. It is not right that we should allow Mahatmaji to be in jail, by not doing such a little work as the enrolling of members. It may be too much to give a rupee; but I ask, is it difficult to give four annas and show your love for the Congress and Mahatmaji? Or are you so confused with arguments of parties, I ask, that you do not know whether you should be members or not? There are volunteers waiting to register your names and I hope you will register in large numbers.

April 30 is fixed for the fulfilment of the Gaya programme as to men and money. Wherever we go we find that the work of enrolling volunteers and collecting has just begun. I hope you will realise your responsibility of completing the programme by the 30th of April. Otherwise the solemn promise mode at Gaya will remain unfulfilled. I hope the people of Behar will not wait for me and Rajendra Prashad to ask them for it. And you will have to give your quota by the 30th of April. If we fail in this, it will again open the period of controversy and then some more time will be wasted. If you want to be saved from this criminal waste of time you must fulfil your share. This year again you will have to put a number of men into prison so that the people may not go to sleep. If you do not do that your work will be tenfold more difficult next year.

We have got to put men into prison to continue our glorious record. We have to put our heroes in jail to show that we prefer jail to slavery. We have to put our brethren in jail to show that ours is not a mere gambler's desire for Swaraj, not the reformer's desire for reform, but it is a dying man's desire for life. Like a drowning man's struggle to get to the shore, like a thirsty man's desire for water, like a hungry man's for food, to must our desire for Swaraj be. But you may ask, 'Are we really drowning'? Why then I will tell you this. I do not know whether we are all drowning. But it is a fact that our Budget showed a deficit of 100 crores during the last 5 years. Since the war began our debts have increased by 300 crores. We all know that 270 crores were spent not in irrigation or any other productive project but absolutely on unproductive things. I know that for the last few years the Government which was called paternal was spending more than it was able to get from the country. But I ask why should this nation spend more than it is able to get? Because it spent every year 60 crores over an army which would not have been necessary if we had Swaraj. Then people would not have lived in fear of Government and Government in fear of people: and there would have been no necessity of spending this 60 crores.

If they required an army for defending themselves against invaders they would have trained the people left them to defend their country when there was any necessity. That is a fortunate nation which has no

> need to keep a standing army. But if it is not done so, it is because the Government thinks it will not be able to exist. That is why the Government has to keep an army and the people have to tax themselves for it. That is why the poor man has to pay more for salt, sugar, and matches than what he can afford. Are you not convinced that we are all drowning? But reason will not convince us. It is only the instinct of freedom that will save us. Never before did any nation know of such a clear weapon as the one which Mahatmaji has given us. If you do not want to allow this weapon to nut you must keep it active. We have no fear of Behar, united and sympathetic as it is. I believe that Behar will lead the movement in future. I am not flattering. I judge the tree by its fruit such could leaders as Behar has produced be possible if the people were not so. I hope you will fulfil your quota of men and money soon today or tomorrow. I wish to remind you again that you should not go away from here with any money that you have with you. I have no shame to beg of you. But it is not we that beg. It is your country and mother, your future Government, that is begging of you.

Unworthy Squabbles

The following paragraphs are called from C. Rajagopalachari's speech at Ajmer:

> We are here in the centre of the present so-called struggle about the conversions. This struggle I tell you is not really a struggle between Hinduism and Islam at all. It is not possible that in these days of mutual understanding of each other's religion there can be any real struggle between Hinduism and Islam. The greatest truth which Hinduism teaches to its followers is that all ways lead to the same heaven. There can be no possible doubt over this point in the mind of any one who has studied the Bhagavad Gita. Indeed, as I understand it, it is wrong for a Hindu to

go and interfere with any man's religious convictions, and I do not think that in these days when Muslims have better understood Hinduism that they bear the same attitude towards Hinduism today as they once bore towards idolatry in general.

The present disturbance is, as I understood, due to the consciousness of weakness, of each party in its own mind, and not really to love of religion. The Hindu is afraid that be it politically weak and the Muslim is afraid that he is numerically weak and hence these mutual attempts at gaining numbers. How can we increase our strength by mutual adjustment when all our strength is wanted against a common enemy? While the Hindu believes that he will become stronger than the Muslim or the Muslim believes that he will become stronger than the Hindu, both fail to sec that they are weaker before the common enemy.

As far as I have seen in my experience it is not possible really to convert a Muslim to Hinduism or a Hindu to Islam. It is only possible to convert people who are doubtful and who are not a strength to either religion.

I know also that no force or fraud is being used. For I know that our beneficent Government will prevent force. As a matter of fact we imagine we are working under strength of Hinduism. But really, we are working under the shameful guarantee of peace which the police station gives us. We take license from the police station that we may go to breach our religion and that our brother thought he is angry may not come and be at us. It is under that sort of license that we have to breach. It is true that we do not take license in writing but every act that we do is really done under such license. On any day the Magistrate can serve us with a notice that in such and such a place we cannot go to preach Hinduism. And on that day we are bound to stop preaching our vaunted Hinduism. So also any Muslim preacher who goes to make Muslims of Hindus goes under such license from the Government and when any Government Magistrate thinks fit he may also be stopped from preaching his religion.

If we tried to get Swaraj by force we might be afraid of force and therefore, minorities should be afraid of majorities. But we are training ourselves in a discipline which makes the numerically weak as strong as the big. The weakest of our communities will be able to enforce its influence on our society under Swaraj. Not even the scavenger need despair but they will be able to command terms under the Swaraj Government. If we ask seven crores of Muslims not to be afraid of twenty crores of Hindus, is it not a shame that twenty crores of Hindus should be afraid of seven crores of Muslims? If twenty crores of Hindus are afraid that 7 cores of Muslims may become 8 eight crores. I am afraid, I cannot conceive of such a nation being brave and able to rule India. It is merely a confession of weakness, and not real political effort. What is the history really of true religion? It is a history of sacrifice. But secret political quarrels do not make up religious efforts. Where do you get most encouragement from for this work of Hindu-Muslim dispute? That will indicate to you the real course of encouragement. This Government has succeeded in setting Muslims quarrelling with Hindus over posts and offices, in the Punjab. You do not really get help from people who are bent upon religion but from people who are out really for posts. I appeal, therefore, with all the earnestness I am capable of to my friends and leaders here not to go on with this quarrel.

I am told by some that Muslims do not care for Swaraj, but only care for the Khilafat. But if you were true politicians you should know that the Khilafat question is greater than Swaraj. Swaraj is only the right to govern India, but Khilafat is the right to control

England in its foreign affairs. Is if not a greater thing to have Swaraj and control over foreign affairs than to have Swaraj only? We cannot get Khilafat restored before we get Swaraj, because the Khilafat is greater than Swaraj. If we are able to alter the treaty between England and Turkey it follows that we rule ourselves. Some people believe that the Khilafat question will be closed with the Angora treaty and that thereafter the Muslims will give up the fight for Swaraj. This is really because we Hindus are ignorant of the Khilafat question. What is the Khilafat question? The most important thing is the freedom of Jazirat-ul-Arab. It is true that nationalist Turkey might be Forced to agree to a treaty. But Islam in India cannot agree to a treaty unless Arabia, Palestine and Syria are free from non-Muslim control. And the will be done only when India is strong enough to wrench Swaraj from England. I ask, therefore, my Hindu brethren not to be nervous about these matters. After we get Swaraj I promise you a fair field for all tournaments and wrestling. But now the enemy is seeking to enter the *akhada* and help one against the other. If we want really to wrestle we must first make sure to buy our *akhada*, that akhada is Swaraj. Let us, therefore, first finish this first duty and than look to other things.

On Cow Slaughter

Thanks to God that He gave us more wisdom and less ambition! We desire to 'strengthen' Hinduism. And after our latest efforts, today Hinduism is weaker than ever it was during the last few years. Hinduism has lost the support which it had secured from Islam by sacrifice and love, and has earned the positive ill will of thousands of Muslims. We had been silently winning convert to the universal creed of love, the vital part of Hindu Dharma. Islam in India had begun to look on old animosities and misunderstandings as ugly dreams of a night that was over. It had begun to identify itself with the single truth. Never before was a more successful silent conversion. But now in trying to win a few men to the forms of Hinduism, we have lost or are fast losing all our previous conquests of the spirit. Gaining in form we are losing a thousands-fold in substance.

We seek to save the cow. But the vision of the coming slaughter is before my eyes, and who can say that we have not been the cause of it all, by our foolish pride and our mistaken attempts to strengthen ourselves. We may have plans of our own. But the moist eves of thousands of dumb creatures led to slaughter not as symbols of sacrifice, but in anger against us during the next Id will turn their piteous gaze at us; and if we have a conscience, we would feel their silent reproach.

We will have to admit before the Father of all that it was we that brought them to torture and death by our unwisdom and uncalled for arrogance of creed. We indulge in hatred and we suffer; but the unfortunate cow suffers more. If we wake up not soon, our folly will flow red with cruelty.

Why do I reproach only the Hindu folly, and why do I not point my finger of complaint at the Muslim for his lapses from the right path? Because I am not so pure. I am not so strong as I must be before claiming to chastise him. I am a Hindu and have a claim and birth-right to speak harshly (in love) to my Hindu brethren. But the man who had by his love and sacrifice and work earned the right to chastise all without distinction of creed or race or community is a prisoner in a solitary cell and India cannot have him in her hour of need.

Unless God give us the courage and the wisdom to see the truth and be led by our peerless leader from inside his prison, breaking down by our loyally and our affection the bars and gates erected by cruel authority.

(C. *Rajagopalachari*)

We Cannot Submit

I cannot understand the contention that the resolution adopted by the All India Congress Committee does not violate the principle embodied in the resolution of Gaya Congress in regard to boycott of Councils. It entirely nullifies the Gaya Congress resolution, whose primary purpose was to defeat the elections of this year. The mandate of the Congress was a positive direction to effect the boycott. On the other hand the Committee's resolution if accepted would make a boycott impossible. It actually recommends a course which will result in the country voting for candidates on the ground that they are Congressmen. The Committee's resolution is, therefore, in flat defiance of the Congress. The present Working Committee has issued a statement that the mandate of the Congress, maintaining the boycott of Councils, remains untouched. It is futile to claim that the Congress resolution remains untouched, when every step is taken to make it a dead letter. To curry the mandate to the people, propaganda was absolutely necessary. I think the revolution of the Congress and the All India Congress Committee's compromise cannot stand together except by casuistry. All Congressmen and Committees have to decide whether they will accept the All India Committee's decision or the Congress resolution. I feel that we should prepare and give effect to the Congress resolution, it is not enough merely to stand aside. We must do our best to reaffirm the national rejection of the present system of Government by refusal to participate in the scheme of Reforms imposed upon us.

I feel very strongly that if we accept the All India Congress Committee's resolution there will be no programme before the country next December or afterwards, except consideration of amendments, to the Reforms Act drafted by the new Councils party. I, therefore, think it my duty to resist the All India Congress Committee's decisions and to ask the people to carry out the Gaya resolution. We have been taken from step to step in a downward course. The Councils party in the Congress did not content themselves with propaganda inside the Congress, but actually revolted. We were, thus, forced to accept the revolt as a fact and make terms with the rebels.

Now in December we will be forced to consider, amend and adopt the Council programme of the rebel party. We must stop this downward career somewhere. We must reject the All India Committee's decision and choose to be loyal to the Congress. I can understand that some provinces on account of particular conditions prevailing, may not undertake the work of the boycott of Councils; but we cannot submit to a total reversal of the policy of boycott of Councils throughout India.

(C. *Rajagopalachari*)

Monday

The status decreed for India in the British Empire is one which it is impossible for her to accept. India would rather be segregated as a whole from the Great Empire than allow her children to be untouchables. The Imperial policy has been made clear with brutal frankness by the South African Prime Minister. He has laid down a programme for not only preventing future Indian immigration but for mercilessly wiping out the existing Indian population by depriving them of political and municipal liberties, trade and property rights, and by locating them outside the towns. This programme, there is no doubt, will be carried out without serious objection on the part of the British Government and soon become the general policy of all the British Dominions.

The Kenya decision is the symptom of a great Imperial conspiracy for racial domination. It is a chastisement and a warning from God for our faltering steps. There is no way but grim determination to sacrifice everything and to achieve freedom for India, as the necessary foundation and the first condition of honour and equality abroad. Every Indian irrespective of community or political party should join in the great demonstration on twenty seventh August.

A word to English merchants and traders. The suspension of business called for on the 27th August, is a non-party demonstration. Is it too much to appeal to every Englishman, who is on the side of India in this struggle, to demonstrate his sympathy and non-racial Catholicism by joining in the general demonstration? From the earliest times Indian rulers allowed you perfect freedom to settle and trade among her people, and you are now here by reason of that same hospitality. It is your turn now to support our suffering children abroad and obtain for them the liberties they are asserting in the national demonstration, and suspend your business on Monday the 27th August, when the Indian cars will be all closed. It will be an achievement of good-will, worthy of your best traditions and a noble example to the whole Empire. It will make the straggle a truly religious and irresistible battle. On the other band, if you keep your shops open and compel your employees to attend business in spite of the National *hartal*, the racial character of the Kenya decision will be emphasised and your action will support the White Imperialist policy.

The National *hartal* will be successful as a demonstration of Indian sentiment in spite of English traders in India keeping aloof. Your non-participation will be a defeat of those who still fondly build on Christ. But if even a few among you join, the cause of Religion and Truth will have triumphed.

(C. *Rajagopalachari*)

Address at Karnataka Conference

Following are the extracts from the presidential address delivered at the Second Karnatak Provincial Conference, by C. Rajagopalachari:

> I shall not detain you with any lengthy address. I shall not attempt to exhaust all the topics that engage the public attention, and crave your permission to leave many things untouched. Obviously, late in November, with the coming sessions of the Congress approaching us fast, it is not necessary or advisable to take up questions that must find final solution only in the Indian National Assembly. We cannot, however, at a Conference like this, fail to give public expression to widespread feelings on some topics, at least as an indication of opinion which may be useful in shaping the decisions at Cocanada. But the main business of the Conference is to organise your province for the work before you.
>
> The Congress suspended propaganda on the Council boycott and permitted those who were convinced of the utility of entering the Councils to do so. This Compromise was agreed to as a necessary evil. We deliberately allowed this breach in the fortifications, but we should not let it widen into anything bigger. Respect and tolerance for difference of opinion is an essential feature of all Gandhian methods including non-cooperation. We should not prevent any nun from acting according to his convictions. The Moderates and other cooperators enjoyed this liberty, and the Swaraj Party too had the same liberty. But they wanted something more than respect and tolerance. The hold

of the Congress and the non-cooperation programme over the people was so great that they wanted on our part a suspension of action according to our own conviction, in order that they may have fuller opportunities to put their own beliefs into practice. Rightly or wrongly, for the take of peace this was done. But we cannot be led further into a path which we are convinced is contrary to the essential principles of non-cooperation. We cannot permit the Congress to be identified with the activities of any group inside the legislatures. For the sake of peace we sacrificed a splendid opportunity to organise the most striking national answer to the Salt Tax, to Kenya and to Nabba. For the sake of peace we gave up the golden opportunity of confirming our hold on the voters and to educate them in the Gandhian principles. If we but compare the educative value of the boycott campaign of 1920 with what has been done by the Swaraj Party this year in getting themselves returned we can see how much has been sacrificed by us. But not to regret the past which cannot be recalled, and to turn to the future, let us not allow ourselves to be dragged into the counter programme any further. There is no doubt there is grave danger. We do not know the further programme of the Swaraj Party. They may wait till another general election for getting their full strength, or for the Congress to give up the Triple Boycott. They may join other members in the legislatures and try parliamentary methods from total obstruction down to cooperation euro-discriminate opposition. They may join the Convention proposed by Mrs. Besant and await the fate of a newly drafted Constitution. But the Congress cannot take any part, active or passive, in any of their proceedings. Unless this is rigidly laid down, the Congress would be led to a repudiation of the great non-cooperation programme.

The political situation has been taxing Congressmen to the uttermost point. The dynamic force of the great tide raised by Mahatmaji seems to have spent itself out. Ideals and methods which in the freshness of first promulgation by the great Mahatma roused surging reaction in the hearts of men, seem now by very reiteration to have lost their magic. Everyone wants something new and newer yet every day. The old truths fail to impress men. The great expectations and hopes that beyond up the spirit of the people at first and created an unexampled energy have yielded to a sense of disappointment and failure. Doubt and circumspection reign in the place of courage and hope. Knowledge and experience have made people wiser but also more apprehensive of failure and unwilling to act.

Our enemies whose first shock and surprise at the revolution aided our efforts and encouraged us to push our campaign on with vigour, have now naturally regained their stability and rallied themselves to a more effective defence against us. People, thus, feel that the Government is stronger today than they were during the earlier days of non-cooperation. The situation is in every way more difficult than it was in the first phase of our revolution. Mahatmaji himself found the difficulty developing, and was trying to meet it. No wonder that after be was taken away from us, lesser men find the problem difficult.

While on the one hand those who stand by Mahatmaji's programme are faced with this situation, the forces that never believed in the Gandhian method of suffering and non-violence have taken advantage of the inertia to reassert themselves. Men, who were compelled by the irresistible force of the national upheaval to adopt the Gandhian programme against their real political convictions, have thrown off the oppressive spiritual burden, and are seeking to interpret and shape the programme into a form of political resistance more suitable to their own temper and convictions. The forms are retained but the guiding principle is different. Not love but hatred; not *ahimsa* but violence such as can be put forth; not self-suffering but cleverly organised embarrassments of the enemy with the minimum amount of suffering one our part; this is the easy Satyagraha sought to be interpreted and practised by the new school of practical non-cooperators. To these folk the basic law is that men is a non-spiritual being, essentially selfish and violent, who can only be compelled by pain and punishment to respect others; whereas the whole basis of the Gandhian method is a truth that men is essentially good and spiritual, and responds to love, not to fear; to sympathy, not to punishment.

The German Government too attempted to sustain Gandhism on a basis of hatred and organised embarrassment without the life-giving Gandhian principle of love and suffering. They ordered non-violent resistance on a large scale. The Government supported the population and reduced suffering to a minimum. The attempt was gigantic and seemed near to success, but failed. German resistance was not Gandhian Satyagraha even as the very best mechanical engine is yet not a living thing.

Non-cooperation interpreted as mere political embarrassment is far from Satyagraha, and is foredeemed to failure or relapse into futile agitation, pure and simple. You can no more set up non-violent coercion of this kind into a Irving force, than make a living man out of an electrified mechanism. Such non-violence will be nothing more than second-rate violence and will have to acknowledge its weakness. Only if we have the courage and the faith of Gandhi according to his own interpretation, can we organise his movement as an irresistible battle of the Spirit against the Devil. Suffering, maximum; love of the enemy, true and genuine, the love and pity that filled Christ's eyes with tears as he was fed to Golgotha — not suppressed hatred, finding legal and constitutional shape but feeding its endless vicious circle all the same — without these non-cooperation and Civil Disobedience can be of no avail, indeed cannot live for long, even as political formulae.

In my opinion, the one and only way out of the present situation is the Constructive Programme. Back to Nagpur, as Maulana Mohammed Ali beautifully put it. It may be difficult to light a fire with damp sticks. I do not know how many of you have had experience of the depression and the agony of lighting a fire with damp firewood. To work the Constructive Programme now is very much like such a process. But it must be done if the cooking is to be done and the household kept going. Other programmes may be easier to catch, may lock more glorious, may indeed be necessary now and then, but the first and the main work is this work of construction sketched at Bardoli. Even the Constructive Programme includes more things than can be at once strenuously concentrated upon. I would ask people tomorrow it down for the present in practical working and widen it with progress. Spinning in every house is the one programme I would ask you now to concentrate upon. That the Charkha means non-violence, means removal of untouchability, means saving the people from the curse of drink, means social service, means Hindu-Muslim unity, means the whole of Gandhian Reform, is not a mere figure of rhetoric but is actual realisable fact. The Charkha and active strenuous propaganda for establishing the doctrine of non-violence must be our programme. Do not speak, about the Charkha but actually spin and get people to spin.

Speak boldly, frankly and fully upon non-violence. Non-violence is losing the universality and firmness of conviction which Mahatmaji has secured for it. The assaults upon it are too many. We must re-establish it firmly upon the throne of the people. This is the great secret of Hindu-Muslim unity in India. The creed of non-violence alone can establish Hindu-Muslim unity on a firm basis. No committees of arbitration, no mixed panchayats will achieve much. Readymade panchayats for deciding disputes will only create disputes where none existed before. That is our experience of the establishment of courts and consequent increase of litigation. Allopathic treatment will fail here as elsewhere. The constant insistence and spread of the fundamental doctrine of non-violence is the only remedy and the only hygiene for healthy-communal life and unity. We have been too long treating non-violence as a Gandhian idiosyncrasy in an otherwise practical programme, giving to it a condescending toleration and nothing more. In truth, however, it the bone of the whole programme, that which gives it strength to oppose the violence of the Government and the anarchy of the people, the most vital part of it, without which the rest will crumble to pieces. Peace and order are necessary for our movement. The essential implication of the Gandhian Revolution is that the Dharma of non-violence must be established as a substitute for the Tyranny which is now policing the country. If we do not work for this the tentacles of the existing Government will continue to hold us in its grip.

I have described the difficulties of the situation, and insist on what I deem to be the only right path before as. The difficulty of problem — the stalemate as some would call it — was only to be expected. Unless we won the whole war in our first campaign this second and more difficult phase was inevitable. It need not depress us. This nation wants freedom, will surely want tomorrow even if it is apathetic today; and when it wants freedom, it is bound to have it without doubt. Our difficulties are not in the methods we have employed being unsuitable or inadequate or in the strength of the enemy. It is only the subsiding of the hunger for freedom that makes work difficult. Let us attend to this mainspring of action. The rest will take care of itself. I am convinced that this great nation is bound to see its own good, to see that freedom is life, and that slavery is hunger, misery and death. I am convinced that for our freedom there is no way but the Gandhian way. I am convinced that the nation is bound to take it up tomorrow if not today, and reach its appointed goal, even if it puts it by for a while now. There is no need to feel depressed or sad. Nothing can be more foolish than the assumption that non-cooperation is dead. What is the meaning of the death of non-cooperation? Is it that not having achieved success by it, the Indian Nation will abandon it us a political weapon, or that the Indian Nation abandons the gold of freedom? Neither can ever be true.

I am certain that the Ali Brothers can revive the life, and raise the tide once more at of old. They can take the word of Mahatmaji and speak at with authority scourging the idle and the needless and giving hope and strength to the faithful and the diligent. They can transform the conditions, as no one else can.

I have not referred to many a topic but I should not close without a word about Nabha. Nabha is a belated recrudescence of Dalhousieism. People have been be fooled by phrases like Sovereign British Government, Suzerain Power, Feudatory State, and the like. Indian Princes may be weak, may be deprived of their armies may be controlled and emasculated by treaties, but in law they are free and sovereign like the Government of India. There are many little states in Europe now which are at weak as Hyderabad or Mysore or even as Nabha or Patiala. But a neighbouring Government does not go and claim the right to depose the ruling Government for maladministration. This process is tolerable only in past history as one of the many wrong things that made the British Empire in India, even like the forgery of Clive or the extortions of Hastings. But we cannot tolerate a repetition of it now when we are masters of our own time and its moralities. Whether Nabha voluntarily abdicated or was compelled, is beside the point. He was either forced or scared into abdication. Coercion of one kind or another is there. What kind, does not matter. If there was maladministration, the British Administrator has no greater legal or moral right than you or I to take charge of the State. We must see to it that the people of a State are the only tribunal entitled to dethrone a Rajah and they are the only authority entitled to elect a Board of Regency to govern in the place of a Sovereign dethroned for misrule. The Congress which stands for popular rights and liberties and whose function it to prevent encroachments upon these, must consider the British Administrator's in road into Nabha as but an act of unconstitutional violence and must help to resist it. The Sikhs are fighting it bravely, and when the call for general help comes, there can be no doubt as to our duty.

The battle has spread outside Nabha. War has been declared on the Gurudwara Parbandhak Committee, and the Akali organisation is sought to be crushed. The battle is accepted and India will stand behind the S.G.P.C.

In this connection I must deplore one capital departure from the principles which guided the Akalis hitherto and led them to victory. The Guru-ka-bagh fight was fought according to strict Gandhism without defence in Court and with faith in the efficacy of suffering. The engagement of lawyers and the offer of defence in the present campaign is a retrograde step. Guru-ka-bagh is a victory of Gandhism pure and unsullied. I know the object is not to save themselves from punishment but only to expose the Governmental misdeeds. But truth and suffering are their own propaganda. Defence and the doctrine of suffering are incompatible. Engagement of lawyers, and non-

> cooperation are incompatible. The propaganda and publicity of cross-examination are a fatal substitute far the self-lustre of truth and suffering, even as Parliamentary obstruction is a fatal substitute for non-cooperation.

Great Test

The Congress has given a clear and unqualified mandate for concentration on the constructive programme. It remains now to be seen whether the workers will be loyal to the Congress and carry out the mandate. The next few months are without any exaggeration a critical period in the history of our national movement. Success or failure depends on how we now respond. These few months will be marked by no excitement or demonstration; yet during this period we shall be put to the severest test. Will India really round the banner of non-cooperation again and show that steady work and strength which will at once render foreign domination impossible and plant Swarajya on unshakable foundations? This is the question upon the answer to which the history of our movement now depends.

Our workers, not the most cruel caviller will deny, have these four years stood the most trying strain bravely and patiently, with faith and courage and steadfast purpose worthy of the glorious motherland. Now will they be tried more sorely than ever. It pleases him that rules nations that we should pass through a further ordeal to prove our claim to freedom. Our sufferings and privations are at breaking point. 'How long?' Is the cry of many a weary soul. Gladly would they welcome others taking their place in the struggle so that they might put their knapsacks down and rest their weary flesh for a time. But this cannot be the last and greatest trial we must go through, and if it pleases God successfully.

Constructive work and nothing else now. Other things however tempting, however speedy-looking and attractive shall not take us out of the path of construction which the Congress with one voice has ordered. It is not without deep and anxious thought that such restless souls, spirits that thirst for freedom immediate and quick and would never count the cost like the All Brothers have asked in clear and unambiguous terms for concentration on the constructive programme. No distraction of any kind should be permitted to imperil the quick fulfilment of the programme. The courage of silent work should be given the fullest play.

"I am fed up with three years of politics. Let me go to my village. I shall take a Panchama boy into my house and sit at the spinning wheel. Let me go", said a weary fighter yesterday. "God bless you" said I, "it is the very thing wanted."

Sincere souls instinctively find the truth which logic and reasoning often fail to reach. Now is the time for every Congress worker to be an example to others like my weary friend. Select your village and spend all your time. Let the people see in your action the faith that is in you, that Swaraj shall be won through the charkha even as Bapu promised us. Sit in peace and spin. You need not go to the people, for the people will come to you. In your village you will verily see Swarajya building itself round you like King Arthur's palace built to music.

I look upon the Cocanada Congress as a Congress that opened the Charkha year — a year that will see Bapu's desire fulfilled. Ask no questions about the wage value of spanning, no queries about economics and politics, but get up in the morning and spin religiously for at least a half hour. Do this for the sake of Congress whatever be your politics, whatever be your day's task. To me this is the great message of the Congress that met and dispersed at Cocanada. Set up the Charkha. All the communities touchable and untouchable will gather round it. The sweet music of it will dispel all jealousies and all anger.

"Even if I fall in everything else," I remember the Master saying one day, "if I restore the ancient cloth of India to her people, I shall have fulfilled the mission of my life." Let us prepare this fulfilment as our great welcome to him upon his release from prison.

(*C. Rajagopalachari*)

A Correction

I am reported in most papers to have said in moving my resolution at Cocanada that the Council boycott was alive and not dead, as in the case of schools and courts. A misplaced fullstop has altogether reversed what I said. I said that the triple boycott was alive and not dead. I pointed out that in the case of schools and courts, the boycott was there as long as we sought to maintain national schools and arbitration courts, though we suspended aggressive propaganda. I then proceeded to say in a new sentence, that as in the case of schools and courts even in respect of Councils the boycott was there, because dissociating ourselves from the Government Legislatures we sought to make the Congress a true and powerful national assembly.

An Appeal

Sisters and Brothers! You are aware of the proceedings of the Indian National Congress at Cocanada and the resolution adopted there. I know that many of my comrades were dissatisfied and thought that the resolution was not strong enough. I desire however to point out, that the resolution is clear in respect of four matters: one, the immediate work before us is constructive work; two, the fundamental basis of our programme, viz. the triple boycott is affirmed; three, we have been just and fair to the Swarajya Party; four, we have secured essentials without sacrificing peace.

The Cocanada Congress has given a definite and clear lead to concentration on constructive work. Let us take it up and put forth immediate, sustained effort this year. Let us not allow doubts and disputations to take up our time and energy. The charkha is the one immediate programme. In the fulfilment of this one programme lies our loyalty to Mahatmaji.

(*C. Rajagopalachari*)

Debate at Cocanada

[The debate in the Cocanada Congress centred round the following resolution. Below are the speeches made by Mr. C. Rajagopalachari in moving the resolution and in replying to the debate].

Resolution

This Congress reaffirms the non-cooperation Resolutions adopted at Calcutta, Nagpur, Ahmedabad Gaya and Delhi.

Since doubts have been raised by reason of the non-cooperation Resolution adopted at Delhi with regard to Council entry, whether there has been any change in the policy of the Congress regarding the policy of the Triple Boycott, this Congress affirms that the principle and policy of that Boycott remain unaltered.

This Congress further declares that the said principle and policy form the foundation of constructive work, and appeals to the nation to carry out the programme of constructive work as adopted at Bardoli and prepare for the adoption of Civil Disobedience. This Congress calls upon every Provincial Congress Committee to take immediate steps in this behalf with a view to the speedy attainment of our goal.

C. Rajagopalachari's Speech

In moving the resolution he said:

> The Congress is determined upon non-cooperation. We have to decide what part of the non-cooperation programme we should work during the year, and in what manner we have to act under the leadership of Maulana Mohammed Ali during the next twelve months.

Constructive Programme

We all know what he wants us to do so far as he himself is concerned. He has told you already that we must concentrate on the constructive programme adopted at Bardoli not merely in policy, but in day today work, with strenuous effort. I, therefore, want you to accept that programme of work and if you do so, one part of the proposition that I place before you must be approved. You must decide upon carrying out the constructive work which is part of the non-cooperation programme.

(*C. Rajagopalachari*)

National Movements

Khilafat Movement

During the First World War, Turkey fought on the side of Germany and Austria against the Allied Powers. Turkey was defeated and was forced to accept the Treaty of Severes according to which the Turkish Empire was to be dismembered and various parts of the empire were to be handed over the France and England as mandates.

The Sultan of Turkey, Abdul Majid was also the Khalifa, or the head of the Islamic religion. The Indian Muslims were very much agitated over the dismemberment of Turkish Empire and the future of the institution of Khilafat. In 1919, they organised Khilafat Movement in India demanding the preservation of the integrity of the Turkish Empire and the retention of the institution of Khalifa. Shaukat Ali, and Muhammed Ali, popularly known as Ali Brothers led the movement. Abul Kalam Azad and Dr. Ansari also were prominent leaders.

Mahatma Gandhi considered it a suitable occasion to make a common cause with Muslims and secure their participation in the freedom struggle against the British Government. In 1919, he presided over the All India Khilafat Conference at Delhi. He asked the Hindus to cooperate wholeheartedly in the Khilafat Movement in order to win the Muslims for ever.

In 1920, another conference was held at Allahabad which was attended by Motilal Nehru, Tej Bahadur Sapru and Mrs. Annie Besant. In 1921, in the Khilafat conference held at Karachi, it was declared that Indian Muslims owed allegiance to the Sultan of Turkey and that they would not rest content until the Khilafat demands were completely fulfilled.

But in due course, the movement collapsed. Turkey accepted a revised peace treaty with liberal conditions. The people themselves abolished the office of Khalifa and declared Turkey a Republic. The Indian Muslims were disappointed at such developments.

The Khilafat Movement fomented religious fanaticism among Indian Muslims. It resulted in a series of Hindu Muslim riots in 1926. It also resulted in the Mopla rebellion in Malabar where thousands of Hindus were either killed or converted to Islam. The wisdom of Gandhiji in supporting the Khilafat Movement is a matter of controversy because Khilafat is not a problem of India.

Non-cooperation Movement

The dismemberment of the Turkish Empire in 1920 roused the feeling of the Indian Muslims. The Hunter Committee Report on Jallianwala Bagh massacres created anger and bitterness against the Government in the minds of the people. Mahatma Gandhi found it the most opportuned time to launch a country-wide agitation for the attainment of self-government.

Nagpur Resolution 1920: Lala Lajpat Rai presided over the Congress session at Calcutta in September 1920 in which the Hunter Committee Report was discussed. Mahatma Gandhi appealed to the Congressmen to adopt a policy of progressive non-violent non-cooperation towards the Government to achieve self-government In spite of opposition from several quarters, Gandhiji's resolution was carried.

In the same year, at the annual Congress session held at Nagpur, the resolution on non-cooperation was confirmed with overwhelming support. The aim of Congress was declared as the attainment of Swaraj instead of self-government within the British

Empire. From then onwards the Congress abandoned its constitutional methods and decided to take up agitational approach with peaceful means.

Non-cooperation Movement 1921-22: Gandhiji and Ali Brothers extensively toured the country and propagated the Nagpur resolution. There was unstinted cooperation between the Muslims and Hindus all over the country. Gandhiji chalked out the following programme of non-cooperation:

1. Surrender of titles, honorary offices and nominated seats in local bodies.
2. Refusal to attend government functions and *darbars.*
3. Withdrawal of children from government schools and colleges and establishing national educational institutions.
4. Boycott of law courts by lawyers and litigants and the establishment of state arbitration courts.
5. Boycott of foreign goods.
6. Not to contest the elections to be held by the Government and not to vote in the elections.
7. Not to accept military service in Mesopotamia.

Gandhiji promised the people 'Swaraj within one year,' and as such there was tremendous response to his clarion call. Several prominent lawyers like Motilal Nehru, Dr. Rajendra Prashad, Vallabhbhai Patel and Prakasam Pantulu gave up their lucrative legal practice and joined the movement. Thousands of students boycotted Government schools and colleges. National colleges and universities were founded at various places. Some of them are the Gujarat Vidya Peeth, the Kashi Vidya Peeth, National College at Calcutta and the National College at Masulipatam.

The 'no-vote campaign' received enormous response from the people. Eighty per cent of the people kept aloof from voting in the elections held in November 1920.

The Congress Party decided to raise a Swaraj Fund of one crore rupees and enlist one crore Congress members. Burning of foreign cloth became a regular programme in public meetings.

Intensification of the Movement: In November 1921, Prince of Wales visited India to congratulate the people for their magnificent contribution to the British War effort. Lord Reading, the Viceroy was determined to make the visit a grand success.

But the Congress gave a call to boycott the programmes of the Royal visitor. There were black flag demonstrations, clashes and bloodshed at Bombay. Calcutta and other places. Enraged by these incidents, the Government resorted to repressive methods and imprisoned Lajpat Rai, C. R. Das and other prominent leaders.

The movement was at its zenith during January 1922. No tax campaign was taken up successfully in the Pedanandipadu Firka of Guntur District. Under the leadership of Vallabhbhai Patel, the farmers of Bardoli Taluk in Gujarat refused to pay the land revenue. The popularity of Mahatma Gandhi was at its highest peak.

Suspension of the Movement 1922: A tragic incident took place at Chauri-Chaura, near Gorakhpur in U.P. on 5th February 1922. When a Congress procession was passing by a Police Station, the mob attacked the station and set it on fire. 21 constables and one sub-inspector were burnt alive. Similar violent incidents were reported from Bombay and Madras. Mahatma Gandhi was overwhelmed with grief over these happenings and called-off the Non-cooperation Movement saying that the masses were not yet ready for a non-violent movement. Even though the movement was withdrawn. Gandhiji was arrested and sentenced for six years' imprisonment.

Estimate: Non-cooperation Movement is a turning point in the Indian freedom struggle. Professor Coupland complemented that "Gandhi converted the nationalist movement into a revolutionary movement." Gandhi made Congress a dynamic organisation.

Griffiths, in his book "Modem India," remarked: "Gandhi taught India a new self-respect, which could be content with nothing less than self-government. He inspired his countrymen with a readiness to suffer in the cause of their country...."

The Non-cooperation Movement had far-reaching effects on the Indian political system. The founding of national schools and colleges, the boycott of foreign goods, the use of khadi the setting up of Panchayats to settle legal disputes — all these programmes began to eat into the vitals of the British rule in India. Gandhiji could achieve what many other leaders put together could not do.

But several Congress Leaders like C. R. Das, Motilal Nehru and Dr. B. S. Moonje condemned the action of Mahatma Gandhi in calling-off the movement. They criticised that Gandhi committed a blunder when the movement reached its zenith. Those who deviated from the Gandhi's policy left the Congress and formed the Swaraj Party.

Swaraj Party

Mahatma Gandhi suspended the Non-cooperation Movement on 12th February 1922 because of violent incidents taken place at Chauri Chaura. The Government arrested him and sentenced him to imprisonment. Prominent Congress leaders condemned Gandhiji for calling-off the movement. Motilal Nehru, C. R. Das, Subhash Chandra Bose and others were languishing in jails.

A section of the Congress leadership felt that the idea of boycotting elections and refraining from contesting the elections to the Central and State Legislative Councils, as ordained by Mahatma Gandhi, resulted only in the capture of Legislative Councils by opportunists, self-seekers and supporters of the British Government. The Government was telling the world that their repressive policies had the support of the elected members of the Legislatures. Therefore, leaders like C. R. Das and Motilal Nehru wanted that the Congress should follow a policy of *Council-entry*. The opponents of the advocates of council-entry were termed as *No-changers*.

Formation of Swaraj Party: The annual session of the Indian National Congress was held at Gaya in December 1922 and it was almost a battle ground between the advocates of the council entry and the No-Changers. C. R. Das presided over the conference. The Changers were led by C. Rajagopalachari and Dr. Ansari. The session opposed the council-entry and passed a resolution proposing to start limited Civil Disobedience Movement.

C. R. Das tendered his resignation then and there. He and Motilal founded the Swaraj Party on 1st January 1923. The

Swarajists declared that their aim was to wreck the Constitution of 1919 from within the Councils. They wanted to follow the method of opposing every measure of the Government on the floor of the Legislative Councils, with the ultimate aim of achieving Swaraj or Home Rule, within the British Umpire.

Achievements of the Swarajists: The Swarajists fought the elections of 1923. They secured majority of seats in the Central Provinces, became a dominant party in Bengal, United Provinces and Bombay. In the Central Legislative Council, they won 45 out of 145 seats. As leader of the opposition in the Central Legislative

Council, Motilal Nehru did commendable work. With the cooperation of other elected members, the Swarajists were able to refuse leave to introduce the entire Finance Bill in 1924-25. The Governor General resorted to his power of "certification" to restore the Bill.

In 1924, the Swarajists demanded the release of Gandhi who was seriously ill and the Government conceded to their demand.

Split within the Swaraj Party: In course of time, leaders like Madan Mohan Malaviya and Lala Lajpat Rai felt that the policy of obstructionism followed by the Swaraj Party was doing more harm to the Hindus. Some of the Swaraj Party leaders developed weakness for power and positions. They started accepting membership in the Legislative Committees,

Motilal Nehru agreed to be a member of the Skeen Committee which was set up to report on the Indianisation of the Army. Lajpat Rai became the deputy leader of the Central Legislative Swaraj Party. Vithal Bhai Patel was elected Chairman of the Central Legislative Assembly. S. B. Tambe, the Swaraj Party leader of Central Provinces accepted the Executive Councillorship.

In 1926, there was a split in the Swaraj Party. Madan Mohan Malaviya and Lala Lajpat Rai formed the Nationalist Party which worked in cooperation with the Hindu Mahasabha.

Relations with Congress: Gandhiji was released from jail in 1924. He granted full freedom to the Swarajists to pursue their own policy in the Legislative Councils. The Congress confined its work to constructive and social reform programmes. The Swarajists and no-changers maintained cordial relations.

Jallianwala Bagh Massacre

Circumstances Leading to the Massacre

The First World War was over on 11th November 1918. Tilak and Annie Besant demanded self-government for India after the war. But the Montford Reforms were very much disappointing for Indian leaders. Only dyarchy was introduced in the provinces and responsible government was not constituted at the centre. The people were utterly disappointed over the post-war developments. They suffered heavily on account of high prices, low wages and shortage of essential commodities.

Rowlatt Act: To suppress the people's unrest, the Government wanted to arm itself with drastic powers. For this purpose the Viceroy constituted a Committee under the Chairmanship of Sydney Rowlatt, an English Judge to recommend measures to deal with acts of sedition.

On the basis of the proposals made by Rowlatt, the Government of India passed the infamous "Anarchical and Revolutionary Crimes Act of 1919" which was popularly known as the Rowlatt Act. It empowered the Government to suppress freedom of the people, to arrest and detain suspected persons without warrant and imprison them without trial. Mahatma Gandhi asked the people to express their resentment through *hartals* and public meetings against the Rowlatt Act.

Conditions in the Punjab: The Government imposed prohibitory orders on Mahatma Gandhi and stopped him from entering the Punjab. The people got infuriated and resorted to violence. There was *hartal* all over the Punjab. There were violent and terrorist activities in various parts of the province. In such conditions, the Government arrested and deported without warrant, the Congress Leaden, Dr. Satya Pal and Dr. Kitchlu. Their internment worsened the situation. People decided to hold a public meeting in the Jallianwala Bagh, in the city of Amritsar to express their strong resentment over the oppressive measures of the Government.

Jallianwala Bagh Massacre: A mammoth public meeting was convened on 13th April 1919, at Jallianwala Bagh. Sir Michael

O'Dyer was the Lt. Governor of Punjab during that crucial period. He entrusted the responsibility of Law and Order of Amritsar to an army official. Brig-General, O'Dyer, who promulgated Section 144 of Cr. P.C., and banned all processions and meetings in the city of Amritsar. In spite of such prohibitory orders, nearly 20,000 men, women and children assembled at the appointed time and held the meeting to denounce police atrocities.

O'Dyer surrounded the meeting place with Indian and British troops along with two armoured cars. As the proceedings commenced. Dyer ordered his troops to *fire till the ammunition exhausted.* Within a span of one hour, 380 persons were killed on the spot and 1,500 were wounded. The corpses were trampled under the feet of the horses and the wounded were not given medical aid. Dyer issued 'crawling order' in the streets of Amritsar. Martial Law was imposed. People were flogged, fined and imprisoned in large numbers. Military resorted to bombing at Gujranwala to disperse the crowds. The whole of Punjab was under turmoil.

Consequences: The whole country was shocked at the wholesale slaughter of hundreds of unarmed men at Amritsar. Rabindranath Tagore renounced his knighthood to express his indignation. The Indian Press demanded the impeachment of O'Dyer.

The Government appointed an Enquiry Committee under the Chairmanship of Hunter. Dyer said that he resorted to large scale massacre because his aim was to crush the morale of the people and thereby he wanted to produce a deterrent effect on the whole of the Punjab.

The Hunter Committee viewed that Dyer used strength beyond the necessary. He was also censured by the Secretary of State for India. The Jallianwala Bagh tragedy emitted shock waves throughout the country and it opened a new chapter in the Freedom Movement of India.

Muddiman Committee

The British Government was affected by the Swarajists. In 1924 (February) the Government set up the well-known

Muddiman Reform Enquiry Committee under the chairmanship of the House Member, Sir Alexander Muddiman, to report on the working of the dyarchy.

In the Muddiman Committee, thus, appointed some Indian members were invited to join. Pt. Motilal Nehru declined the offer while Sir Tej Bahadur Sapru and M. A. Jinnah joined. The committee was retained; investigations were made in the working of the Act of 1919, but the official found it difficult to agree in its findings with the non-official majority.

The Muddiman Committee did not submit a unanimous report. The majority view was that the existing Constitution was working in most provinces and was affording valuable political experience. A detailed recommendations were made for improving machinery of the Government.

The minority view was that dyarchy has absolutely failed and could not succeed at all in the future. It was only a fundamental change of the Constitution which could bring about an improvement. The minority reports condemned the system of dyarchy as one unworkable system and stressed the need for its early abolition. The Government accepted majority view and proceeded with the considerations of its recommendations.

In September 1925, the Report of Muddiman Committee was brought on the floor of the Central Legislature for discussion. Pandit Motilal Nehru delivered a brilliant speech. He moved a resolution which was carried by an overwhelming majority in the teeth of Government's opposition. The resolution demanded, among other things that:

1. Certain immediate changes in the Government of India Act of 1919, and
2. A Round Table Conference to prepare a detailed scheme for the approval of the Central Assembly. This scheme would revise the existing Constitution so as to make the government responsible to the legislature.

The government paid no heed to the resolution and on 24th January 1926. Lord Reeding expressly declared that the British Parliament would not be coerced by such resolutions.

Simon Commission

In 1927, Lord Birkenhead, the Secretary of State for India announced that appointment of the Indian Statutory Commission under the Chairmanship of Sir John Simon with six more British Parliament members to assist him. This was popularly known as the Simon Commission.

Reasons for Appointment of the Commission: In the Government of India Act of 1919, it was provided that a Statutory Committee would be appointed to go into the working of the Act and the representative institutions in the British Indian provinces. Accordingly, such a Commission ought to be constituted in 1929. But it was propound by two years because the conservative Government in England wanted to take the credit for itself since General Election was due to be held in England in 1929.

The Congress leaders boycotted the Simon Commission because no Indian member was included in it. Motilal Nehru looked upon the Commission as a mere 'eye wash'. Only a section of the Muslims League and the Anglo-Indians made representations to the Commission.

The Congress leaders held black flag demonstrations and observed *hartal* wherever the Commission visited. Lala Lajpat Rai was assaulted by the police and subjected to severe *lathi* blows in Lahore. A few days later, he succumbed to the injuries. At Lucknow, Govind Vallabh Pant and Jawaharlal Nehru suffered the police excesses. At Madras, Tanguturi Prakasam emerged as the leader of the masses during anti-Simon demonstration.

Recommendations of the Commission: Some leaders of the Justice Party, Indian Liberal Federation and certain Muslim organisations met the Commission and gave their evidences. The Simon Commission made the following recommendations to the British Government:

1. Complete autonomy should be given to the provinces with over-riding powers to the Provincial Governors.
2. Federal Government should be formed at the centre comprising of the British India and the Native States.
3. Provincial Legislative Councils should be enlarged.

4. The Governor General should select and appoint the members of his Cabinet.
5. The High Courts should be under the administrative control of Indian Government.
6. Sindh and Orissa should be formed into separate provinces.

Nehru Report

Lord Birkenhead, the Secretary of State for India was of the opinion that the Hindu-Muslim differences were unbridgeable and the leaders of the two communities could never come to an understanding in respect of the future constitutional set up for India. He justified the non-inclusion of Indian members in the Simon Commission and speaking in the House of Commons, threw a challenge to the Indian leaders to produce an agreed Constitution and submit it to the British Parliament for consideration.

The Indians took it as a challenge and an all party meeting was convened at Bombay in May 1928 under the presidentship of Dr. M.A. Ansari. The conference appointed a committee under the chairmanship of Motilal Nehru to consider and determine the principles for the Constitution of India. Sir Tej Bahadur Sapru, Subhash Chandra Bose, M. S. Aney, Sardar Mangal Singh, Sir Ali Imam, S. Qureshi and G. R. Pradhan were its members.

Nehru Report: The Committee submitted its report after three months. Popularly known as Nehru Report, it envisaged a Constitution for India basing on the following principles:

1. India should have a full responsible government on the model of the self-governing Dominions.
2. Sindh should be made a separate province (with its Muslim majority). Northwest Frontier Province should be given the status of a Governor's province.
3. Separate electorates for Muslims should be discarded and they should be given only "reservation" of seats in the provinces where they were in minority, and also in the centre. No weightages should be allowed to the Muslims. The non-Muslims also should be given reservation of seats in the North-West Frontier Province.

4. The Indian Government should be federal in character and the Native States should be invited to join it.
5. The Constitution would provide for 19 Fundamental Rights for the Indian citizens.
6. The Governor General would be the King's Representative. He was free to choose the Prime Minister. He would appoint the other ministers on the advice of the Prime Minister. The same provisions would apply to the Provincial Governors.
7. There would be bi-cameral legislature at the Centre. The lower house was to be elected on the basis of adult franchise.
8. The Governor General should act on the advice of his Executive Council. The Governors also should act likewise.
9. The residuary powers would vest with the Centre.

The Nehru Reports was submitted to the All Parties Conference held at Lucknow in August 1928. The nationalist Muslims like Abul Kalam Azad and Dr. M.A. Ansari supported the Nehru Report. But some other Muslim leaders like the Agha Khan criticised the report because it repudiated the Lucknow Pact of 1916 regarding weightages and separate electorates.

Jinnah's Fourteen Points

The Nehru Report was very much criticised by the fanatic Muslim leaders like Agha Khan and Mohammed Shafi. They considered it as a "death warrant" to the Muslim community because it recommended joint electorals for the Hindus and Muslims. The Report suggested to discard the separate electorates and weightages which were given to Muslims in 1909 and 1919.

Muhammed Ali Jinnah left for England in May 1928 and returned after six months. In March 1929, the Muslim League session was held at Delhi under the Presidentship of Mr. Jinnah. In his presidential address to the delegates, he consolidated the Muslim viewpoints under fourteen items and these ideas became popular as Jinnah's 14 points in the coming years. The following were some of the significant demands made by him:

1. India should have a federal Constitution with residuary powers vested in the provinces.

2. In the Central Legislature, the Muslim representation should not be less than one-third.
3. The separate electorates should be continued for providing representation to the communal groups.
4. No bill or resolution should be passed in any legislature if three-fourth of the members of any community in that legislative body opposed it as being injurious to the interests of that community.
5. No Cabinet should be formed either at the Centre or in any province, without at least one-third of the ministers being Muslims.
6. Sindh should be separated from the Bombay Presidency.
7. Any territorial redistribution should not in any way affect the Muslim majority in the Punjab, Bengal and North-West Frontier Province.
8. Muslims should be provided adequate share in the administrative services.
9. Adequate share for Muslims should be provided in the Government services subject to the requirements of efficiency.
10. Safeguards should be provided for the promotion of Muslim culture, education, language, religion, personal laws and charitable institutions.

Jinnah's fourteen points created a permanent cleavage between the Congress and the Muslim League. Some national minded Muslims left the League and formed "The Nationalist Muslim Party" in July 1929. The Muslim Leaguers clamoured for a separate homeland for Muslims.

Civil Disobedience Movement

First Phase

The Labour Party came to power in England and Ramsay MacDonald became the Prime Minister. In 1929, he expressed his hope that India would soon attain the Dominion Status. The Viceroy Lord Irwin declared that a Round Table Conference would be held to bring about agreement among the political leaders. But nothing was done to that effect.

The country was simmering with agitation when Simon Commission visited India. In the Calcutta Session of Congress, in 1928, Gandhiji declared that he would lead a movement for complete independence of Dominion Status was not granted before the end of 1929.

Under the Presidentship of Jawaharlal Nehru, Congress session was held at Lahore on the banks of the Ravi on 31st December 1929. On that historic occasion it was resolved that nothing less than "Complete Independence" should be the goal of the Congress.

The All India Congress Committee was authorised to launch upon a programme of Civil Disobedience including non-payment of taxes. It was decided to celebrate 26th January as Independence Day every year all over the country.

Gandhiji Started the Movement — 6th April 1930: The Congress Working Committee empowered Gandhiji to launch the Civil Disobedience Movement at the time and place of his own choice. In March 1920, along with 78 followers, he walked 240 miles starting from Sabarmati Ashram and reached Dandi, a place on the western sea coast. He violated the Salt Laws by picking up salt lying on the beach. He urged the people to manufacture contraband salt, to picket the liquor shops, to burn foreign cloth and boycott the Government services, schools and colleges.

Responding to his clarion call, hundreds of government servants left their jobs. A number of legislators tendered their resignations. Peasants refused to pay taxes to the government. Students left their schools and colleges. Huge public meetings were held all over the country. Thousands of volunteers courted arrest by breaking the salt laws. It appeared as if the country was in complete revolt.

The Muslim League and its leaden remained aloof from the Civil Disobedience Movement. The bulk of the Muslim population did not participate. The nationalist Muslims under the leadership of Khan Abdul Ghaffar Khan (Frontier Gandhi) and Abul Kalam Azad courted arrests and suffered imprisonment.

Repressive Measures of the Government: Mahatma Gandhi was arrested on 5th May. His place was taken by Abbas Tyyabji as the leader of the movement. When he was also arrested, Sarojini

Naidu took up the responsibility. Subhash Chandra Bose was sentenced to one year's imprisonment. Jawaharlal Nehru courted arrest along with thousands of volunteers. The participation of women was significant. In the city of Delhi alone 1,500 women were arrested. In the Central Provinces, Satyagraha was started against forest laws. The Gurkha soldiers committed atrocities against the people in the Midnapur District. The Garhwali riflemen refused to open fire on the Pathan volunteers of Peshawar.

Lord Irwin, the Viceroy realised that the movement had the people's support and could not be suppressed by repressive methods. He made efforts to establish cordial relations between the British and the Congress. The Report of Simon Commission was made public on 7th June, 1930. Lord Irwin declared that a Round Table Conference of Indian leaders would be held in London on 12th November.

The Congress leaders made it clear that unless the British granted a "National Government responsible to the people," they would not participate in the discussions at London. The British Government was not prepared to accept the proposal. Therefore, the First Round Table Conference was held at London without the Congress participation.

Gandhi-Irwin Pact — 5th March 1930: Ramsay MacDonald declared that Responsible Government at the Centre would be given if on agreement was reached regarding "safeguards" and "federation." He desired that Congress also should participate in the Round Table Conferences.

It was found that the Civil Disobedience Movement had undermined the respect for law and order in the country. Gandhi also found that the enthusiasm of the people was diminishing day by day. He was also perturbed by the separatist attitude of the Muslim League. All these circumstances favoured compromise with the Government.

On 5th March 1931, the Gandhi-Irwin Pact was signed. Gandhiji agreed to discontinue the Civil Disobedience Movement, to stop the boycott of British commodities and to participate in the Second Round Table Conference which was intended to draft a Constitution on the basis of federation, responsibility and safeguards for minorities, etc.

On the Government side, Lord Irwin agreed to release the political prisoners who were imprisoned during the movement, to withdraw the Ordinances promulgated during that period, to permit people living near the sea coast to manufacture salt free of duty and permit peaceful picketing of liquor and opium shops.

Criticism: It was criticised that Mahatma Gandhi did not demand the release of terrorist prisoners like Sardar Bhagat Singh, Sukh Dev and Raj Guru who were to be executed on 23rd March 1931 in connection with the Lahore Conspiracy case. Gandhi did not agree to identify himself with the revolutionary prisoners.

The Gandhi-Irwin Pact was endorsed by the Congress in its annual session at Karachi and authorised Gandhi to represent it in the Second Round Table Conference.

Round Table Conferences

In 1930, Labour Party swept the polls and Ramsay MacDonald formed the Cabinet in England. He expressed his wish that Indian leaders would come to a compromise regarding the constitutional reforms to be introduced in India. Irwin, the Viceroy, announced the intention of the Government to hold Round Table Conferences to find out a solution to the Indian problem.

The Congress leaders; declared that they would not take part in the conferences unless National Government responsible to the people was granted to India. As the Viceroy refused to concede to any such demand, the Congress leaders refused to participate in the First Round Table Conference. Instead, the Congress continued the Civil Disobedience Movement which was launched under Gandhiji's leadership in April 1930.

The First Round Table Conference: The First Round Table Conference was held in London at St. James Palace from 12th November 1930 to 19th January 1931. It was attended by 89 distinguished persons representing Indian Liberal Federation, Muslim League, Hindu Maha Sabha, Depressed classes and the Native States. Sir Akbar Hydari, Sir Mirza Ismail and Maharajah of Bikaner were some of them. Ramsay MacDonald declared that responsible Government at the Centre would be formed if the Indian people agreed for "safeguards" and "federation." The

Government realised that nothing substantial could be achieved unless the Congress participated in the discussion.

Gandhi-Irwin Pact: The Viceroy realised the need of enlisting the cooperation of the Congress for the success of the Round Table Conferences. He ordered the release of Gandhi and other Congress leaders from imprisonment. He held talks with Gandhiji which lasted for fifteen days which culminated in the Gandhi-Irwin Pact. According to it, Gandhi agreed to call of the Civil Disobedience Movement and to participate in the Second Round Table Conference for drafting a Constitution based on federation, responsibility, and safeguards for minorities. On the Government side, the Viceroy agreed to withdraw all ordinances and release the political prisoners.

Second Round Table Conference: Before leaving to London, Gandhi wanted to find a solution to the Hindu-Muslim question. He tried to placate the Muslims by agreeing for separate electorates. But the Muslim League leaders were harping upon the 14 points of Jinnah and were demanding separate homeland for Muslims. Gandhi sailed for England with a hope of resolving the deadlock there.

The Second Round Table Conference was held in September 1931. 107 delegates representing British India and the Native States attended.

The discussions were held on the proposed federation for India. The Indian Princes were ruling over 601 states comprising of 2/5 of Indian territory and 1/4 of Indian population. The Princes stoutly opposed the idea of federation since they would lose their personal power and privileges if they joined the federation.

Regarding the representation and safeguards for minorities, the problem became more complicated. Dr. B. R. Ambedkar, the leader of the depressed classes, demanded separate constituencies for the Scheduled Castes who numbered 50 millions or one-seventh of the total population. Speaking before the Minorities, Committee Gandhi expressed his anguish over such a demand and said that the depressed classes were part of the Hindu society. The Maharajah of Darbhanga and Rajah of Bobbili, the two big zamindars wanted safeguards for the Indian land-holders. No agreement was reached on the Hindu-Muslim problem. The conference was abruptly adjourned without coming to any settlement. Gandhi felt humiliated over the unpleasant end of the conference.

Communal Award

After his return to India, Gandhiji restarted the Civil Disobedience Movement in the country. Foreign cloth and liquor shops were picketed. Payment of land revenue was withheld. The Government issued new ordinances to exercise emergency powers. Gandhiji was put behind the bars.

On 17th August 1932, Ramsay MacDonald announced the "Communal Award". According to it, the depressed classes were treated as a minority community and they were allotted separate communal electorates. While they were also entitled to contest from general constituencies earmarked for Hindus, they were allotted separate electorates. Only the voters of those communities alone could vote for them.

The Communal electorates would be continued for Muslims, Sikhs, Christians and Anglo-Indians as before.

Poona Pact

As a protest against the Communal Award announced by the British Prime Minister, Mahatma Gandhi went on fast unto death from inside the Yervada jail. He opposed the move to separate the Depressed Classes from the rest of the Hindu society. The fast began on 20th September.

Moved by the critical situation, the Hindu and Harijan leaders like Dr. B. R. Ambedkar, and Madan Mohan Malviya met at Poona and came to an understanding. They agreed not to demand separate electorates for the depressed classes. But instead, they would be granted reservation of seats in the Central and Stale Legislatures. The members of the depressed classes who were voters in a general constituency were to form an electoral college which was to elect a panel of four candidates for each reserved seat. The general electorate would choose one of those four.

It so happened, that while Ramsay MacDonald's award gave only 71 seats to the depressed classes, the Poona Pact gave them 148 seats. The agreement was readily accepted by the Government.

Third Round Table Conference: The Third Round Table Conference was held in November 1932. The Congress did not participate in it. It prepared the concrete plan to be submitted to the Parliament. The Parliament constituted a Joint Select Committee whose recommendations formed the basis for the Government of India Act of 1935.

Civil Disobedience Movement

Second Phase

When Gandhiji returned to India on 28 December 1931 after the failure of the Second Round Table Conference, he had to face an ugly situation. The then Viceroy Lord Willingdon resorted to suppression and repression against the nationalists. Gandhiji felt very much for this condition. Hence, he sent a telegram expressing great regret at the oppressive measures undertaken by the Government and seeking an interview with Lord Willingdon. But he refused to grant interview. On the other hand, he issued four ordinances which completely restricted the freedom of the Indians. Gandhiji then gave the signal for the resumption of the Civil Disobedience Movement.

Thousands of Congressmen including Khan Abdul Gaffar Khan, the leader of the Red Shirt Volunteers' Body, Jawaharlal Nehru, Gandhiji, Sardar Vallabhbhai Patel and other leaders were arrested and sent to the jails. Congress offices were brought under the custody of the Government. Everywhere the police resorted to lathi-charges and firing to disperse the crowds of the Movement. Thousands of houses, hundreds of farms, a large number of cattles and lot of furnitures and enormous household properties were destroyed or confiscated.

In spite of all measures of repression, the Movement spread like wildfire and gained great momentum. Many meetings and demonstrations were held. Boycott of British goods was an important part of the programme. It was made a penal offence. So people began to preach "Buy Indian things." Even for this propagation some Indians were sent to jail. People refused to pay taxes; everywhere national flags were hoisted. At the same time the Congress Session was held at Delhi. It reiterated the resolution on complete independence.

Gandhiji's Fast

While the struggle was going on in the country, the British Prime Minister MacDonald announced his decision on the communal problem on August 17, 1932. From the jail he immediately wrote to the Prime Minister about his decision to fast unto death if the Award was not revoked. The Prime Minister turned his deaf ears. So Gandhiji began his fast from Yervada Jail on 20 September 1932. Addressing the Hindu Community he said, "If the Hindu mass mind is not prepared to banish untouchability, root and branch, it must sacrifice me without the slightest hesitation." To save Gandhiji's life, Congress leaders such as C. Rajagopalachari, Dr. Rajendra Prashad, Malaviya and others met Dr. Ambedkar at Poona and concluded the Poona Pact on 25 September 1932. Gandhiji broke his fast on the very next day. Thus, Mahatmaji's fast gave a great fillip to the movement for the eradication of untouchability. The Poona Pact provided that the Scheduled Castes would forego their separate electorates and contest themselves with the general Hindu electorates. It gave the Scheduled Castes 148 seats out of the general electorate seats in the various Provincial Legislatures. They were to be given sufficient representation in the Local Bodies and the Public Services. In this way this Pact created a conducive and cordial atmosphere between the Congress and the Scheduled Castes.

The Movement drugged on till May, 1934. But Gandhiji was suddenly released from Jail on May 8, 1933. He suspended the Movement for 12 weeks. He devoted all his energy to the work of Harijan uplift and for that purpose undertook a tour of the country. The outbreak of a terrible earthquake in Bihar which caused terrible damage diverted the attention of Gandhiji. So he advised all Congressmen to suspend the Movement for Swaraj and leave it to him. Thus, the heroic struggle which began in 1932 came to an end.

The White Paper

The British Government issued in March 1935, a small document known as the White Paper. It gave in detail the working basis of the new Constitution with a dyarchy at the centre and a responsible Government in the Provinces. It was condemned by the Indians. A Joint Select Committee was appointed to examine the White Paper Report. A Bill was drafted on the basis of its examination and introduced in the House of Commons on 5th February 1935.

Sir Samuel Hoare, Secretary of State for India was in charge of the Bill. The Labour members tried to amend the Bill in such a way as to recognise explicitly India's right to Dominion status. The diehards led by Winston Churchill tried to introduce reactionary elements into the bill.

However, the Bill was passed by the House of Commons on 4th June 1935. It was introduced in the House of Lords on 6th June 1935. The Bill received the Royal Assent on 2nd August 1935 as Government of India Act, 1935.

The Act of 1935 and Working of Provincial Autonomy

In the forgoing pages we have seen already that as a result of the three Round Table Conferences, the White Paper was published and finally it led to a Bill. This Bill became an Act -- The Government of India Act on 2 August 1935.

Provisions

1. The Act provided for an All India Federation of both British India and the Princely States. Princely States were given option to join the Federation. The Indian States were to send 125 members to the Federal Assembly and 104 members to the Council of States. The provinces were to send 250 members to the Federal Assembly and 156 members to the Council of States. The members from the Indian States were to be nominated by the rulers, but those from the provinces were to be elected on communal lines.

   There was no simple division of powers between the Centre and the Slates. There were three lists, viz. the Federal List, the Provincial List and the Concurrent List. Because of the introduction of Dyarchy at the centre, the Federal List was further subdivided into the Reserved and Transferred subjects.

The residuary powers were given to the Governor General. The Federal Legislature consisted of the Governor General and two chambers — the Federal Assembly and the Council of States.

The Federal Government was authorised to pass laws on the subjects given in the Federal List. The subjects given in the Provincial List were within the powers of Provincial Legislature. Both the Federal Legislatures and the Provincial Legislatures could pass laws on the subjects given in the Concurrent List. Federal subjects were to be administered by a Council of not more than ten ministers and reserved subjects (defence, foreign relations, ecclesiastical affairs, etc.), by not more than three Councillors responsible to the Governor General alone. The Federal Ministry was to administer all the Federal Departments except the above mentioned reserved departments.

2. The Federal Legislature was to be bicameral, consisting of the Federal Assembly and the Council of States. The duration of the Federal Assembly was five years. On the expiry of that period, it was to be automatically dissolved. However, the Governor General was given the power to extend its life.

   The Council of State was a permanent body. One-third members were to retire after every 3 years. Members from States were nominated by the rulers. The representatives from British India were to be elected. On communal lines the Hindu, Muslim and Sikh members were to be elected.

3. The Indian Legislatures had restricted powers. In Army Act, Air Force Act and law affecting the Royal Family the Legislatures had no power at all. Besides there were many non-votable items in the budget over which the Federal Legislature was given absolutely no control.

4. The Act of 1935 abolished the India Council of the Secretary of State. The Secretary of State was given advisers.

5. Under this Act, a Federal Court with jurisdiction over the States and the Provinces was to be established. There were one Chief Justice and two puisne judges. Having

both original and appellate jurisdiction, it was to be the highest court in India.

6. The same Act sought to establish the Reserve Bank of India and the Federal Railway Authority.
7. Under the Act of 1935, the Governor General played a pivotal role in the Central Executive. In short there was no control from London when the Governor General and the Governors acted according to the advice and consent of their ministries.
8. In live Act there was a provision for elaborate safeguards. These safeguards were very essential for responsible Government as well as of self-government.
9. The most important feature of the Act of 1935 was the provision of provincial autonomy. It was a definite and significant improvement on the Act of 1919. There was no reserved subjects with the Governors. Even then there was no full-fledged responsible government in the provinces. The Act abolished dyarchy and introduced autonomy in the Provinces. Under the Act, the Provincial Executive consisted of the Governor and the ministers who were mode responsible to the Provincial Legislature. The governors enjoyed substantial powers which would often destroy the working of Provincial Autonomy. Hence, their special responsibilities, discretionary powers and the responsibility to the Governor General evoked bitter criticism from Indian nationalists who had desired the establishment of a truly responsible government.

   The Act of 1935 did not set up Provincial Legislatures of a uniform pattern. Of them eleven had Bicameral Legislatures; remaining five had unicameral legislatures. The bicameral legislatures were to consist of the Legislative Assemblies and the Legislative Councils and the unicameral Legislatures had only the Legislative Assemblies.

   Members of the Legislative Assemblies were elected directly through communal or racial electorates. The Legislative Councils were permanent bodies. One-third of the members retired at the end of every third year.

Majority of them were elected members. The rest were nominated by the Governor at his discretion.

The Provincial Legislatures were competent to pass legislation on all matters included in the Provincial List. They had the power to legislate on items included in the Concurrent List so long as such legislation did not conflict with central law.

Congress Reaction to the Act

This Act of 1935 was severely condemned and criticised by the Nationalists and other sections of the people in spite of its vast improvement over the Act of 1919. The safeguards and reservations were interpreted strictly and enforced vigorously since they would have killed the soul of responsible Government. The Governor General and the Provincial Governors were given vast powers according to the Act. By these powers they could intervene in almost every sphere of administration.

Hence, they could veto legislation; they could legislate on their own authority; they could do anything they wanted. In short they could oppose the popular ministries also. Many important subjects were given to them so as to enable them to exercise their full control. This Act was hardly an inviting prospects; the Congress was justified in strongly condemning and rejecting it.

Second World War and the Congress

The Second World War broke out on 1st September 1939. It had immense impact on the Indian freedom struggle. It acted as a catalyst for the final withdrawal of the British from the Indian subcontinent.

Resignation of Congress Ministries, October 1939: In 1937, elections were held for the Legislative Assemblies on the basis of 1935 Act. The Congress contested the elections though it expressed its disapproval for the Act of 1935. It formed ministries in seven out of eleven provinces, namely, U.P., C.P., N.W.F. Province, Bihar, Orissa, Madras and Bombay. The Muslim League headed the ministries in Sindh and Bengal whereas Unionist Party formed ministry in the Punjab. There was a coalition ministry in Assam.

When the World War broke out in Europe, Lord Linlithgow, the Viceroy, proclaimed that India was at war with Germany. He did so without consulting the Indian leaders. As a protest the Congress ministries resigned in October 1939. Muslim League was jubilant over the incident, and celebrated "the Deliverance Day" on 2nd December 1939.

Muslim League's Demand for Pakistan

The Demand for Pakistan, March 1940: Jinnah presided over the Lahore session of the Muslim League and declared that division of India into two autonomous states was the only solution to the Indian problem. He asserted that it was a matter of life and death for the Muslims to achieve a homeland consisting of Muslim majority provinces. Liaquat Ali Khan, the General Secretary of the League observed that Pakistan would include the N.W.F.P., Baluchistan, the Punjab, Sindh, Bengal and Assam.

August Offer

The August Offer of Lord Linlithgow: Hitler overran France in June 1940 and started aerial bombardment of Great Britain. England was very much in need of external help. The Congress leaders demanded the formation of the National Government at the Centre as a precondition to extend cooperation to the British Government during the war.

Lord Linlithgow turned down their demand. Instead, he issued a statement on 8th August, 1940, popularly known as the 'August Offer'. Therein, he offered to expand the Governor General's Executive Council by including Indian leaders. He said that a Constitution-making body would be set up after the war was over. The Congress expressed its disappointment and rejected the offer.

Individual Satyagraha, October 1940: The Congress leaders were disappointed because their demand for the formation of a provisional Government was not conceded to by the Viceroy. Gandhi decided to launch individual Satyagraha because freedom of speech against war effort was denied. On 17th October, 1940, Acharya Vinoba Bhave, a trusted follower of Gandhi, courted arrest by offering Satyagraha and opposing the war-effort. The movement continued for five months and hundreds of volunteers and leaders were sentenced to imprisonment.

Japan's Entry into the War — December 1941: On 7th December 1941, Japan entered the world war by bombarding Pearl Harbour and destroying one-third of the American Navy. In a lightning way, she conquered Indo-China, Thailand, Malaya, East Indies and Burma. The theatre of war came to the eastern borders of India. The Japanese planes dropped bombs over Calcutta, Vishakhapatnam and Kakinanda. The situation on the eastern front aggravated the political situation in the country.

Free India Government: Subhash Chandra Bose, a veteran Congress leader suddenly disappeared from Calcutta in January 1941 and made his way to Berlin. He contacted the Nazi leaders and secured their help in organising the Indian War Prisoners into the Indian National Army. Later he sailed to Japan in a German submarine and sought the Japanese support in his plan to liberate India from the British yoke. He formed a provisional Government of free India at Singapore. His armies crossed the Indo-Burma border and entered Manipur and Chittagong. But they were defeated and captured prisoners by the British armies at a later stage.

Cripps' Proposals

Cripps' Mission — March 1942: As Japan was conquering the South-East Asiatic countries one after another, Chiang-Kai-Shek, the President of Republic of China and Roosevelt, the American President realised the need of securing India's voluntary cooperation in the war efforts. They brought pressure on Winston Churchill to find out solution for the Indian problem. The British Premier also felt the urgency of breaking the political deadlock. He deputed Sir Stafford Cripps to conduct direct discussions with the leaders of Indian political parties. On 22nd March 1942, he arrived in Delhi and made the following proposals to the Indian leaders.

1. After the war was over, India would become a Dominion under the British Empire. It would be on equal status with other Dominions.
2. Soon after the war, steps would be taken to set up a Constituent Assembly to frame a new Constitution for India.

3. Provision would be made for the participation of the Indian States in the Constitution-making body.
4. If any province of British India was not willing to accept the new Constitution such province could remain separate from the Indian Union.
5. During the war, the Viceroy's executive council was to consist entirely of the members of the Indian political parties. They would manage all departments except defence.

Prof. Coupland described the Cripps' proposals as the declaration of Indian independence. Mahatma Gandhi called it "a post dated cheque on a bank that was obviously failing." Congress wanted National Government immediately whereas Cripps promised Dominion status after the war. Hence, Congress rejected the proposals. The Muslim League also rejected them because the demand for partition was not approved.

Quit India Movement

Quit India Movement — August 1942: Japan was knocking at the gates of Assam and the pro-Japanese feeling was very much growing in the country. The Congress leaders wanted to make use of the anti-British atmosphere by giving a clarion call to the people. The British Government was determined not to lose her hold on India during the war. They offered Dominion Status for India after the war whereas the Congress demanded National Government endowed with all powers. The Congress leaders were deadly opposed to the Japanese conquest of India. But at the same time they were unwilling to cooperate with the British Government for the defence of the country, unless the political power was handed over to the Indian leaders immediately.

On 8th August, the All India Congress Committee met at Bombay and passed a resolution urging the British to handover power to a provisional Government and quit the country forthwith. It was said that such an independent government headed by the Indian leaders would alone resist the foreign aggression/properly.

The Government arrested all the Congress leaders throughout the country and put them behind the bars. The Quit India Movement began on its own accord and it was not launched. The

Congress leaders did not spell out any plan or procedure to be implemented by the people. Soon after their arrest, people resorted to violence and tried to paralyse the administration. There was mob fury, lawlessness, riots and disorders in the British Indian provinces. Communications were disrupted and telephone wires were cut-off. The Government put down the movement ruthlessly within a few weeks. About 60,000 people were arrested throughout the country. Jinnah appealed to all Muslims to keep aloof from the movement. Dr. B. R. Ambedkar, the leader of the Depressed Classes described the mass disobedience movement of Gandhi as irresponsible and insane.

Rajagopalachari's Formula

To solve the political problem between the Congress and the League, Chakravarthi Rajagopalachari, a veteran leader of the Congress formulated a scheme in April 1944. It came to be known as 'C.R. Formula' or 'Rajaji Formula'. Accordingly:

1. The League was to endorse the Indian demand for independence,
2. The League was to cooperate with the Congress in the formation of Provisional Interim Government,
3. At the end of the War, a commission would be appointed to demarcate the areas having a Muslim population in absolute majority,
4. In the areas thus demarcated a plebiscite would be held on the basis of adult franchise. It would decide the issue of separation from Hindustan,
5. In the event of separation, a mutual agreement would be entered into for safeguarding essential matters such as defence, communication, commerce, etc.,
6. The transfer of population, if any would be absolutely on a voluntary basis.

The Rajaji Formula was rejected by Jinnah and the Muslim League. He desired to have the six provinces of Sindh, Punjab, Baluchistan, the North-West Frontier Province, Bengal and Assam. Moreover it disturbed Gandhiji. The Gandhi-Jinnah talks commenced on 9 September 1944, and continued till the 27th but they failed to reach any agreement.

Then Bhulabhai Desai, the leader of the Congress Party in the Central Legislative Assembly, and Liaquat Ali Khan, the Deputy Leader of the Muslim League also tried to resolve the political deadlock. It was called Desai-Liaquat Pact. It too failed in its object of solving the problem.

Wavell Plan and the Shimla Conference

In May 1945, pressure was brought upon Winston Churchill from various quarters to take steps to win over the goodwill and support of the Indians. It led to the publication of a White Paper, popularly called the Wavell Plan on 14 June 1945.

The then Viceroy of India was Lord Wavell. The Plan was named after him as Wavell Plan. Its proposals were: (i) the re-Constitution of the Executive Council at the centre by the nomination of members selected from the leaders of the various Indian political parties on the basis of party between the Hindus and the Muslims; (ii) Except Viceroy and the Commander-in-Chief all the members of the Executive Council would be Indians.

Lord Wavell summoned a conference at Shimla on June 25, 1948 to execute his plan. In accordance with the plan, the arrested leaders and other members of all parties were released. Invitation was extended to all. Maulana Azad attended the Conference on behalf of the Congress. But like all other previous attempts to solve the political deadlock, the Shimla Conference ended in a failure. It broke down because of the intransigence of Mr. Jinnah.

In spite of this Lord Wavell conferred with Jinnah. Gandhi and other leaders to save the Conference from failure. But the Viceroy announced the failure of the Conference on July 14. The Congress insisted the Viceroy to implement the plan without the cooperation of the League. But he refused to do so. This only encouraged the League still further to have its own way in the direction of achieving Pakistan.

Fresh Election: On 30th April 1945, Hitler committed suicide. The Germans laid down arms and signed a document of unconditional surrender on 7th May. Atom bombs were dropped on Hiroshima and Nagasaki. On 14th August the Japanese announced their unconditional surrender.

The Labour Party came to power in England with comfortable majority. Clement Attlee was elected Prime Minister. This even had far-reaching effect on the Indian political situation. Attlee announced his Government's intention of early realisation of full self-government in India.

Lord Wavell declared that the Government would soon convene a Constitution-making body. As a first step, he announced holding of fresh elections to the Central and Legislative Assemblies.

The Elections were held in January 1946: In the Central Legislative Assembly, out of 102 elected seats, the Congress captured 56, the Muslim League 30 and the others 40. Out of 11 Provincial Legislative Assemblies, the Congress secured majority of seats in 8 provinces — Assam, Bihar, Bombay, C.P., Madras, N.W.F.P., Orissa and U.P. The Muslim League won majority in Sindh, Bengal and the Punjab. It is significant that the Muslim League captured 426 of the 492 seats allotted to the Muslims and the Congress won 930 out of 1595 general seats in the eleven Provincial Legislative Assemblies. These elections indicated that the Muslims all over the country were favouring the partition of India.

Thus, the Second World War created the necessary circumstances for the transfer of power to the Indian political leaders, soon after the war was over.

Cabinet Mission Plan

The Second World War aggravated the political situation in India. The entry of Japan into the war, the formation of the Azad Hind Fauj by Subhash Chandra Bose and the Quit India Movement created political deadlock in the country. The coming of Labour Party to power in England soon after the war helped the peaceful transfer of power to the Indian political parties. Clement Attlee declared the policy of his Government in favour of the early realisation of complete self-Government in India.

The Cabinet Mission Plan — 16th May 1946: Clement Attlee deputed three members of his Cabinet to discuss with the Indian leaders regarding the future constitutional set up in India. The mission consisted of Lord Pattrick Lawrence, the Secretary of

State, Sir Stafford Cripps, the President of the Board of Trade and A. V. Alexander, the First Lord of Admiralty. They held parleys with the Indian leaders at Shimla on 5th May 1946. The talks broke down on 12th May. The Cabinet Mission announced the following plan on May 16th, 1946:

1. The formation of Pakistan was rejected.
2. The Union of India would embrace both British India and the Indian States.
3. The All India Union Government would deal with foreign affairs, defence and communications only.
4. All the remaining powers would be vested in the provinces.
5. The All India Union Legislature would be composed of equal proportions from Hindu majority and Muslim majority provinces with representatives of Indian States.
6. The British Indian provinces were to be formed into A, B and C group. Each group was to have an executive and legislature. Each group was to have a Constitution for itself and for the provinces comprising it. Madras, Bombay, U.P., Bihar, C.P. and Orissa came under Group A. The Punjab, N.W.F.P. and Sindh came under group B. Assam and Bengal came under group C.
7. A Constituent Assembly was to be formed immediately to frame a Constitution for India.
8. An Interim Government was to be formed with the representatives of the main political parties.

The talks broke down because the Muslim League insisted on the division of India as a pre-condition for the transfer of power to the Indian hands. Pandit Nehru was opposed to the grouping of provinces.

Interim Government — 2nd September 1946: Jawaharlal Nehru was elected Congress President in July 1946. Lord Wavell invited him to join the Interim Government. On 2nd September, the Congress formed the Government with 12 members, including 3 Muslims. Nehru became the Vice-President of the Interim Government with Viceroy as President. Sardar Patel look up to Home portfolio.

In the beginning the Muslim League refused to join the Interim Government because partition was not accepted. Later, on 24th October, five Muslim members joined the Cabinet. Liaquat Ali Khan became the Finance Minister. From the very beginning the Muslim Leaguers followed obstructionist tactics and created hurdles at every step of the functioning for the Government.

Direct Action by Muslim League — 16th August 1946: Muhammad Ali Jinnah fixed 16th August as "Direct Action Day." The Muslim League wanted to show its strength and create terror in the Hindu minds by resorting to violence and bloodshed. With the approval and support of Suhrawardy, the Muslim League leader of Bengal, the great Calcutta killings took place. About 7,000 Hindus were killed and their properties looted in Calcutta alone. The Police and the army passively observed the massacre. Similar atrocities were committed on the Hindus in Naokhali and Tipperah towns of East Bengal. Thousands of Hindus left their hearths and homes and fled to Bihar. The stories of sufferings related by these men and women roused a spirit of revenge among the Hindus who retaliated against the Muslims of Bihar. On 6th November, Mahatma Gandhi left for East Bengal to create communal harmony. The riots spread to Punjab, North-West Frontier Province and Sindh. Serious disturbances took place in Lahore, Amritsar, and Karachi. Tens of thousands of Hindus were migrating to India from the western provinces.

Formation of Constituent Assembly: The Constituent Assembly to frame a Constitution under the Cabinet Mission Plan was concerned on 14th November 1946. The members were elected indirectly by the Provincial Legislative Assemblies. But Jinnah declared boycott of Constituent Assembly by the Muslim League members. He stated that the creation of Pakistan alone would solve the problem and a separate Constitution for Pakistan should be framed.

Mountbatten Plan

Lord Mountbatten arrived in Delhi on 22nd March 1947 to replace Wavell. He held consultations with the Congress, Muslim League and Sikh leaders. He found that the differences between the Congress and Muslim League leaders were unbridgeable. He came to the conclusion that the partition was the only solution for the communal problem. On June 3rd, he announced the following plan which was simultaneously proclaimed by Attlee in London.

1. Pakistan would be formed consisting of Sindh. West Punjab and East Bengal. Referendum would be held in N.W.F.P., British Baluchistan and Silhet district in Assam to decide whether the people in those areas would prefer to join Pakistan or otherwise.
2. The existing Constituent Assembly would frame Constitution for the Indian Union. A separate Constituent Assembly representing the areas of Pakistan would be formed to prepare Constitution for Pakistan.
3. The provinces of Bengal and Punjab were to be partitioned into the Hindu majority and the Muslim majority areas on the basis of 1941 census. The Muslim majority parts of those provinces were to be included in Pakistan and the Hindu majority parts would remain with India.

The Muslim League was jubilant over the Mountbatten's plan and formally accepted it. The Congress leaders agreed for partition reluctantly. But unfortunately they never thought of safeguarding the lives and properties of the Hindu minority left in Pakistan. Hence, the partition created the gigantic problem of rehabilitating the lakhs of Hindus who were driven out from Pakistan.

Indian Independence Act

On the basis of the June 3rd plan of Mountbatten, the British Parliament passed the Indian Independence Act. According to it, India was to be partitioned into two dominions with effect from 15th August 1947. Each dominion was to decide whether it would remain as member of the British Commonwealth or not. The Native States were freed from all their obligations to the Crown. The post of Secretary of State for India was abolished. The two Dominions were to frame Constitutions for themselves through separate Constituent Assemblies.

On the occasion of the attainment of independence, Pandit Nehru said: "Long years ago we made a tryst with destiny, and now the time comes when we shall redeem our pledge, not wholly or in full measure, but substantially. At the stroke of the mid-night hour, when the world sleeps. India will awake to life and freedom."

Partition of India

After the war, when the British Government announced their intention of transferring power to the Indian hands, the Muslim League demanded that the British should first divide the country before leaving India. On 16th August, 1946 the Muslim League started "Direct Action" to achieve Pakistan. They killed hundreds of Hindus and looted their properties. They created terror in the country so that the peace loving and non-violent Congress leaders would concede to their demand.

Gandhi visited East Bengal to bring about harmony between the Hindus and Muslims. When the Congress leaders accepted Mountbatten's plan to partition the country, Mahatma Gandhi gave his approval unwillingly.

The non-violent Satyagraha weapon of Gandhiji could awaken millions of people against the oppressive foreign rule. He made freedom struggle, a mass movement. But when he had to face the stubborn Muslim League leaders, he utterly failed. His policy of appeasement did not satisfy them. He could not foresee the dangerous consequences of the atrocities committed by the Muslim leaguers. Ultimately he surrendered to the League's demand of partition, against his conscience.

On the eve of Independence, a Press Correspondent told Gandhiji. "Independence is your crown", for which Gandhiji replied "But, partition is my cross".

Indian National Democratic Congress

The Congress Reform Committee (CRC) was formed by a group of dissidents that left the Indian National Congress in the Madras State. The CRC was led by C. Rajagopalachari, who had been defeated by Kamaraj in the inner-party disputes over leadership of the Congress in Tamil Nadu. CRC was formed just one month before the 1957 elections to the Lok Sabha and the Madras state legislative assembly.

Soon CRC began cooperation with the All India Forward Bloc of U. Muthuramalingam Thevar. The CRC-AIFB combine contested 59 seats in the assembly election (54 candidates from CRC, 5 candidates from AIFB. One of the five AIFB candidates, P. K. Mookiah Thevar, stood as a CRC candidate). There was also an informal understanding with the Communist Party of India, which decided not to contest against the CRC in some constituencies.

The CRC-AIFB combine formulated a 12-point election manifesto. The CRC-AIFB alliance emerged as the major opposition alliance in these elections, but could not defeat the Congress government. CRC won 14 seats and AIFB three. Half of the seats won were from the Ramnad and Madurai districts.

Following the election, a joint 'CRC opposition' group was formed in the legislative assembly. This was done to counter the bid of the Dravida Munnetra Kazhagam (which had 16 seats) to hold the post of leader of opposition. Soon five independent assembly members joined the CRC opposition group. V. K. Ramaswamy Mudaliar was elected leader of the 'CRC opposition'.

On September 28-29, 1957 CRC held a state conference and reconstituted itself as the Indian National Democratic Congress. Notably, U. Muthuralingam Thevar, one of the inaugural speakers of the event, was arrested just after having delivered his speech.

In March 1959 elections to the Madurai municipality was held. An alliance of INDC, AIFB, CPI and the Dravida Munnetra Kazhagam was formed. Forward Bloc members stood as INDC candidates, denoting that the Tamil Nadu state unit of that party has virtually merged into INDC. 12 INDC candidates, 12 CPI candidates and 2 DMK candidates were elected against only 10 of the Congress. This was the first time the Congress lost its hold over the municipality after Independence. The INDC-AIFB-CPI-DMK front only lost in three constituencies were they had nominated independent candidates.

In July 1959 INDC merged into the Swatantra Party. Albeit representing virtually opposite positions on the left-right scale, the cooperation between the Forward Bloc and the Swatantra Party continued in the state. Forward Bloc members of the Tamil Nadu assembly sat in the Swatantra group and the group was led by Forward Bloc leader P. K. Mookiah Thevar.

Swatantra Party

The Swatantra Party (swatantra meaning 'free' or 'independent' in Sanskrit) was a political party in India founded by Chakravarti Rajagopalachari and N. G. Ranga in August 1959. The party opposed the Nehruvian socialist outlook of the Congress Party by advocating free enterprise, opposing the so-called Licence-Permit Raj, and ending India's economic autarky by courting Western investment. In 1960 Rajaji and other Swatantra leaders wrote about why Swatantra Party had to be formed despite having worked closely with Nehru to obtain independence for India:

The 21 principles of the Swatantra Party manifesto were on broadly classical liberal lines.

Swatantra Party did not fare badly in the first general elections after its formation. It received 6.8 per cent of the total votes and 18 seats in the third Lok Sabha (1962-67). It emerged as the main opposition in four states - Bihar, Rajasthan, Gujarat and Orissa. It became a significant force in some regions of India and became the single largest opposition party in the mid-1960s in Parliament with 8.7 per cent of the total votes and 44 seats in the Fourth Lok Sabha (1967-71). In 1971, it secured only 8 seats in the Lok Sabha with 3 per cent of the votes. After Rajaji's death in 1972, it declined rapidly. It was also associated in the public mind with wealthy industrialists and former maharajas. The Swatantra experiment of liberalism ended in 1974 by merging with Bharatiya Kranti Dal (led by Charan Singh), a coalition of left-wing, right-wing, and Hindu opponents of Congress Party rule.

Madras Presidency Days

At its greatest extent, Madras Presidency included much of southern India, including the present-day Indian State of Tamil Nadu, the Malabar region of North Kerala, Lakshadweep Islands, the Coastal Andhra and Rayalaseema regions of Andhra Pradesh, Brahmapur and Ganjam districts of Orissa and the Bellary, Dakshina Kannada, and Udupi districts of Karnataka. The presidency had its capital at Madras (now known as Chennai). Madras Presidency, also known as Madras Province and also known officially as Presidency of Fort St. George, was a province of British India.

The Presidency had its origins in the Agency of Fort St George established by the British East India Company soon after the purchase of the village of Madraspatnam in 1639. However, there have been Company factories at Machilipatnam and Armagon ever since the early-1600s. Madras was upgraded to a Presidency in 1652 before reverting to its previous status as an Agency. In 1684, Madras was elevated to a Presidency once again and Elihu Yale was appointed its first President. From 1785 onwards, as per the provisions of the Pitt's India Act, the ruler of the Presidency of Fort St George was styled Governor instead of President and was made subordinate to the Governor General at Calcutta. Madras made a significant contribution to the Indian independence movement in the early decades of the 20th century. Madras was the first province in British India where the system of dyarchy was first implemented. The Presidency was dissolved when India became independent on August 15, 1947. On January 26, 1950, when the Republic of India was inaugurated, Madras was admitted as one of the states of the Indian Union.

Madras was one of the three provinces originally established by the British East India Company as per the terms of the Pitt's India Act. The head of state held the title of Agent from 1640 to 1652 and 1655 to 1684, and President from 1652 to 1655 and 1684 to 1785, and Governor from 1785 to 1947. The judicial, legislative and executive powers are rested in the Governor who is assisted by a Council whose Constitution has been modified by reforms enacted in 1861, 1909, 1919 and 1935. As per the Montague-Chelmsford reforms of 1919, a system of dyarchy was established and regular elections were conducted till the outbreak of the Second World War. The head of the government was known as Prime Minister. In 1908, the province comprised 22 districts each under a District Collector. Each district was further subdivided into *taluks* and *firqas*. The smallest unit of administration was the village.

Government of India Act of 1935

The Government of India Act of 1935 abolished dyarchy and ensured provincial autonomy. It created a bicameral legislature in the Madras province. The Legislature consisted of the Governor and two Legislative bodies — a Legislative Assembly and a Legislative Council. The Assembly consisted of 215 members who were further classified into General seats and those reserved for special communities and interests:

General	116
Scheduled Castes	30
Mohammadans	28
Indian Christians	8
Women	8
Landholders	6

Contd...

Commerce and Industry	6
Labour and Trade Unions	6
Europeans	3
Anglo Indians	2
University	1
Backward areas and tribes	1

The Legislative Council Consisted of a minimum of 54 and a maximum of 56 members. It was a permanent body not subject to dissolution by the Governor and one-third of its members retired every three years. 46 of its members were elected directly by the electorate while the Governor could nominate 8 to 10 members. The break down of seats in the Council were as follows:

General	35
Mohammadans	7
Indian Christians	3
Europeans	1
Nominated	8-10

The Act provided for a limited adult franchise based on property qualifications. Seven million people, roughly 15 per cent of the Madras people holding land or paying urban taxes were qualified to be the electorate. Separate ballot boxes were kept for candidates of different political parties. The Congress was allotted the yellow coloured box, while the Muslim League was allotted green coloured box.

Madras Presidency Legislative Assembly Election, 1937

The First legislative assembly election for the Madras Presidency was held in February 1937. The Indian National Congress obtained a majority by winning 159 of 215 seats in the Legislative Assembly. This was the first electoral victory for the Congress in the presidency since elections were first conducted for Madras Legislative Council in 1920. The Justice Party which had ruled the presidency for most of the previous 17 years was voted out of power. The assembly was constituted in July 1937 and C. Rajagopalachari (Rajaji) became the first Congress Chief Minister of Madras.

The Congress also won the election held simultaneously for the Legislative Council. The victory in Madras was the Congress' most impressive electoral performance in all the provinces of British India. The Congress Government that was formed after the elections lasted till October 1939, when it resigned protesting India's involvement in the Second World War. The next election was held in 1946.

Issues and Campaign

The Justice Party had been in power in Madras for 17 years since 1920. Its hold on power was briefly interrupted only once in 1926-28 when P. Subbarayan was a non-affiliated Chief Minister.

Unpopularity of the Justice Government

The Justice Government under the Raja of Bobbili had been steadily losing ground since the early-1930s. It was beset with factional politics and its popularity was eroding slowly due to the autocratic rule of Bobbili Raja. The Raja was inaccessible to his own party members and tried to destroy the power and influence of the District level leaders who were instrumental in the party winning power earlier. The Suthanthira Sangu, in its issue dated February 26, 1935 explained the destruction of the power of local bodies:

> The Local Boards Act has been recently amended, taluk boards have been abolished, a district board has been bifurcated and attempts have been made to bifurcate other boards, which are hostile to him... He is superseding municipalities, which do not bow to his authority, removing chairmen not liked by him and trying to forfeit the liberty of these bodies by the appointment of Commissioners.

The Justice party was seen as the collaborative party, agreeing with the British Government's harsh measures. Its economic policies during the Great Depression of the 1930s were also highly unpopular. Its refusal to decrease the land revenue taxation in non-Zamindari areas by 12.5 per cent was hugely unpopular. The Bobbili Raja, himself a Zamindar, cracked down on the Congress protests demanding reduction of the revenue. This further reduced the popularity of the Justice Party. The Governor of Madras, Lord Erskine reported to the then Secretary of State Zetland in February 1937, that the peasants in South India had become fed up with the Justice Party and "every sin of omission or commission of the past fifteen years is put down to them [Justice Party]". The affluent lifestyle led by the Justice ministers at the height of the Great Depression were sharply criticised by the Madras Press. They drew a monthly salary of Rs. 4,333.60 when compared to Rs. 2,250 per month the ministers in the Central Provinces received. This invoked the ire of the Madras press. The newspaper India wrote:

> Is not Rs. 2,000 enough for Madras ministers, who were only second-rate *vakils* (lawyers) in the *mufassal* (rural areas)? When the poor are suffering for want of money, they are drawing fat salaries? What an injustice?.. When the country is on fire, when the axe of retrenchment has fallen on the poor and when the people are experiencing intense suffering under the heavy burden of taxation, the Madras Ministers have started on their tours immediately after passing the budget.

Even the European owned newspaper The Madras Mail which had been the champion of the earlier Justice Governments was sickened by the ineptitude and patronage policies of the Bobbili Raja administration. On 1 July 1935, it wrote in its editorial: if the Justice Party is really determined upon reorganisation... the spoils system must go. The extent of the discontent against the Justice Government is reflected in an article of Zamin Ryot:

> The Justice Party has disgusted the people of this presidency like plague and engendered permanent hatred in their hearts. Everybody, therefore, is anxiously awaiting the fall of the Justice regime which they consider tyrannical and inauguration of the Congress administration... Even old women in villages ask as to how long the ministry of the Raja of Bobbili would continue.

Resurgence of the Congress

The Swaraj Party which had been the Justice party's main opposition merged with the Indian National Congress in 1935 when the Congress decided to participate in the electoral process. The Madras Province Congress party was led by S. Satyamurti and was greatly rejuvenated by its successful organisation of the Salt Satyagraha and Civil Disobedience Movement of 1930-31. The Civil Disobedience Movement, the Land Tax reduction agitations and Union organisations helped the Congress to mobilise popular opposition to the Bobbili Raja government. The revenue agitations brought the peasants into the Congress fold and the Gandhian hand spinning programme assured the support of weavers. Preferential treatment given to European traders brought the support of the indigenous industrialists and commercial interests. The Congress had effective campaigners like Satyamurti and Rajaji while the Justice party had only Arcot Ramaswamy Mudaliar to counter them. The Congress election manifesto was populist in nature and promised to reduce land revenue taxes, to ensure decent working conditions and wages for the labourers, low rents and all around prosperity. It even appealed to the Europeans who had reserved seats in the Assembly. It also appealed to the nationalist sentiment of the populace. Commenting on the Congress's manifesto, the Indian Annual Register said:

> The promises made in the election manifesto by the congress, while seeking suffrage, roused hopes, that the Congress government, if voted to power, would give relief to them. Perhaps the Agrarian distress forced the Indian National Congress to give up the policy and programme of non-cooperation and to undertake the responsibility of Government under a hated act.

The Congress campaign was effective and targeted all sections of the population like peasants, workers, weavers and businessmen. Against it the Justice party had no definite programme or policies. It could only harp on the Brahmin domination in Congress. Amidst the backdrop of the Great Depression and economic distress their charge was not effective. Satyamurti utilised the services of popular actors like Chittor V. Nagaiah and K. B. Sundarambal for the election campaign. In particular Sundarambal vigorously campaigned for the Congress. Satyamurti also produced a campaign film directed by A. Narayanan of Srinivasa Cinetone. It featured the speeches of Rajaji, Satyamurti and other Congress leaders. But the film was banned by the colonial government. The coloured box system enabled the most organised party — the Congress to have uniform slogans through out the presidency. The slogan "vote for Gandhi and the yellow box", was very popular and helped the party to mobilise its supporters.

Other Parties

The other parties contesting the election were the Madras Province Muslim League (MPML) headed by Jamal Mohammed, the People's Party of Madras started by Raja of Pithapuram (a breakaway faction from the Justice Party) and the Muslim Progressive Party led by Nawab C. Abdul Hakim and S. M. Pasha.

Results

Party wise break up of seats in the Madras Legislative Assembly:

Total Number of Seats: 215

Inc	*Seats*	*Jusp*	*Seats*	*Others*	*Seats*
Indian National Congress (INC)	159	Justice Party (JUSP)	18	Madras Province Muslim League (MPML)	11
Southern India Chamber of Commerce	1	Nattukottai Nagarathar Association	1	European Commerce	3
		Justice Supported Parties	2	Anglo Indians	2
				Muslim Progressive Party	1
				People's Party of Madras	1
				Others	1
				Independents	15
Total (1937)	**160**	**Total (1937)**	**21**	**Total (1937)**	**34**

Note: The Nattukottai Nagarathar Association and Southern India Chamber of Commerce were seats reserved for Indian Commerce (businessmen). Nagarathar Association seat was won by Rajah Muthiah Chettiar (allied with Justice Party) and the Southern India Chamber of Commerce seat was won by T. T. Krishnamachari of Congress.

Analysis

Causes for Defeat: The victory of Congress over the Justice Party has been ascribed to various reasons. N. Ram, Editor-in-Chief of The Hindu and Robert L. Hardgrave, Professor Emeritus in the Humanities, Government and Asian Studies at University of Texas, Austin attribute the defeat of the Justice party to its collaboration with the British Government. According to Hardgrave:

> The Justice Party had strangled itself on the rope it had woven: Support of the British Raj had brought it to power, but with the impact of national self-consciousness and aspiration for Swaraj, its imperial connection brought its defeat.

Dr. David A. Washbrook, Senior Research Fellow of History at Trinity College, Cambridge and Andre Béteille say the elitist nature of the Justice Party members caused its defeat. Marguerite Ross Barnett attributes the Justice party's defeat to two causes — (1) The loss of Dalit and Muslim support, and (2) Flight of the social radicals to the Self-Respect Movement. According to P. Rajaraman:

> ...internal dissension, ineffective organisation, inertia and lack of proper leadership led the Justice Party along the path of decline.

Notable Losses

Many incumbent ministers of the Justice Government were defeated in this election. The chief minister Raja of Bobbili was defeated by V. V. Giri of Congress by a margin of over 6,000 votes in the Bobbili Assembly Constituency. Other prominent Justice losers included Kumararaja of Venkatagiri, P. T. Rajan, A. P. Patro and the Raja of Ramnad.

Government Formation

The elections were held and the results declared in February 1937. Rajaji was elected as the leader of Congress Legislature Party (CLP) in March 1937. Despite being the majority party in the Assembly and the Council, the Congress was hesitant to form a Government. Their objections stemmed from the special powers given to the Governor by the Government of India Act of 1935. According to the act, the Governor was given: (1) special responsibilities in the area of Finance, and (2) control and absolute discretionary powers over the Cabinet in certain other issues. The Governor had the power to overrule the Cabinet. The Congress refused to accept power (in all the six provinces where they had won) with such caveats .The Governor of Madras, Lord Erskine, decided to form an interim provisional Government with non-members and opposition members of the Legislative Assembly. V. S. Srinivasa Shastri was first offered the Chief Ministership of the interim government but he refused to accept it. Eventually an interim Government was formed with Kurma Venkata Reddy Naidu of the Justice Party as Chief Minister on 1 April 1937. Congress leaders like S. Satyamurti were apprehensive about the decision to not accept power. They carried out a campaign to convince Congress High Command (Gandhi and Nehru) to accept power within the limitations set by the Government of India Act. They also appealed to the British Government to give assurances that the Governor's special powers will not be misused. On 22 June, Viceroy Linlithgow issued a statement expressing the British Government's desire to work with the Congress in implementing the 1935 Act. On 1 July, the Congress Working Committee (CWC) agreed to form Governments in the provinces they had won. On 14 July, Rajaji was sworn in as the Chief Minister. The first legislative assembly convened for the first time on 15 July and elected Bulusu Sambamurti and A. Rukmani Lakshmipathi as the Speaker and Deputy Speaker respectively.

Kurma Venkata Reddy Naidu's Cabinet

Council of ministers in K. V. Reddy Naidu's interim provisional Cabinet (1 April - 14 July 1937):

Minister	*Portfolio*
Kurma Venkata Reddy Naidu	Chief Minister, Public, Revenue and Legal
A. T. Panneerselvam	Home and Finance
M. A. Muthiah Chettiar	Local self government
K. Venkataswamy Naidu	Religious Endowments and Registration
P. Kalifulla Sahib Bahadur	Public Works
M. C. Rajah	Development
R. M. Palat	Education and Public health

Chief Ministership of Rajagopalachari

C. Rajagopalachari (aka Rajaji) was a Chief Minister of erstwhile Madras Presidency of British India and Tamil Nadu of Independent India. He was the first Indian National Congress member to assume office in Madras Presidency.

He served as a Chief Minister for two terms spanning about 5 years. He was elected as a Chief Minister after 1937 elections in Madras Presidency and served till 1939. He was also the first Chief Minister to serve the Madras State after first elections held after Indian independence. His second term lasted from 1952 till 1954.

Rajagopalachari's Cabinet

Council of Ministers in Rajagopalachari's Cabinet (15 July 1937 - 29 October 1939):

Minister	*Portfolio*
C. Rajagopalachari	Chief Minister, Public and Finance
T. Prakasam	Revenue
P. Subbarayan	Law and Education
V. V. Giri	Labour and Industries
Bezawada Gopala Reddy	Local Administration
T. S. S. Rajan	Public Health and Religious Endowments
Maulana Yakub Hasan Sait	Public Works
V. I. Munuswamy Pillai	Agriculture and Rural Development
S. Ramanathan Pillai	Public Information and Administration Reports
Kongattil Raman Menon	Courts and Prisons

Changes:

- On 7 January 1939, Raman Menon died and C. J. Varkey, Chunkath was inducted into the Cabinet. Education portfolio was transferred from Subbarayan to Varkey and instead Subbarayan was given additional charge of Courts and Prisons.

First Term

Election Win: Elections to the Madras Legislative assembly and legislative council was conducted in 1937. This was the first election conducted after the creation of a bicameral legislature by Government of India Act of 1935. Indian National Congress won 159 of the 215 seats in the assembly and 27 of the 56 seats in the council. Despite being the majority party in the Assembly and the Council, the Congress was hesitant to form a Government.

Their objections stemmed from the special powers given to the Governor by the Government of India Act of 1935. According to the act, the Governor was given special responsibilities in the area of Finance and control and absolute discretionary powers over the Cabinet in certain other issues. The Governor had the power to overrule the Cabinet. The Congress refused to accept power (in all the six provinces where they had won) with such caveats.

The Governor of Madras, Lord Erskine, decided to form an interim provisional Government with non-members and opposition members of the Legislative Assembly. V. S. Srinivasa Shastri was first offered the Chief Ministership of the interim government but he refused to accept it.

Eventually an interim Government was formed with Kurma Venkata Reddy Naidu of the Justice Party as Chief Minister on 1 April 1937. Congress leaders like S. Satyamurti were apprehensive about the decision to not accept power. They carried out a campaign to convince Congress High Command (Gandhi and Nehru) to accept power within the limitations set by the Government of India Act.

They also appealed to the British Government to give assurances that the Governor's special powers will not be misused. On 22 June, Viceroy Linlithgow issued a statement expressing the British Government's desire to work with the Congress in implementing the 1935 Act.

On 1 July, the Congress Working Committee (CWC) agreed to form Governments in the provinces they had won. On 14 July, Rajaji was sworn in as the Chief Minister.

Cabinet

Council of Ministers in Rajagopalachari's Cabinet (15 July 1937 - 29 October 1939):

Minister	*Portfolio*
C. Rajagopalachari	Chief Minister, Public and Finance
T. Prakasam	Revenue
P. Subbarayan	Law and Education
V, V. Giri	Labour and Industries
Bezawada Gopala Reddy	Local Administration
T. S. S. Rajan	Public Health and Religious Endowments
Maulana Yakub Hasan Sait	Public Works
V. I. Munuswamy Pillai	Agriculture and Rural Development
S. Ramanathan Pillai	Public Information and Administration Reports
Kongattil Raman Menon	Courts and Prisons
C. J. Varkey, Chunkath	Education

Changes:

- On 7 January 1939, Raman Menon died and C. J. Varkey, was inducted into the Cabinet. Education portfolio was transferred from Subbarayan to Varkey and instead Subbarayan was given additional charge of Courts and Prisons.

Prohibition

Rajaji introduced The Prohibition Act in September 1937. This was the first time it was ever introduced in India. In order to offset the loss of revenue, he also introduced sales tax for the first time. The Act penalised manufacture, traffic in and consumption of liquor and intoxicating drugs in areas of Presidency it was introduced. It was first introduced in his home district of Salem on 1 October 1937. It was to be expanded to Chittoor and Cuddapah districts on 1 October 1938 and to North Arcot district in 1 October 1939. A provision was included in the Bill at the insistence of the Governor that British officials to be exempted from the Prohibition.

Government had a system to grant permits to individuals who consume foreign liquor. The Governor had given an order that all Europeans who apply for liquor licenses to be granted one. People could travel to areas in Presidency where the Prohibition was not enforced for consumption of liquors. There was system to regulate licensed clubs, wine for religious purposes in Churches, and brandy in Hospital for Medical purposes. Licenses were also given for toddy tapping.

Temple Entry Act

Rajaji who initially supported the idea of a Temple Entry Bill proposed by M. C. Raja in January 1938 backed off later and instead, supported the passage of Malabar Temple Entry Act. The Act paved the wave for entry of Harijans in temple in Malabar regions if the caste Hindus in the particular area did not object to it. M. C. Raja filed a complaint to Gandhi in disappointment to this modified Act. His government later passed Temple Entry Authorisation and Indemnity Act in 1939.

Second Term

Election Win: The 1952 election, the first election in Tamil Nadu after Indian independence produced no party with a clear majority. However, Indian National Congress emerged as the biggest party. Rajaji was invited by Sri Prakasa to form the Government on 1 April 1952 and was sworn in on 10 April 1952. He refused to run for a by-election and the Governor nominated him for the assembly's upper house (Legislative Council). In July 1952 he was able to win a vote of confidence with the support of 200 members with 151 opposing the confidence motion.

Cabinet

Minister	*Portfolio*
C. Rajagopalachari	Chief Minister, Public and Police
A. B. Shetty	Health
C. Subramaniam	Finance, Food and Elections
K. Venkataswamy Naidu	Religious Endowments and Registration

Contd...

Minister	***Portfolio***
N. Ranga Reddi	Public Works
M. V. Krishna Rao	Education, Harijan Uplift and Information
V. C. Palanisami Gounder	Prohibition
U. Krishna Rao	Industries, Labour, Motor Transport, Railways, Posts, Telegraphs and Civil Aviation
R. Nagana Goud	Agriculture, Forests, veterinary, Animal Husbandry, Fisheries and Cinchona
N. Sankara Reddi	Local Administration
M. A. Manickavelu Naicker	Land Revenue
K. P. Kuttikrishnan Nair	Courts, Prisons and Legal Department
Raja Sri Shanmuga Rajeswara Sethupathi	House Rent Control
S. B. B. Pattabirama Rao	Rural Welfare, Commercial Taxes and Scheduled areas
D. Sanjeevayya	Cooperation and Housing

Changes:

- The portfolios of Agriculture, Forests, Fisheries, Cinchona, Rural Welfare, Community Projects and National Extension Schemes were handed over to M. Bhaktavatsalam on October 9, 1953.
- C. Subramaniam was given the additional portfolios of education, information and publicity.
- V. C. Palaniswamy Gounder was put in charge of Veterinary, Animal Husbandry and Harijan welfare.

Hereditary Education Policy

The Modified Scheme of Elementary Education or New Scheme of Elementary Education or Madras Scheme of Elementary Education called by its critics as Kula Kalvi Thittam (Hereditary

Education Policy), was an abortive attempt at education reform introduced by the Indian National Congress Government of the Madras State, led by C. Rajagopalachari (Rajaji) in 1953. The scheme proposed the introduction of two shifts or sessions in elementary schools. In one session regular teaching would be done and during the second session, the students would be sent home to learn the occupations of their parents. It became controversial and was accused of being a casteist scheme to perpetuate the caste hierarchy. The opposition to the scheme was led by the Dravida Munnetra Kazhagam (DMK). Public opposition and internal dissent within the congress led to the deferment of the scheme. The discontent it triggered among the Congress legislature members forced the resignation of Rajaji as Chief Minister. The scheme was dropped completely by Rajaji's successor Kamaraj in 1954.

Impact

The 1937 elections marked the start of the Indian National Congress' participation in the governance of India. In the Madras Presidency, it also marked the beginning of Rajaji's ascendancy in the Congress Legislature Party. Though it was Satyamurti who had led the election campaign, he gave up the leadership of the Legislature to Rajaji in accordance to the wishes of the national leaders of the Congress in Delhi. This election also marked the beginning of Congress dominance in the politics of Madras Presidency and later the Madras State. Except for an interlude during 1939-46, the Congress would go on to rule Madras uninterrupted till 1967. The Justice Party was demoralised by its defeat and the Raja of Bobbili temporarily retired from active politics. The party remained in political wilderness and eventually came under the control of Periyar E. V. Ramaswamy in 1938 and transformed into the Dravidar Kazhagam in 1944.

Modified Education Policy

The Background

According to the 1951 Census of India, the literacy rate in the Madras State was 20.86 per cent. During fiscal year 1950-51, the Madras State Government spent 68.79 crore Rupees (68,79,00,000) — about 11.5 per cent of total revenues for the state — for Elementary education. The enrolment rate for children of school-going age was around 47.8 per cent. The Directive Principles of the Indian Constitution require the Indian state to provide education to all citizens. In accordance to this directive, in 1950 the Madras State's Directorate of Public Instruction prepared a ten year plan to provide education to all children of school-going age.

This plan called for an allocation of one crore (Rs. 1,00,00,000) per year for enrolling five lakh additional students for the next ten years. Against this, the actual allocation in 1950-51 was only rupees five lakh (Rs. 5,00,000). The cost of educating a student was estimated to be around Rs. 22.80 per year, out of which the government's contribution was only Rs. 16.30. Out of the 12,22,775 students who had enrolled in standard I in 1946-47, only 4,61,686 (37%) had reached the Standard V in 1950-51. It was against this background, the Congress party with Rajaji as chief minister took power on 10 April 1952.

Modified Scheme of Elementary Education

The Modified Scheme of Elementary Education or New Scheme of Elementary Education or Madras Scheme of Elementary Education called by its critics as Kula Kalvi Thittam (Hereditary Education Policy), was an abortive attempt at education reform introduced by the Indian National Congress Government of the Madras State, led by C. Rajagopalachari (Rajaji) in 1953. The scheme proposed the introduction of two shifts or sessions in elementary schools. In one session regular teaching would be done and during the second session, the students would be sent home to learn the occupations of their parents. It became controversial and was accused of being a casteist scheme to perpetuate the caste hierarchy. The opposition to the scheme was led by the Dravida Munnetra Kazhagam (DMK). Public opposition and internal dissent within the congress led to the deferment of the scheme. The discontent it triggered among the Congress legislature members forced the resignation of Rajaji as Chief Minister. The scheme was dropped completely by Rajaji's successor Kamaraj in 1954.

Earlier Attempts at Change

In 1939, during Rajaji's first term as Chief Minister of the Madras Presidency, the girl students of standards III to V and those belonging to Scheduled Castes had been allowed to attend school for only three hours a day and spend the rest of the day helping their parents. In the academic year 1949-50, during the Chief ministership of P. S. Kumaraswamy Raja, an experimental shift system had been introduced in ten taluks and later expanded to other areas as an optional measure. Schools which adapted this system functioned in two shifts or sessions. Teachers who worked during both sessions were paid an additional allowance of 10 Rupees per month. However this system was not widely adopted and by 1951 only 155 elementary schools (out of a total 38,687) in the state were functioning in shifts.

Reasons Stated for the Reform Attempt

- The cost of educating all children in the 6-12 age group would be enormous. Besides enrolment, more than half of the elementary schools lacked proper infrastructure. The reform attempted to increase the number of school-going children within the financial limitations faced by the Government.

- There was an acute shortage of teachers. The state had an average of less than three teachers for five standards per school. There were 4,108 single-teacher schools and more than 60 per cent of the schools with five standards had less than four teachers.
- This poor student-teacher ratio was putting a strain on the teachers and led to students being made to stay in school for longer hours. This directly contributed to the high drop out ratio. This plural teaching had to stopped without hiring new teachers.
- Rajaji favoured Gandhi's Basic Eduction Scheme over the existing elementary education system. He stated that he wanted to reduce the unemployment amongst educated people. The Basic education system called for learning through living and training in self reliance.
- The retention rate of 37 per cent (between 1947 and 1951) had to be improved by making schools attractive to students of poorer sections.

Proposals in the New Scheme

The Modified Scheme of Elementary education proposed the following changes in the school system:

- Reduction of School hours from five hours per day to three.
- Introduction of shifts — the students were to be divided into two batches and the school would function in two sessions. Each session will be of three hours duration, consisting of four periods of 40 minutes each, with not less than two intervals totalling 20 minutes. The sessions will be arranged to suit local conditions. One batch will attend only one session a day. There were to be six working days per week.

- No dilution of the previous syllabus and no reduction in duration for subjects like Language, Elementary Mathematics, Nature Study, Drawing, History, Geography, Hygiene, Civics, Moral Instruction and Singing.
- The second session in which the students would be out of school was to be utilised for obtaining the objectives of the basic education system — learning through living and training in self-reliance.
- During the out of school session, the girl students were to learn house keeping from their mothers in their home environment. The boys were supposed to learn farming or other crafts from their respective fathers.
- Boys whose parents did not belong to occupational groups, were to be sent to work in farms or with other craftsmen in their villages.
- In addition to the learning the students were to be utilised in service to the village like building sheds, laying bricks, attending to village sanitation, improving roads, etc.
- The out of school session would have no strict attendance or work requirements.

Implementation

The Rajaji Government introduced the new elementary education scheme in all schools in the non-municipal (rural) areas for the academic year 1953-54. It was planned that eventually the scheme would be extended to 35,000 of the total 38,687 schools in the state. However due to public opposition, it was put on hold on 29 July 1953 and dropped altogether on 18 May 1954.

Opposition

From the beginning, the scheme attracted heavy opposition from the Dravidian movement led by Periyar E. V. Ramaswamy. The Dravidar Kazhagam organised a conference in Erode protesting the scheme's introduction. The teachers' unions also opposed their move as they were not consulted before implementation. They also resented the increase in working hours without any increase in pay. The DMK seized the opportunity and started a campaign against the scheme. They dubbed the scheme as the Kula kalvi thittam (Hereditary/Caste Education Scheme) and as the Acharyar Education Scheme. The Dravidian movement viewed the scheme as an attempt to preserve and perpetuate caste based discrimination through official means. Rajaji and his education minister M. V. Krishna Rao responded with a counter campaign in the scheme's defence. They gave speeches and made broadcasts in the All India Radio explaining their position. The month of June 1953 saw aggressive propaganda efforts by both the proponents and opponents of the scheme. On 13 July 1953, the DMK executive committee met and decided to conduct a marial (blockade) agitation outside the Chief Minister's residence. EVK Sampath was nominated to lead the agitation. This agitation was part of a three pronged attack on the Government's policies by the DMK. On 14 July 1953, a possession led by Satyavani Muthu was organised to protest the scheme. Its destination was Rajaji's official residence at Bazullah road, T. Nagar. It was stopped by the police as it was unlicensed. The next day (15 July 1953) the confrontation heated up with the Government introducing a motion in the Legislative Assembly for implementing the scheme from the academic year 1953-54. On the same day another DMK procession was stopped before it could reach T Nagar. In the next fifteen days as many as twenty such processions were attempted by the DMK.

Deferment

By the end of July, public opinion started to turn against the scheme and at least four public petitions were tabled in the Legislative Assembly about the scheme. On 29 July 1953, M. V. Krishna Rao, the minister for education moved an motion for considering the new scheme. After a discussion, Communist leader K. P. Gopalan moved a motion to drop the scheme. The house was deadlocked with 138 ayes to 138 noes on dropping the scheme. The speaker of the assembly J. Shivashanmugam Pillai used his casting vote to defeat the motion. A second motion to defer the scheme and refer it to a committee of experts was moved by K. R. Vishwanatham. This motion passed with 138 ayes against 137 noes. The Scheme was stayed and the Parulekar Committee was commissioned to review the scheme.

Parulekar Committee

On 20 August 1953, the Government passed an order to constitute a committee of experts for reviewing the scheme. The committee was composed of Prof. RV. Parulekar, Director of Indian Institute of Education Bombay, as the Chairman; Dr. B. B. Dey, Retired Director of Public Instruction, Madras; Prof. Mohammad Mujeeb, Vice-Chancellor of the Jamia Millia University as members and S. Govindarajulu Naidu, the former Director of Public Instruction, Madras, and the then Director of Public Instruction, Andhra Pradesh, as the Member Secretary. The Parulekar committee submitted its report on 23 November 1953. It found the scheme to be sound and endorsed the Government's position. It made additional recommendations including extending the scheme to rural areas, opening as many as 4,000 new schools, revising the existing curriculum, providing training and remuneration to the craftsmen involved.

Cancellation

The opposition campaign was successful in creating doubts about the scheme in the minds of the general public. There was dissent within the Congress party and Kamaraj wanted Rajaji to withdraw the scheme as it was unpopular amongst the public and with the party members. On 20 October 1953, forty Congress Legislative Assembly members led by K. Rajaram Naidu, sent a memorandum to Nehru objecting to Rajaji's unilateral conduct. Among the issues they raised was his refusal to budge on the education scheme issue. But Rajaji refused to drop the scheme. On 8 November 1953, Congress lost the by election for the Kangayam constituency by a narrow margin.

Pressure mounted from within the party to drop the scheme. Faced with defeat in the annual election of the Congress Legislative Party, he decided to quit. His preferred successor C. Subramaniam was defeated by Kamaraj in the CLP election on 31 March 1954. Rajaji resigned and Kamaraj took over as chief minister on 13 April 1954. This effectively ended the prospects of the new education scheme. On 18 May 1954, the new education minister C. Subramaniam announced in the assembly that the scheme was being dropped. The reason stated for the dropping was that the necessary acceptance, support and cooperation of the people were not forthcoming for the scheme and the atmosphere was not propitious for the success of the scheme.

Meanwhile, the composite Madras State had been reorganised along linguistic lines. The state of Andhra had split from Madras on 1 October 1953. The Andhra Government constituted an Elementary Education Committee with Dr. B. Kuppuswamy as chairman to review the elementary education situation. The Kuppuswamy committee report recommended the rejection of the Modified Elementary Education Scheme. In 1954, the Andhra state cancelled the scheme.

Criticism

The main arguments made against the Modified Scheme of Elementary Education were:

- That the scheme was casteist by design. It aimed to preserve and perpetuate the caste hierarchy by ensuring that children took up their parents' profession. It was designed to ensure Brahmins alone got positions and authority.
- That it intended to reduce the schooling imparted to children by not monitoring them during out of school sessions.
- That it would increase the workload of teachers as it would increase their working hours and force them to handle more children without the appointment of new teachers and without an increase in their pay.
- That it was undemocratic and dictatorial as Rajaji had not consulted his Cabinet or the assembly in his decision to implement the scheme (In Rajaji's own words — *This is an executive matter, no law is involved*).
- That it was deliberately targeted at rural children alone to keep them from getting an education.

Writing in *Viduthalai* on 17 November 1953, Periyar denounced the scheme as a Brahiminical conspiracy:

> "This educational policy is a casteist educational policy. This has to be opposed and abolished... Is this educational scheme not a reconstruction and

> protection of varnashrama? ...who physically labours and slaves in the name of caste? Only we, who are called shudras ...should we keep doing the caste occupation while brahmins alone get positions, employment, authority and go higher and higher? ...is this justified? ...we don't think physical labour is disgraceful, but why should we alone do that work?....
>
> ...How much of opposition to Rajaji's minister post? Though the situation is such that his post can topple any day. If he can manage all that and still have a tight grip, what is it for? Only to save his race, only for the protection of the Brahmin society. As long as he is in power, he wants to fill up Brahmins in all the places. He wants to repress the Shudras, and with that motive alone he remains in power. Among us we do not have this mind, this feeling, this racial fanaticism! He fights for the welfare of the Brahmin race..."

In another Viduthalai article written on 26 February 1954, he vowed to destroy the scheme by any means:

> "Rajaji says that people in the villages do not need education. He has said that the student in the village should cut hair, he should wash clothes, and he should make pots and pans. The village school is only for three hours duration, the rest of the time our children should graze donkeys, this is called the New Primary Education Scheme. We organised a conference in Erode only to oppose this educational scheme. Can we keep looking at law and democracy in such a situation? The work will be successful only through a great revolution. Though 100, 1000 of us will have to be sacrificed, we need to be prepared. That is why even I gave a three months notice; and said that if they want to shoot, let them shoot. I am going to start a struggle. This educational scheme has to be destroyed by all means."

He kept up his harangue even after Rajaji resigned and C. Subramaniam became the new Education minister. On 17 April 1954 he wrote:

> "Rajaji did this only because of the fear that the position of his society will disappear. If the Vanaan washes clothes, if the Paraiyan beats the drums, if the Chakkili stitches shoes, if the Ambattan shaves, only then they will get the feeling that they are a low caste. If they also get educated and come ahead, the highness of the upper castes will disappear. So, Rajaji interfered in the basics by introducing a 3-hour occupational education...
>
> ...The servant of this Rajaji, C. Subramanian was the one who raised his hand to say that Shudras don't need communal representation. Those who had gone on the merit of our votes were sitting there like the five Pandavas during Draupadi's disrobing. All this takes place in this country. If it had been another country, four or five (death) anniversaries would have been observed for such people. When it is so, how can we fight legally?"

The Andhra Elementary Education Committee Report also rejected the Modified Scheme and recommended an approach similar to the one eventually adopted by the Kamaraj Government.

Defence and Endorsements

During and after his tenure as Chief Minister, Rajaji defended his scheme vigorously. He derided the critics as people who did not want to do physical labour:

> "The opposition to the scheme comes mainly from those who do not want to do any physical labour. There are others who ask whether there will be any examination in the crafts. That may come or may not come. But I would like you to ponder over one factor. Are not the children of parents with an educational tradition at an advantage now over children whose

> parents have no education at all? Should an examination in crafts be held, will not the children of illiterate artisans score over the other class of children? In that way will not the handicap of the poor man's children be removed? The new system gives a chance to the backward people to progress. I would, therefore, appeal to you all to support the scheme or at least desist from opposing it."

About the casteist angle of the criticism, he reasoned that it was because of him being the author of the scheme:

> "It is indeed regrettable that it should be said that there is a big conspiracy behind the new scheme. Probably because i am its author, some people suspect there is something behind it ...If some other person would have done it, by God's grace, everyone might have accepted it and the scheme might have worked successfully... I made similar suggestions over 30 years ago."

After the Kamaraj Government scrapped the scheme, he again defended it as:

> "My plan was based on the conviction — which was confirmed by educational officers of highest rank and experience — that three hours attendance was quite adequate for the purpose and would leave nothing out of the present elementary school instruction."

Replying to Papanasam MLA Swayam Prakasam's concerns over the scheme, then Prime Minister, Jawaharlal Nehru offered his endorsement to the scheme:

> "As for the education policy which Rajaji has sponsored, I cannot speak for conditions in Madras. But that policy is an aspect of Basic Education which is the proved policy of our Government. The Madras proposals, as you know, were referred to a special High-powered Committee of Educationists. They expressed their approval of them.... At the Governors' Conference recently, the Madras proposals were not

> directly discussed, but the present system was discussed and thoroughly disapproved of and generally the basic system was approved."

India's President Rajendra Prashad offered his support in a letter written to the Governor of Madras — Sri Prakasa — on 9 June 1953:

> "I have read with great interest both the speech of Rajaji and the scheme of education in primary schools in rural areas. I have felt great dissatisfaction with the present scheme of things so far as education is concerned... with the large number of graduates and under graduates we are turning out from year to year are without any employment... most of them are unemployable...
>
> This scheme fits them at any rate for their parents' work or for the work people have been doing in their own place. With education it may be hoped that they would be able to do that work better. I there look forward with great hope and enthusiasm to this experiment."

The Central Advisory Board of Education, passed a resolution endorsing the scheme during its 21st Meeting held in February 1954:

> "The Central Advisory Board of Education has given careful consideration to the Modified Scheme of Elementary Education formulated by the Madras Government. It is of the opinion that the Scheme represents a welcome attempt to bring education within the reach of a large majority of children and thus help in the achievement of the constitutional directive about the provision of universal Primary Education. The Board is also satisfied that the reduction of school hours from five to three will not necessarily affect the education of children adversely, provided the out-of-school activities which are an integral part of the education of children are implemented under controlled conditions. The Board

also appreciates the attempt made in the Scheme for bringing education into closer contact with the life of the community and this gives it a practical bias which is at present lacking in ordinary Primary Schools.

The Board would, however, like to point out that the arrangements made for the out-of-school activities of the children need to be carefully supervised on the lines suggested by the Parulekar Committee and their success critically assessed from time to time. Further, the Board would like to place on record its definite opinion that this Scheme is valuable as an interim measure only, because, sufficient funds are not at present available for providing education to all the children and that the proper pattern of education for the country is Basic Education which would offer full-time co-related education to children in which teaching of craft as well as of other school subjects will be provided under proper educative conditions in the school itself, which will serve as a community centre where the school and the community are brought into an organic relationship.

The Board would also recommend that other States may conduct similar experiments under controlled conditions. (The Madras Government have since intimated their decision to discontinue their modified scheme of Elementary Education)"

The Legacy

The Modified Scheme of Elementary Education even after being dropped had the unintended consequence of bringing primary education to Lakhs of school children in Tamil Nadu. Rajaji's successor Kamaraj was ever mindful of the fact that it was the issue of primary education that caused his predecessor's downfall. Knowing the public opposition to Rajaji's scheme he took the diametrically opposite approach in providing education to Tamil Nadu's children — imparting free and compulsory education till the age of 14. He set up a commission under R. M. Alagappa Chettiar to examine the means for providing compulsory primary education.

Instead of sending children away from the school, the committee recommended active Government intervention to bring more children into the schooling system by building new schools and abolishing school fees. This approach was successful and by the end of Kamaraj's tenure as Chief Minister in 1963, enrolment in primary schools had been doubled.

6

Anti-Hindi Agitations in Tamil Nadu

The first anti-Hindi agitation was launched in 1937, in opposition to the introduction of compulsory teaching of Hindi in the schools of Madras Presidency by the first Indian National Congress government led by C. Rajagopalachari (Rajaji). This move was immediately opposed by E. V. Ramaswamy (Periyar) and the opposition Justice Party (later Dravidar Kazhagam). The agitation, which lasted three years, was multifaceted and involved fasts, conferences, marches, picketing and protests. The government responded with a crackdown resulting in the death of two protesters and the arrest of 1,198 persons including women and children. The mandatory Hindi education was later withdrawn by the British Governor of Madras Lord Erskine in February 1940 after the resignation of the Congress Government in 1939.

The anti-Hindi agitations of Tamil Nadu are a series of agitations that happened in the state of Tamil Nadu (formerly Madras State and part of Madras Presidency) during both pre- and post-Independence periods. The agitations involved several mass protests, riots, student and political movements in Tamil Nadu, and concerned the official status of Hindi in the state and in the Indian Republic.

Adoption of an official language for the Indian Republic was a hotly debated issue during the framing of the Indian Constitution after India's independence from Britain. After an exhaustive and divisive debate, Hindi was adopted as the official language of India with English continuing as an associate official language for a period of fifteen years, after which Hindi would become the sole official language. The new Constitution came into effect on 26 January 1950. Efforts by the Indian Government to make Hindi the sole official language after 1965 were not acceptable to many non-Hindi Indian states, who wanted the continued use of English. The Dravida Munnetra Kazhagam (DMK), a descendant of Dravidar Kazhagam, led the opposition to Hindi. To allay their fears, Prime Minister Jawaharlal Nehru enacted the Official Languages Act in 1963 to ensure the continuing use of English beyond 1965. The text of the Act did not satisfy the DMK and increased their skepticism that his assurances might not be honoured by future administrations.

As the day (26 January 1965) of switching over to Hindi as sole official language approached, the anti-Hindi movement gained momentum in Madras State with increased support from college students. On 25 January, a full-scale riot broke out in the southern city of Madurai, sparked off by a minor altercation between agitating students and Congress party members. The riots spread all over Madras State, continued unabated for the next two months, and were marked by acts of violence, arson, looting, police firing and lathi-charges. The Congress Government of the Madras State, called in paramilitary forces to quell the agitation; their involvement resulted in the deaths of about seventy persons (by official estimates) including two policemen. To calm the situation, Indian Prime Minister Lal Bahadur Shastri gave assurances that English would continue to be used as the official language as long the non-Hindi speaking states wanted. The riots subsided after Shastri's assurance, as did the student agitation.

The agitations of 1965 led to major political changes in the state. The DMK won the 1967 assembly election and the Congress Party never managed to recapture power in the state since then. The Official Languages Act was eventually amended in 1967 by the Congress Government headed by Indira Gandhi to guarantee the indefinite use of Hindi and English as official languages. This effectively ensured the current "virtual indefinite policy of bilingualism" of the Indian Republic. There were also two similar (but smaller) agitations in 1968 and 1986 which had varying degrees of success.

The Backdrop

The Republic of India has hundreds of languages. According to the Census of 2001, there are 1,635 rationalised mother tongues and 122 languages with more than 10,000 speakers. During the British Raj, English was the official language. When the Indian Independence Movement gained momentum in the early part of the 20th century, efforts were undertaken to make Hindustani as a common language to unite various linguistic groups against the British Government. As early as 1918, Mahatma Gandhi established the Dakshin Bharat Hindi Prachar Sabha (Institution for the Propagation of Hindi in South India). In 1925, the Indian National Congress switched to Hindustani from English for conducting its proceedings. Both Gandhi and Jawaharlal Nehru were supporters of Hindustani and Congress wanted to propagate the learning of Hindustani in non-Hindi speaking Provinces of India. The idea of making Hindustani or Hindi the common language, was not acceptable to Periyar, who viewed it as an attempt to make Tamils subordinate to North Indians.

Agitations of 1937-40

The Indian National Congress won the 1937 elections in Madras Presidency. Rajaji became the Chief Minister on 14 July 1937. He was a supporter of propagating Hindi in South India. On 11 August 1937, within a month of coming to power, he announced his intention to introduce Hindi language teaching in secondary schools by issuing a policy statement. On 21 April 1938, he issued a government order (G.O.) making the teaching of Hindi compulsory in 125 secondary schools in the Presidency. Periyar and the opposition Justice Party led by A. T. Panneerselvam immediately opposed the move. They started state wide protests against Rajaji and Hindi.

The agitation was backed by Periyar's Self-respect Movement and Justice Party. It also had the support of Tamil scholars like Maraimalai Adigal, Somasundara Bharathi, K. Appadurai,

Mudiyarasan and Ilakkuvanar. In December 1937, Tamil Shivite scholars were among the first to announce their opposition to the Hindi teaching in the Saiva Sidhandha Maha Samaja conference at Velur. Women also participated in the agitation in large numbers. Moovalur Ramamirtham, Narayani, Va. Ba. Thamaraikani, Munnagar Azhagiyar, Dr. Dharmambal, Malar Mugathammaiyar, Pattammal and Seethammal were some of the women who were arrested for participating in the agitation. On 13 November 1938, the Tamil Nadu Women's Conference was convened to demonstrate women's support for the movement. The agitation was marked by anti-Brahmin sentiments as the protesters believed Brahmins were attempting to impose Hindi and Sanskrit over Tamil. Despite the general anti-Brahminism of the agitation, a few Brahmins like Kanchi Rajagopalachari also participated in the movement. The Tamil speaking Muslims in the Madras presidency supported the agitation (in contrast to the Urdu speaking Muslims, who supported the propagation of Hindi). The agitation was marked by fasts, protest marches, processions, picketing of schools teaching Hindi and government offices, anti-Hindi conferences, observing an anti-Hindi day (1 July and 3 December 1938) and black flag demonstrations. It was active in the Tamil speaking districts of the Presidency — Ramnad, Tinnevely, Salem, Tanjore and North Arcot. During the course of the agitation, two protesters — Thalamuthu and Natarajan — lost their lives in police custody.

The ruling Congress Party was divided on the Hindi issue. While Rajaji and his supporters stuck to their position, Sathyamurti and Sarvepalli Radhakrishnan were against it. They wanted Rajaji to make Hindi optional or to provide a conscience clause for allowing parents to withhold their children from Hindi Classes. But Rajaji was firm in his stance. The police response to the agitation grew progressively brutal in 1939. During the agitation, a total of 1,198 protesters were arrested and out of them 1,179 were convicted (73 of those jailed were women and 32 children accompanied their mothers to prison). Periyar was fined 1,000 Rupees and sentenced to one year of rigorous imprisonment for inciting "women to disobey the law" (he was released within six months on 22 May 1939 citing medical grounds) and Annadurai was jailed for four months. On 7 June 1939, all those arrested for participating in the agitations were released without explanation.

Rajaji also organised pro-Hindustani meetings to counter the agitators. On 29 October 1939, the Congress government resigned protesting the involvement of India in the Second World War, and the Madras provincial government was placed under Governor's rule. On 31 October, Periyar suspended the agitation and asked the Governor to withdraw the compulsory Hindi order. On 21 February 1940, Governor Erskine issued a press communique withdrawing compulsory Hindi teaching and making it optional.

Agitations of 1946-50

During 1946-50, there were sporadic agitations against Hindi by the Dravidar Kazhagam (DK) and Periyar. Whenever the government introduced Hindi as a compulsory language in schools, anti-Hindi protests happened and succeeded in stopping the move. The largest anti-Hindi agitations in this period occurred in 1948-50. After India obtained independence in 1947, the Congress Government at the Centre urged all states to make Hindi compulsory in schools.

The Congress Government of Madras Presidency under Omandur Ramaswamy Reddiar complied and made Hindi compulsory from the academic year 1948-49. It also introduced a minimum mark qualification in Hindi for the promotion of students to higher classes. Periyar once again launched an anti-Hindi agitation. The 1948 agitation was supported by former Congress nationalists like M. P. Sivagnanam and Thiru. Vi. Ka, who recanted their earlier pro-Hindi policies. On 17 July, the DK convened an all party anti-Hindi conference to oppose the compulsory Hindi teaching.

As in the agitation of 1938-40, this agitation was also characterised by strikes, black flag demonstrations and anti-Hindi processions. When Rajaji (then the Governor General of India) visited Madras on 23 August, the DK staged a black flag demonstration protesting against his visit. On 27 August, Periyar and Annadurai were arrested. The Government did not change its position on Hindi and the agitation continued. On 18 August Periyar and other DK leaders were arrested again. A compromise was reached between the government and agitators. The government stopped the legal action against the agitators and they in turn dropped the agitation on 26 December 1948. Eventually, the government made Hindi teaching optional from the academic year 1950-51. Students who did not want to learn Hindi were allowed to participate in other school activities during Hindi classes.

Official Languages and the Indian Constitution

The Indian Constituent Assembly was established on 9 December 1946, for drafting a Constitution when India became independent. The Constituent Assembly witnessed fierce debates on the language issue. The adoption of a "National Language", the language in which the Constitution was to be written in and the language in which the proceedings of the assembly were to be conducted were the main linguistic questions debated by the framers of the Constitution.

On one side were the members from the Hindi speaking provinces like Algu Rai Shastri, R. V. Dhulekar, Balkrishna Sharma, Purushottam Das Tandon, (all from United Provinces), Babunath Gupta (Bihar), Hari Vinayak Pataskar (Bombay) and Seth Govind Das (Central Provinces and Berar). They moved a large number of pro-Hindi amendments and argued for adopting Hindi as the sole National Language. On 10 December 1946, Dhulekar declared "People who do not know Hindustani have no right to stay in India. People who are present in the House to fashion a Constitution for India and do not know Hindustani are not worthy to be members of this assembly. They had better leave."

The pro-Hindi block was further divided into two camps: the Hindi faction comprising Tandon, Govind Das, Sampurnanand, Ravishankar Shukla and K. M. Munshi; and the Hindustani faction represented by Jawaharlal Nehru and Abul Kalam Azad. The adoption of Hindi as the national language was opposed by members from South India like T. T. Krishnamachari, G. Durgabai, T. A. Ramalingam Chettiar, N. G. Ranga, N. Gopalaswamy Ayyangar (all belonging to Madras) and S. V. Krishnamurthy Rao (Mysore). This anti-Hindi block favoured retaining English as official language. Their views were reflected in the following pronouncement of Krishnamachari:

> We disliked the English language in the past. I disliked it because I was forced to learn Shakespeare and

> Milton, for which I had no taste at all. If we are going to be compelled to learn Hindi, I would perhaps not be able to learn it because of my age, and perhaps I would not be willing to do it because of the amount of constraint you put on me. This kind of intolerance makes us fear that the strong Centre which we need, a strong Centre which is necessary will also mean the enslavement of people who do not speak the language at the centre. I would, Sir, convey a warning on behalf of people of the South for the reason that there are already elements in South India who want separation..., and my honourable friends in U.P. do not help us in any way by flogging their idea of "Hindi Imperialism" to the maximum extent possible. So, it is up to my friends in Uttar Pradesh to have a whole India; it is up to them to have a Hindi-India. The choice is theirs.

After three years of debate, the assembly arrived at a compromise at the end of 1949. It was called the Munshi-Ayyangar formula (after K. M. Munshi and Gopalaswamy Ayyangar) and it struck a balance between the demands of all groups. Part XVII of the Indian Constitution was drafted according to this compromise. It did not have any mention of a "National Language". Instead, it defined only the "Official Languages" of the Union:

> Hindi in Devanagari script would be the official language of the Indian Union. For fifteen years, English would also be used for all official purposes (Article 343). A language commission could be convened after five years to recommend ways to promote Hindi as the sole official language and to phase out the use of English (Article 344). Official communication between states and between states and the Union would be in the official language of the union (Article 345). English would be used for all legal purposes — in court proceedings, bills, laws, rules and other regulations (Article 348). The Union was duty bound to promote the spread and usage of Hindi (Article 351).

India became independent on 15 August 1947 and the Constitution was adopted on 26 January 1950.

Language Commission

The adoption of English as official language along with Hindi was heavily criticised by pro-Hindi politicians like Jana Sangh's founder Syama Prashad Mukherjee, who demanded that Hindi should be made National language. Soon after the Constitution was adopted on 26 January 1950, efforts were made to propagate Hindi for official usage. In 1952, the Ministry of Education launched a voluntary Hindi teaching scheme. On 27 May 1952, use of Hindi was introduced in warrants for judicial appointments. In 1955, in-house Hindi training was started for all ministries and departments of the central government. On 3 December 1955, the government started using Hindi (along with English) for "specific purposes of the Union".

As provided for by Article 343, Nehru appointed the First Official Language Commission under the chairmanship of B. G. Kher on 7 June 1955. The commission delivered its report on 31 July 1956. It recommended a number of steps to eventually replace English with Hindi (The report had dissenting notes from two non-Hindi members — P. Subbarayan from Madras State and Suniti Kumar Chatterji from West Bengal). The Parliamentary Committee on Official Language, chaired by Govind Ballabh Pant was constituted in September 1957 to review the Kher commission report. After two years of deliberations, the Pant Committee submitted its recommendations to the President on 8 February 1959. It recommended that Hindi should be made the primary official language with English as the subsidiary one. The Kher Commission and the Pant Committee recommendations were condemned and opposed by from non-Hindi politicians like Suniti Kumar Chatterji, Frank Anthony and P. Subbarayan. The Academy of Telugu opposed the switch from English to Hindi in a convention held in 1956. Rajaji, once a staunch supporter of Hindi, organised an All India Language Conference (attended by representatives of Tamil, Malayalam, Telugu, Assamese, Oriya, Marathi, Kannada and Bengali languages) on 8 March 1958 to oppose the switch and declared "Hindi is as much foreign to non-Hindi speaking people as English is to the protagonists of Hindi."

As the opposition to Hindi grew stronger, Nehru tried to reassure the concerns of non-Hindi speakers. Speaking in the parliamentary debate on a bill introduced by Anthony to include English in the Eighth Schedule, Nehru gave an assurance to them (on 7 August 1959):

> I believe also two things. As I just said, there must be no imposition. Secondly, for an indefinite period — I do not know how long — I should have, I would have English as an associate, additional language which can be used not because of facilities and all that... but because I do not wish the people of non-Hindi areas to feel that certain doors of advance are closed to them because they are forced to correspond — the Government, I mean — in the Hindi language. They can correspond in English. So I could have it as an alternate language as long as people require it and the decision for that — I would leave not to the Hindi-knowing people, but to the non-Hindi-knowing people.

This assurance momentarily allayed the fears of the South Indians. But the Hindi proponents were dismayed and Pant remarked "Whatever I achieved in two years, the Prime Minister destroyed in less than two minutes".

DMK's Anti-Hindi Policies

The Dravida Munnetra Kazhagam (DMK) which split from the Dravidar Kazhagam in 1949, inherited the anti-Hindi policies of its parent organisation. DMK's founder Annadurai had earlier participated in the anti-Hindi agitations during 1938-40 and in the 1940s. In July 1953, the DMK launched an agitation for changing the name of a town — Dalmiapuram — to Kallakudi. They claimed that the town's name (after Ramkrishna Dalmia) symbolised the exploitation of South India by the North. On 15 July 1953, M. Karunanidhi (later Chief Minister of Tamil Nadu) and other DMK members erased the Hindi name in Dalmiapuram railway station's name board and lay down on the tracks. In the altercation with the Police that followed the protests, two DMK members lost their lives and several others including Karunanidhi were arrested.

In the 1950s DMK continued its anti-Hindi policies along with the secessionist demand for Dravidistan. On 28 January 1956, Annadurai along with Periyar and Rajaji signed a resolution passed by the Academy of Tamil Culture endorsing the continuation of English as the official language. On 21 September 1957 the DMK convened an anti-Hindi Conference to protest against the imposition of Hindi. It observed 13 October 1957 as "anti-Hindi Day". On 31 July 1960, another open air anti-Hindi conference was held at Kodambakkam, Madras. In November 1963, DMK dropped its secessionist demand in the wake of the Sino-Indian War and the passage of the anti-secessionist 16th Amendment to the Indian Constitution. But the anti-Hindi stance remained and hardened with the passage of Official Languages Act of 1963. The DMK's view on Hindi's qualifications for official language status were reflected in Annadurai's response to the "numerical superiority of Hindi" argument: "If we had to accept the principle of numerical superiority while selecting our national bird, the choice would have fallen not on the peacock but on the common crow."

Official Languages Act of 1963

As the deadline stipulated in Part XVII of the Constitution for switching to Hindi as primary official language approached, the central government stepped up its efforts to spread Hindi's official usage. In 1960, compulsory training for Hindi typing and stenography was started. The same year, India's President Rajendra Prashad acted on the Pant Committee's recommendations and issued orders for preparation of Hindi glossaries, translating procedural literature and legal codes to Hindi, imparting Hindi education to government employees and other efforts for propagating Hindi.

To give legal status to Nehru's assurance of 1959, the Official Languages Act was passed in 1963. In Nehru's own words:

> This is a Bill, in continuation of what has happened in the past, to remove a restriction which had been placed by the Constitution on the use of English after a certain date, i.e. 1965. It is just to remove that restriction that this is placed.

The Bill was introduced in Parliament on 21 January 1963. Opposition to the Bill came from DMK members who objected to the usage of the word "may" instead of "shall" in section 3 of the Bill. That section read: "the English language may... continue to be used in addition to Hindi". The DMK argued was that the term "may" could be interpreted as "may not" by future administrations. They feared that the minority opinion would not be considered and non-Hindi speakers' views would be ignored.

On 22 April, Nehru assured the parliamentarians that, for that particular case "may" had the same meaning as "shall". The DMK then demanded, if that was the case why "shall" was not used instead of "may". Leading the opposition to the Bill was Annadurai (then a Member of the Rajya Sabha). He pleaded for an indefinite continuation of the status quo and argued that continued use of English as official language would "distribute advantages or disadvantages evenly" among Hindi and non-Hindi speakers. The Bill was passed on 27 April without any change in the wording. As he had warned earlier, Annadurai launched state wide protests against Hindi.

In November 1963, Annadurai was arrested along with 500 DMK members for burning part XVII of the Constitution at an anti-Hindi Conference. He was sentenced to six months in prison. On 25 January 1964, a DMK member, Chinnasamy, committed suicide at Trichy by self immolation, to protest the "imposition of Hindi". He was claimed as the first "language martyr" of the second round of the anti-Hindi struggle by the DMK.

Nehru died in May 1964 and Lal Bahadur Shastri became Prime Minister of India. Shastri and his senior Cabinet members Morarji Desai and Gulzari Lal Nanda were strong supporters of Hindi being the sole official language. This increased the apprehension that Nehru's assurances of 1959 and 1963 will not be kept despite Shastri's assurances to the contrary.

Concerns over the preference of Hindi in central government jobs, civil service examinations and the fear that English would be replaced with Hindi as medium of instruction brought students into the anti-Hindi agitation camp in large numbers. On 7 March 1964, the chief minister of Madras State, M. Bhaktavatsalam at a session of the Madras Legislative Assembly recommended the introduction of Three-language formula (English, Hindi and Tamil) in the state. Apprehension over the Three-language formula increased student support for the anti-Hindi cause.

Agitation of 1965

As January 26, 1965 approached, the anti-Hindi agitation in Madras State grew in numbers and urgency. The Tamil Nadu Students anti-Hindi Agitation Council was formed in January as an umbrella student organisation to coordinate the anti-Hindi efforts. The office bearers of the council were student union leaders from all over Madras State including P. Sreenivasan, K. Kalimuthu, Na. Kamarasan, Seyaprakasam, Ravichandran, Tiruppur. S. Duraiswamy, Sedapatti Muthaiah, Durai Murugan, K. Raja Jmad, Navalavan, M. Natarajan and L. Ganesan.

Several student conferences were organised throughout the state to protest against Hindi imposition. On 17 January, the Madras State anti-Hindi Conference was convened at Trichy and was attended by 700 delegates from Madras, Maharashtra, Kerala and Mysore. They called for the indefinite suspension of Part XVII of the Constitution. The Home and Information and Broadcasting ministries of the central government (headed by Nanda and Indira Gandhi respectively) upped the ante and issued circulars for replacing English with Hindi from 26 January.

On 16 January, Annadurai announced that 26 January (also the Republic Day of India) would be observed as a day of mourning. Chief minister Bhaktavatsalam warned that the state government would not tolerate the sanctity of the Republic day blasphemed and threatened the students with "stern action" if they participated in politics. The DMK advanced the "Day of Mourning" by a day. On 25 January, Annadurai was taken into preventive custody along with 3000 DMK members to forestall the agitations planned for the next day. On 26 January, 50,000 students from Madras city's colleges marched from Napier park to the Government secretariat at Fort St. George and unsuccessfully tried to petition the chief minister.

On 25 January, a clash between agitating students and Congress party workers in Madurai went out of control and became a riot. Rioting soon spread to other parts of the State. Police responded with lathi-charges and firing on student processions. Acts of arson, looting and damage to public property became common. Railway cars and Hindi name boards at railway stations were burned down; telegraph poles were cut and railway tracks displaced. The Bhaktavatsalam Government considered the situation as a law and order problem and brought in para military forces to quell the agitation. Incensed by police action, violent mobs killed two police men. Several agitators committed suicide by self-immolation and by consuming poison. In two weeks of riots, around 70 people were killed (by official estimates). Some unofficial reports put the death toll as high as 500. A large number of students were arrested. The damage to property was assessed as one crore Rupees.

On 28 January, classes in Madras University, Annamalai University and other colleges and schools in the state were suspended indefinitely. Within the Congress, opinion was divided: one group led by K. Kamaraj wanted the government not to impose Hindi on the Tamils; but others like Morarji Desai did not relent. Home minister Nanda agreed with Bhaktavatsalam's handling of the agitation. Rioting continued through out the first week of February and by the second week students lost control of the agitation. Violence continued despite Annadurai's appeal for calm. Efforts were made by both sides to find a compromise. On 11 February, C. Subramaniam and O. V. Alagesan, two union ministers from Madras state, resigned protesting the government's language policy. President Sarvepalli Radhakrishnan refused to accept the Prime Minister Shastri's recommendation that their resignations be accepted. Shastri backed down and made a broadcast through All India Radio on February 11. Expressing shock over the riots, he promised to honour Nehru's assurances. He also assured Tamils that English would continue to be used for centre-state and intrastate communications and that the All India Civil Services examination would continue to be conducted in English.

The Impact

Shastri's assurances calmed down the volatile situation. On 12 February, the students council postponed the agitation indefinitely and on 16 February, C. Subramaniam and O. V.

Alagesan withdrew their resignations. Sporadic acts of protests and violence continued to happen throughout February and early March. On 7 March, the administration withdrew all the cases filed against the student leaders and on 14 March, the anti-Hindi Agitation Council dropped the agitation. Shastri's climbdown angered the pro-Hindi activists in North India. Members of Jan Sangh went about the streets of New Delhi, blackening out English signs with tar. The agitation slowly changed into a general anti-Congress organisation. In the 1967 election, student leader P. Sreenivasan contested against Kamaraj in the Virudhunagar constituency. A large number of students from all over the state campaigned for him and ensured his victory: the Congress party was defeated and DMK came to power for the first time in Madras State.

Official Languages (Amendment) Act of 1967

Amendment Efforts in 1965: Efforts to amend the Official Languages Act according to Shastri's assurances given in February 1965 faced stiff resistance from the pro-Hindi lobby. On 16 February, 55 MPs from 8 different states publicly expressed their disapproval of any change in the Language policy. On 19 February, 19 MPs from Maharashtra and Gujarat voiced their opposition for change and on 25 February, 106 Congress MPs met the Prime Minister to request him not to amend the Act. However, Congress MPs from Madras did not debate the issue on the Parliament floor but met the Prime Minister on 12 March. Congress and opposition parties hesitated to debate the issue in Parliament as they did not wish to make their bitter divisions on public. On 22 February at a meeting in Congress Working Committee, K. Kamaraj pressed for the amendment to Official Languages Act, but received instant opposition from Morarji Desai, Jagjivan Ram and Ram Subhag. The Congress working committee finally agreed to a resolution which amounted to slowing down of Hindisation, strong implementation of the three language formula in Hindi and non-Hindi speaking states, and conduct of the public services exam in all regional languages. These decisions were agreed upon during the Chief Ministers' meeting which was held on February 24.

The three language formula was not strictly enforced either in South or Hindi-speaking areas. The changes to public services exams were impractical and not well received by government officials. The only real concession to the south was the assurance that the Official Languages Act would be modified. However, any effort to follow through with that pledge received stiff resistance. In April 1965, a meeting of a Cabinet subcommittee comprising Gulzari lay Nanda, A. K. Sen, Satyanarayan Sinha, Mahavir Tyagi, M. C. Chagla and S. K. Patil and but no southern members debated the issue and could not come to any agreement.

The subcommittee recommended the continuation of English and Hindi as joint link languages and was not in favour of either quota system or use of regional languages in public services exams. They drafted an amendment to Official Languages Act incorporating Nehru's assurances explicitly. This Bill guaranteeing the use of English in inter-state and state-Union communications as long as desired by Non-Hindi states was approved for discussion by the Speaker on August 25. But it was withdrawn after a bitter debate citing inopportune time due to the ongoing Punjabi Suba movement and Kashmir crisis at that time.

Amendment in 1967

Shastri died in January 1966 and Indira Gandhi became Prime Minister. The election of 1967 saw Congress retaining power with a reduced majority. In Madras State, Congress was defeated and DMK came to power. In November 1967, a new attempt to amend the Bill was made. On 27 November, the Bill was tabled in Parliament; it was passed on 16 December (by 205 votes to 41 against). It received presidential assent on 8 January 1968 and came into effect. The Amendment modified section 3 of the 1963 Act to guarantee the "virtual indefinite policy of bilingualism" (English and Hindi) in official transactions.

Agitation of 1968

The anti-Hindi activists from Madras State were not satisfied with the 1967 Amendment, as it did not address their concerns about the three language formula. However, with DMK in power, they hesitated to restart the agitation. The Tamil Nadu Students' anti-Hindi Agitation council split into several factions. The moderate factions favoured letting Annadurai and the government to deal with the situation. The extremist factions restarted the agitations. They demanded scrapping of the three language formula and an end to teaching of Hindi, abolishing the use of Hindi commands in the National Cadet Corps (NCC), banning of Hindi films and songs and closure of the Dakshina Bharat Hindi Prachara Sabha - the Institution for propagation of Hindi in South India.

On 19 December 1967, the agitation was restarted. It turned violent in 21 December and acts of arson and looting were reported in the state. Annadurai defused the situation by accepting most of their demands. On 23 January 1968, a resolution was passed in the Legislative Assembly. It accomplished the following:

> The Three-Language policy was scrapped and Hindi was eliminated from the curriculum. Only English and Tamil were to be taught, the use of Hindi commands in NCC was banned, Tamil was to be introduced as medium of instruction in all colleges and as the language of administration within five years, the Central Government was urged to end the special status accorded to Hindi in the Constitution and treat all languages equally, and was urged to provide financial assistance for development of all languages mentioned in the Eighth Schedule of the Constitution. These measures satisfied the agitators and normalcy returned by February 1968.

Agitation of 1986

In 1986, Indian Prime minister Rajiv Gandhi introduced the "National Education Policy". This education policy provided for setting up Navodaya Schools, where the DMK claimed teaching of Hindi would be compulsory. The Anna Dravida Munnetra Kazhagam (ADMK) led by M. G. Ramachandran (which had split from the DMK in 1972), was in power in Tamil Nadu and the DMK was the main opposition party. Karunanidhi announced an agitation against the opening of Navodaya Schools in Tamil Nadu. On 13 November, the Tamil Nadu Legislative Assembly unanimously passed a resolution demanding the repeal of Part XVII of the Constitution and for making English the sole official language of the union.

On 17 November 1986, DMK members protested against the new education policy by burning Part XVII of the Constitution. 20,000 DMK members including Karunanidhi were arrested. 21 persons committed suicide by self immolation. Karunanidhi was sentenced to ten weeks of rigorous imprisonment. Ten DMK MLAs including K. Anbazhagan were expelled from the Legislative Assembly by the speaker P. H. Pandian. Rajiv Gandhi assured Members of Parliament from Tamil Nadu that Hindi would not be imposed. As part of the compromise, Navodhaya schools were not started in Tamil Nadu. Currently, Tamil Nadu is the only state in India without Navodhaya schools.

The Impact

The anti-Hindi agitations of 1937-40 and 1940-50 led to a change of guard in the Madras Presidency. The main opposition party to the Indian National Congress in the state, the Justice Party, came under Periyar's leadership on 29 December 1938. In 1944, the Justice Party was renamed as Dravidar Kazhagam. The political careers of many later leaders of the Dravidian Movement, such as C. N. Annadurai and M. Karunanidhi, started with their participation in these agitations. The agitations stopped the compulsory teaching of Hindi in the state. The agitations of the 1960s played a crucial role in the defeat of the Tamil Nadu Congress party in the 1967 elections and the continuing dominance of Dravidian parties in Tamil Nadu politics. Many political leaders of the DMK and ADMK, like P. Sreenivasan, K. Kalimuthu, Durai Murugan, Tiruppur. S. Duraiswamy, Sedapatti Muthaiah, K. Raja Mohammad, M. Natarajan and L. Ganesan, owe their entry and advancement in politics to their stints as student leaders during the agitations, which also reshaped the Dravidian Movement and broadened its political base, when it shifted from its earlier pro-Tamil (and anti-Brahmin) stance to a more inclusive one, which was both anti-Hindi and pro-English. Finally, the current two-language education policy followed in Tamil Nadu is also a direct result of the agitations.

In the words of Sumathi Ramaswamy (Professor of History at Duke University),

> [The anti-Hindi agitations knit] together diverse, even incompatible, social and political interests... Their

common cause against Hindi had thrown together religious revivalists like Maraimalai Atikal (1876-1950) with avowed atheists like Ramaswamy and Bharathidasan (1891-1964); men who supported the Indian cause like T. V. Kalyanasundaram (1883-1953) and M. P. Sivagnanam with those who wanted to secede from India like Annadurai and M. Karunanidhi (b.1924); university professors like Somasundara Bharati (1879-1959) and M. S. Purnalingam Pillai (1866 -1947) with uneducated street poets, populist pamphleteers and college students.

The anti-Hindi agitations ensured the passage of Official Languages Act of 1963 and its amendment in 1967, thus ensuring the continued use of English as an official language of India. They effectively brought about the "virtual indefinite policy of bilingualism" of the Indian Republic.

Significant Works

Literary Works

In Tamil: Rajaji was an accomplished writer both in his mother tongue Tamil. In 1922, he published a book Siraiyil Tavam (Meditation in jail) which was a day-to-day diary about his first imprisonment from 21 December 1921 to 20 March 1922. In 1958, he was awarded the Sahitya Akademi Award for Tamil for his retelling of the Ramayana — Chakravarti Thirumagan.

In 1916, Rajaji started the Tamil Scientific Terms Society. This society coined new words in Tamil for terms connected to botany, chemistry, physics, astronomy and mathematics. At about the same time, he called for Tamil to be introduced as the medium of instruction in schools.

In English

Rajaji was the founder of the Salem Literary Society and regularly participated in its meetings in which he suggested introducing scholarships for Dalit students. He also edited Mahatma Gandhi's newspaper Young India.

In 1951, Rajaji wrote an abridged retelling of the Mahabharata in English, followed by one of the Ramayana in 1957. Earlier, in

1955, he had translated Kambar's Tamil Ramayana into English. In 1965, he translated the Thirukkural into English. He also wrote books on the Bhagavad Gita, the Upanishads, Socrates, and Marcus Aurelius in English. Rajaji often regarded his literary works as the best service he had rendered to the people. In 1958, he established the Bharatiya Vidya Bhavan.

Musical Compositions

Apart from his literary works, Rajaji also composed a devotional song Kurai Onrum Illai devoted to Lord Krishna. This song was set to music and is a regular in most Carnatic concerts. Rajaji composed a benediction hymn which was sung by M. S. Subbulakshmi at the United Nations General Assembly in 1967.

Rajaji was also a strong advocate of Tamil music and lent his support to the Tamil music movement of the 1940s.

Significant Works

- India's flag (1923, Ganesh).
- Plighted word (1933, Servants of Untouchables Society).
- The way out (1943, Oxford University Press).
- The impending fast of Mahatma Gandhi: the issues explained (1944, Servants of Untouchables Society).
- Reconciliation, why and how: a plea for immediate action (1945, Hind Kitabs).
- Ambedkar Refuted (1946, Hind Kitabs).
- The fatal cart and other stories (1946, Hindustan Times).
- Vedanta, the basic culture of India (1949).
- The Indian communists (1955, Cultural Books).
- The good administrator (1955, Government of India).
- Our democracy and other essays (1957, B.G. Paul & Co.).
- Mankind protests: a collection of speeches and statements on atomic warfare and test explosions (1957, All India Peace Council).

- Satyam eva jayate: a collection of articles contributed to Swarajya and other journals from 1956 to 1961, Volume 1 (1961, Bharathan Publications).
- The Art of translation: a symposium (1962, Government of India).
- The question of English (1962, Bharathan Publications).
- Our Culture (1963, Bharatiya Vidya Bhavan).
- Gandhiji's teachings and philosophy (1963, Bharatiya Vidya Bhavan).
- Hinduism, doctrine and way of life (1964, Bharatiya Vidya Bhavan).
- Swatantra answer to Chinese Communist challenge (1964).
- English for unity (1965, Bharathan Publications).
- The unification of cultures: being an address delivered at the Indian Institute of World Culture on 18 August, 1966, under Major-General S. L. Bhatia Endowment Lectureship (1966).
- Stories for the innocent (1967, Bharatiya Vidya Bhavan).
- Bharati, the Tamil poet (Bharathi Tamil Sangam).

Translations

- Bhagavad Gita abridged and explained: setting forth the Hindu creed, discipline and ideals (1949, Hindustan Times).
- Mahabharatha (1950, Bharatiya Vidya Bhavan).
- Sri Ramakrishna Upanishad (1953, Sri Ramakrishna Math).
- Bhaja Govindam (1965, Bharatiya Vidya Bhavan).
- *Kural:* the great book of Tiru-Valluvar (1965, Bharatiya Vidya Bhavan).

Significant Speeches

Independence Day Eve

[His Excellency the Governor General broadcasting to the nation on August 14, 1948].

Jai Hind!

I have the privilege tonight of speaking to you, Dear Brothers and Sisters, all over India who are listening to me, Tomorrow — or rather at midnight today — we·begin the second year of free India. Great have been our troubles after the undertaking of Independence. Insane riots and barbarities and movements of masses of panic-stricken people leaving their homes and their belongings threatened to put an end to all order and rule Problems arising out of the partition and problems created by the sudden break of the nexus that bound the Indian States with the Central authority to whom everywhere the people turned for maintenance of social order and rule, taxed and confounded the ability of the best of our statesmen.

It is easy to be wise after the event and to say that we should have anticipated and prepared for the misfortunes and complications that followed and overwhelmed our people. But men of affairs throughout the world have not blamed us either for not having anticipated them or for the way in which our Government faced them They have complimented us on the way we handled the situation They have paid these compliments not to flatter They are men who have seen trouble in other parts of the world and have the experience to appreciate and to judge fairly.

We have largely restored order to replace the chaos produced by the doctrine of lapse of paramountcy. Brave women workers have achieved the restoration to their homes of more than ten thousand women, Hindus, Muslims and Sikhs, who had been victims of the riots. We have staved off famine and we have kept industry going in spite of recurring conflicts between labour and management.

But it is no good indulging in self-pity or self-praise.

We have to overcome the impediments that still stand in the way of a better life for our people. We have to work for a higher standard of civic sense and a higher standard of production. Character must be improved all-round and fruitful work should increase. The only way for progress is to make conditions which would help these two things, more honesty all-round and more work everywhere.

The greatest of our misfortunes was the passing away of Gandhiji. Those who killed him have done the greatest injury to our country, exceeding what any other enemies of the State have done. He was snatched away from us when he was most wanted.

But it was God's will that some men should be so thoughtless as that, and inflict this grievous injury on our people It is through severe trials that a nation's fibre is strengthened. We have now to work and build without Do we fulfil our purpose by carving statues, painting pictures, printing his effigy on stamps and notes, putting wreaths on the spot where he was killed or where he was cremated? We do all this, and it may be proper we do all this. But we should do more if our worship is not to be an empty form Empty worship is dangerous if it makes us feel we have done all that is due.

We should, as far as in our power lies, do what Gandhiji earnestly trusted we could do. When any doubt or difficulty arises, private individuals and officials of all grades as well as governments should ask themselves the question, what would Gandhiji have advised if he had been alive and if we had gone to him for advice? It is not difficult for us to guess in every case the course he would have advised Let us follow that line honestly and prayerfully, and God will help us.

I would ask citizens constantly to ask themselves Have we given sufficient positive help to our national government? If the answer is doubtful, we should hasten to make up the deficiency. Let us think constructively. The old habit of opposition and intolerance of authority that was natural when we lived under foreign rule has no place now Let us give out of love that respect to the authority and prestige of our own government which the old government was able to extort through force and fear.

We have to work hard, everyone in his job. Every weaver, every peasant, every trader must make up his mind to do his best, each in his own sphere, avoiding deceit, avoiding idleness Public affairs are only the sum-total of private lives. The motherland wants the maximum output of work and mutual trust and honesty.

May God help us and the time come soon when we shall all have realised the vanity of hatred — indeed there is nothing more than vanity in hatred — and the vanity of jealousy and the waste in dishonesty. Soon, let us hope we shall all be at work strenuously cooperating for the whole of India. By India I mean both parts of India There is no conflicting economic interest between the two parts of India, but on the contrary every need for cooperation in order to supplement one another. We shall see this easily when our temporary passions have cooled down, We are free and that does not mean just release from bondage. It means we have become, all of us, citizens of the potential world-state Let us shape our conduct to be worthy of that new status. India has a mission. Our place in Asia, our long and intimate connection with the civilization and culture of the West and last but not least our noble inheritance, our own ancient civilization, these put on US, now that we are free, the duty of playing an effective part in the progress of the world. May God bless us in this, for the whole world is His.

Bande Mataram.

Unveiling of the Portrait of Gandhiji

[Unveiling a portrait of Mahatma Gandhi at the Association of the Council of Scientific and Industrial Research Ministerial Staff on December 4, 1948].

I am very grateful for the sweet words of welcome read by the President of the Association, He said many nice things.

This is one: "Ours is the first Association in the Secretariat which has the honour to greet amongst us the first Indian Governor General of free and independent India."

I think he could have even said that it is the first Association in the Secretariat which has the honour to greet any Governor General! It gives me great pleasure to be asked to meet on intimate terms the young men who are working in the offices in, as they think, a subordinate position.

Many are our difficulties, some of them avoidable, some unavoidable. All can be faced more effectively with patience than without it. That is absolutely certain. Not that I do not understand the difficulties of our young men; those difficulties are not caused by any particular persons whom you can blame now but are inherent in the present condition of our affairs. I have very great pleasure in being with you all on this occasion. I wish this were a more common phenomenon in Delhi. There should be more play, more fun and healthy competition in sports.

I am very glad that Dr. Mukherjee and the head of the Department, Dr. Bhatnagar, are helping you in this matter I would like to help you if you will show how I can do it Members of the ministerial staff of a Scientific Department may not be scientists or doing scientific work.

But any work that facilitates Science is also essential.

Although priests and learned men may be chanting hymns in the main shrine of a temple, the people engaged in sweeping the steps and keeping the courtyard of the temple clean were considered by our saints as equally dead tc God so that they occasionally did that work too, in order to enhance then: own merit. Do not think therefore that you are occupying any humble or humdrum position.

Governors' Conference

[Addressing the Governors' Conference at Government House, New Delhi, on May 8, 1949].

Your Excellencies,

On behalf of myself and on behalf of the Hon'ble the Prime Minister and the Deputy Prime Minister I welcome you all heartily and thank you for undertaking long journeys to meet here today. I do hope you will not mind the inconveniences you are put to by reason of the time of the year you have been asked to meet. It was not possible to have this conference earlier and I tender my apologies for it.

We are meeting as in last year's conference informally. There is no specific official function that this conference can fulfil, but a great deal can be learnt from one another at this informal meeting which you could place at the disposal of your respective Governments. We shall as far as we have time, discuss matters which have been exercising your minds and on which you feel exchange of views would be useful. As Governors you must have watched and appraised with detachment the administration in your respective Provinces and it would be very useful if we frankly discuss such problems as have caused you any degree of concern. The Prime Minister and the Deputy Prime Minister will only be too glad to have the advantage of knowing your mind on those matters so that they could shape their decisions and help good government all over India. Our meeting is not a public conference and there can be the most cordial and frank exchange of views. You should not imagine that you are just figure-heads and can do nothing to affect the governance of the country. Our Prime Minister and our Deputy Prime Minister do not hold that view. They want you to develop influence for good and them expect you to End means for achieving it without friction and without prejudice to the march of democracy.

Subject of course to the limitation of time we could with advantage discuss the following subjects:

1. The law and order position in the provinces.
2. Public Safety legislation.

3. The BSS ban and its aftermath.
4. Unlicensed arms and violent crime prevailing in certain areas.
5. The Communist party and its activities.
6. The Food position.
7. Agrarian legislation.
8. The Labour situation.
9. The Refugee problem.
10. Provincialism and the question of linguistic provinces.
11. Foreign Affairs.
12. The Rules of Business in each province in regard to the Governor and his work.

I should like to say a few words about the historic conference at London at which our Prime Minister was the central figure. We all know with what universal satisfaction the news of his great achievement was received in India It was not just personal joy or pride. There was distinct political satisfaction in all circles. We know what great joy it gave to all people and all parties in Britain, in Ireland, in America and in all the countries of the world that desire the reign of peace and of democracy. But it gave no less satisfaction to thinking people of all classes in India The croakers are few and far between and they are incorrigible We know how this great and historic decision has changed the phase of things all over the world. Gandhiji has indeed made a posthumous conquest of the whole of the British Commonwealth.

In saying this I do not underestimate the achievement of our Prime Minister nor say anything which he himself has not felt. India has worked a historic revolution for the whole of the Commonwealth along with the complete confirmation of its own independence. The moral gain for the British is great, but we have gained no less in demonstrating that the Indian people can forgive, forget and be great, and give in freedom what they resisted when demanded through force. Civilization itself has taken a big step forward in this historic achievement. I am full of joy that I have seen such great things in my life-time. And on behalf of you all as of myself I tender our most cordial and affectionate congratulations to the Prime Minister on the historic part it was given to him to play in this connection.

May his greatness still grow, I am asking the Prime Minister and the Deputy Prime Minister to address us While the international connections of India are very important, our internal affairs are no less important. Indeed the integration of India is the foundation on which our greatness abroad rests and our Deputy Prime Minister has, as all the world knows, done and is still doing a Herculean task. He still requires the goodwill, full understanding and cordial assistance of all to complete his great and difficult task I request him also therefore to say to you a few words on this subject.

Once again I welcome you all.

Swearing-in Ceremony

[His Excellency the Governor General made the following speech at the Swearing-in Ceremony on June 21, 1948, at Government House, New Delhi].

I am very grateful to you all for your participation at this ceremony. Your presence has lifted the occasion from the place of a mere ceremony to that of human fellowship and cooperation.

Speaking objectively, the occasion is undoubtedly historic, for this is the first time that one who belongs to the soil has, in accordance with the wishes of the Prime Minister of India and his Cabinet, been entrusted with the honour and the duties of the Head of the State in India. I owe a debt of gratitude, which I cannot hope to repay, for the signal honour implied in this my installation. I hope I shall act, on every occasion and in every matter, in a manner worthy of the trust reposed in me. The work of my predecessor during his memorable term of office was a marvellous instance of detachment, devotion and energy on the part of one who, though not belonging to India, worked as one belonging to her and did his work in the spirit that is laid down in our scriptures with regard to the task that falls to any one. I come after him but I hope I will be judged by standards suitable to one who is inexperienced either in arms or in diplomacy, unlike my predecessor.

Our problems have multiplied beyond all expectation and are such as may perturb even the most adventurous spirits among us. The only remaining interest in life which moves my colleagues who are entrusted with the charge of the affairs of India is the happiness of our people and the good name of our country. This is the passion that binds them together. They have experience and nobility of character May God enable them to achieve the purpose so dear to their hearts. I shall be proud to render them all such assistance as I can in this position.

India is unchangeably committed to the policy of making everyone within her borders find pride and joy in citizenship irrespective of caste, creed or race. No one will suffer any disability by reason of the community to which he or she belongs.

The days of dynastic rule or domination through force are gone in India. No territorial or racial or religious community can hope to thrive or maintain its happiness through force without the willing and full cooperation of other people and the utmost intercommunication. It is therefore necessary that all communal and territorial isolationism should be abandoned and the best talents in every community should seek to serve the whole State. Communities should spread themselves out rather than build walls round themselves.

Whatever be the technical phraseology which public law may use to describe it, what disturbs the peace of India now is internecine discord pure and simple and it is utter folly.

Our economy has not yet had time to separate into two parts corresponding to the political division to which we have agreed. It is very doubtful if it ever can be so split. We are far too interdependent and whatever we might do, there will yet be vital links that can never be severed. It is folly to quarrel and make into a scene of strife and misery what has been shaped by the pressure of age-long forces into a field of beauty and joy. Let us pray for wisdom and let us do what will make good thoughts grow and save them from being swamped by folly and evil which wait to tempt man.

I have received blessings and good wishes from great and good men in all parts of the world. May these help me to steer clear of error and enable me to be of some service to our people in the great office conferred on me.

New Delhi Municipal Committee

[His Excellency the Governor General received an address of welcome from the New Delhi Municipal Committee on June 25, 1948].

Sir Arthur Dean and Friends,

It is very kind of you to come and say words of welcome to me. I thank you very much indeed, and more than your welcome I thank you for your good wishes, of which I stand very much in need. You have certainly maintained a very high standard of sanitation and services in regard to public amenities. You started as an expert body and have worked for over 32 years now. Let me congratulate you on the task that you have well performed. This is a Central Government enclave, and naturally more emphasis is laid on the efficient performance of expert and public health services than on the development of democratic representation.

This is natural, and marks the difference between a government enclave of this kind and ordinary municipal corporations. I hope that high standards will be maintained in services, whatever may happen to the development of the Corporation itself.

The New Delhi Municipal Committee is sharing the natural history of all metropolitan centres. The old capitals too, I dare say, began as New Delhi began, with beauty, art and plan, and upheavals and catastrophes and difficulties that occurred from time to time brought large influxes of people under the direct protection of the Central Government and in pell-mell fashion. The problems became intricate, houses grew without order, streets formed themselves by accident so to say, and we find old beautiful well-planned capitals becoming more or less like the Old Delhi that we see now. Five hundred years hence, probably New Delhi may become a replica of Old Delhi. Already as you have pointed out, this has begun. Houses have been built which do not come up to your standard of artistic beauty. Let us hope that we shall, through conscious and deliberate effort, prevent deterioration in standards in spite of the pressure that is bound to be brought on all capital cities, pressure of population, trade and commerce. You have done very well.

You have maintained standards in spite of many difficulties, and I congratulate you. I hope I shall be of some service to you in helping you in tiding over your problems.

Thank you once again for your good wishes. Whatever the Constitution of the Committee might be as time advances, the efficiency of municipal services rendered is the essential thing and I hope you will set an example to the rest of India in this respect. Thank you very much for what you have said.

Old Delhi Municipality

[His Excellency the Governor General received an address of welcome from the Old Delhi Municipality on July 11, 1948].

I thank you for your address of welcome. What you have said about the affairs of your Municipality will, I have no doubt, receive the careful attention of the Government. I thank you for what you have said about me.

I have been the recipient of good wishes and the beneficiary of devout prayers of numerous good men and women throughout the country. I stand very much in need of this and I am deeply grateful for it.

We are facing very tough problems, some of which had never before been faced by any Government in the world and have, therefore, to be solved by us without the help of a tried precedent. But it is impossible for us to find persons more worthy of confidence than the tried leaders who have been bearing the burden God has helped us so far to stand the great trials to which we had been subjected.

We have been strengthened in our fibre by reason of these trials, for this is the law of all misfortunes. We are thankful to God for it and we hope to overcome all difficulties and justify our independence by loyal adherence to the principle of progress and the cause of peace in the world.

Gandhiji has left us. But let us remember what he taught, the thing for which he gave up his life. Let us live as brothers although we worship God in different ways following the custom of those that brought us up. It is more important to live like brothers and to help one another than even to beautify our historic city of which we are justly proud. Beauty without love is like a poisonous flower, beautiful to look at, but dangerous to life.

I do not find pleasure in holding the office I hold or in holding any other office at present, but as my colleagues unanimously wanted me to join them now in this capacity, I have agreed. I hope your good wishes and the good wishes of others will enable me to be of some use to the nation.

The ambition to serve the country and to take a spectacular part in improving the lot of the people is natural and worthy. The progress of a from people requires this and it should be encouraged. But during the present troubled times, unity is more important than even emulation in noble purposes I would, therefore, appeal to all to call a truce to all individual and competitive ambition, however noble, and to canalise talent in one stream until we have achieved our immediate objects.

Employment Service

[His Excellency the Governor General made the following speech at the Third Anniversary Celebrations of the foundation of the Employment Service in India at Gurdwara Road, New Delhi, on August 9, 1948].

Sir Jagjivan Ram, Ladies And Gentlemen,

I am very grateful for all the sweat things you have said about me You consider that my coming here is a concession or boon conferred upon you, It is I who should thank you for having done all this, and I rejoice at the good work that has been done by loyal servants of the State The service rendered by this Department, there is no doubt, is of immense importance The normal life of the people was disturbed by the war and by the partition of our country During the war, many had to go and fight as soldiers or help soldiers in various ways. When they return, they have to be placed back in civil life in order that they may carry on after the interruption to their normal We and do not feel that they have been let down by the State Similarly, the disturbance dislocated the lives of many people after the partition They have a right not to be let down and to ask the State to do all in its power to rehabilitate them. What honest men and women desire is opportunity for honest work and to earn their own living. It requires therefore no deep thought or analysis to see that the work this Department is doing is a natural and important part of the work that any government has to do under abnormal conditions.

Government therefore must give you and your colleagues their very sincere thanks for the remarkably good and presentable amount of work that has been achieved. You, Sir, as Minister, are entitled specially to receive thanks from me. We must find it rather embarrassing to compliment one another, but at the same time I must fulfil a duty as head of the State and on behalf of the whole of the people of this land tender their thanks and gratitude to you on this occasion.

This is the third anniversary of this Department. These three years being infant years were years of anxiety The Department has come through it all right and you have shown in the charts hung up in the neighbouring room and literature that these three years have been very active years You have done not only normal work, but have shown great enthusiasm and strenuous industry Otherwise you could not have grown to the size that you have now grown to.

I would ask people interested in this work to study carefully and sympathetically the charts hung in the other room It is only if one looks at anything with sympathy and examines it with attention that he can at all understand it. If you examine the figures in the charts in the right way, all of you will see that in the midst of the enormous amount of anxiety and disturbance we have passed through, the Department has done a great deal of work These inadequate words of mine, I hope, will succeed in putting yet greater enthusiasm in your workers.

The habit of continual opposition to established government tends to persist somewhat. Even now many thoughtless people are inclined to look upon all those who are employed in the administrative services as, if not enemies, parasites who live on the work of other people They think they are in charge of the kitchen and therefore eat more than they serve to other people. This is altogether a superficial and wrong view of things The man who organises productive work and productive service is also a man who works The man who plans, organises or who supervises the distribution of work is also a worker Those who have changed their government into a completely socialist government have no difficulty in understanding this point. But we still have some difficulty in appreciating that the man who sits on a chair in front of a table is a worker at all. All of us are workers. I claim that even I am a fairly industrious and hard worker. To sit still requires a great deal of energy, let me tell you, and a great deal of painful exertion. I can claim to be exerting a great deal in not doing anything, and if I can be called a worker, you can understand how hard Ministers must be working who have to see that nothing goes wrong and who have to take on themselves the blame when anything does go wrong. It is not the men who do the wrong thing who should be allowed to be blamed It is the Ministers who have to take all the blame If the Employment Exchange curve goes down, it is the Minister that takes the blame. He will have to go and set the curve right. I plead that people should be more considerate to those on whom the responsibility of the State has been placed in this transitional stage, when everybody has a desire to be idle and blame others and everybody expects every other man to do his own work. This is a transitional stage when people are bound to be judged very badly all round, but still it is a time when the greatest amount of patience is necessary.

No one is entitled to lose his temper, and I hope that the Labour Minister, whose temper is tried first of all by the labourers, secondly, no less by the Industrialists, thirdly, no less again by those who watch things from their drawing rooms and their own places in life, will be patient. At the, same time I want him to be firm. If in this transitional and critical stage of our national life, we are not firm, we are bound to break and fail. I plead therefore for reasoned patience. I congratulate the Department and everyone concerned and not the least the chart-maker, I congratulate him to be honest and not pull the chart slant-wise and make it tell a comfortable tale when it really warns us. Make it true and let it speak the truth.

At the Jama Masjid Grounds

[His Excellency the Governor General made the following speech in Hindustani at an informal gathering of communities at Jama Masjid Grounds on August 14, 1948].

Anger and retaliation cannot give us happiness. The history of the past twelve months is a record of attempts to achieve happiness through anger and retaliation. If happiness could be achieved by retaliation, today the people of Pakistan and India must both be very happy. But we are not happy We know how far away we are from happiness.

This should teach us a lesson.

Anger and retaliation are the Devil's weapons to keep evil going in this world. Through them the Devil is counteracting the teachings and defeating the purpose of the prophets and the saints.

We should forget what has happened and pray to God that from now on we may live like human beings and brothers to one another You should look upon every woman as a mother or sister and every child as your own child. By hating one another we cannot achieve satisfaction or happiness in our lives. It is only when we begin to help one another that we shall achieve true happiness.

If something wicked takes place somewhere, treat it like plague or cholera, and think of the means to isolate yourself from the infection.

For governmental purposes, our country has been divided into two; but hi trade and economic affairs there is no conflict between Pakistan and India. We should help each other and advance trade and commerce in both States If we help one another we shall both rise in the world and attain great prestige and influence.

Civic Address at Mysore

[His Excellency the Governor General said in reply to the Civic Address presented at Mysore on August 19, 1948].

Your Highness, President and Members of the Municipal Council,

Even though I know a little Kannada, I find myself quite frightened out of my little knowledge of it by the sentiments and words with which you have over-whelmed me. Since yesterday I have been thinking of what I should say to you. I have come to the conclusion that words cannot satisfy what I wish to say and, therefore, it is better that I leave unsaid most of the things I should have liked to say. But I must find some words to express my gratitude, All this pomp and ceremony now paid to me are homage paid to previous history, not to me. I know that the hearts of young and old in this country, here as elsewhere, find exhilaration in the thought that one of themselves should be the recipient of honours hitherto paid, uniformly and in full measure, to people from other countries This gives you pleasure. Let me tell you, it gives me pleasure also in a very objective way which may easily be misunderstood as vanity on my part! But behind all this pomp and all this hospitality which His Highness and you have all conspired to shower on me, without the least reduction in measure from what it had been hitherto to successive Viceroys and Governors-General, I see something which, I am sure, was not there in the old days affection.

I have, to some extent, been myself responsible for your feeling that I am one of your own. I came here from a neighbouring district when I was young and received my education under the care of your Maharaja and Government.

I owe my body to my family but I owe, what is more precious, my mind, to the education that I received here. If I have served the country and if I have deserved all the kind things that you have said in Sanskrit and Kannada in such beautiful language, it is due entirely to the education I received in your State. I belong to a village only less than five miles from your border. It was merely an accident that my village was torn off from this State some time before I was born. I belong to the same plateau on which you live and have grown. I am, therefore, one of you and can understand your particular exhilaration at my attaining to a position which Olive, Wellesley, Dalhousie and others occupied It is wonderful and remarkable how what was once regretted now becomes a cause for increased joy.

We have to deserve this good fortune. The country is free and your own State has now acquired democratic government for itself. I thank the Municipal Commissioners for all the kind words they have showered upon me. It is not for me to say anything about your municipal affairs The beauty of this city is a great example and inspiration to towns and cities all over India. I may say without hesitation, not as an old citizen of Mysore State but as Governor General and an objective judge, that Mysore is really the most beautiful city in India. I have been feeling it all the time since I came here. In fact, I did not get good sleep last night because I was feeling I had just come back from a visit to Fairyland!

The State has now been handed over to a democratic machinery. Successive and able administrators under His Highness' predecessors have built this province to an enviable degree of progress and glory. A new government has taken over responsibility. If I were they, I should not sleep happily My colleagues in the national agitation and struggle must feel a very heavy responsibility.

It is not easy to maintain a State and keep up the level which it has reached through the talent, industry, devotion and patriotism of previous administrators.

You will have to work hard, my dear friends, if you desire that people should not regret the change. It is not enough to be patriotic in the old sense. It is necessary to be patriotic in a new sense. We have to plan anxiously; we have to be straightforward in the execution of our promises and plans. We have to think hard.

Democracy has come when life, individual and national, has become harder than ever before. In one way it may not be very fair to compare the achievements of the older administrators with the work of the new democratic government. People are inclined to think now only about achievements and not difficulties. Yet democracy would be untrue to itself if it did not exert special anxiety to meet the numerous difficulties that face us in the present day and produce results over which people might say: "Well, democracy is not bad after all I" Successive talented administrators were in charge of the affairs of this State to the good luck of the people of the State. They had all the facilities. They had untrammelled power to do what they wished Now, there are difficulties created by democracy itself Nothing can be done which does not satisfy the majority and a larger amount of criticism is brought to bear than ever before. In spite of it, I am sure the patriotism of the people and the patriotism of the workers and the new administrators will all combine to save us from any disappointment.

Patriotism must now be newly defined and understood. In the olden days, it was just struggle and agitation. But now it is as hard as building a new house It requires all the patience of a brick-layer and something more. It requires all the skill of a good engineer and something more. We have, therefore, to work hard It was easy to take over power from His Highness, but it is difficult to realise the duties and fulfil them.

His Highness has been taking me round I was overwhelmed by his kindness and courtesy. All the time, I was thinking whether the hereditary tradition was not, after all, superior to any amount of training. His Highness is young and I am old. All the time I took the high privilege of feeling that I was father and he the son. It gave me continual joy to be sitting by him as a father by his son when he took me over to Brindavan and back. May the Lord of Brindavan protect him and protect you!

Gymkhana of the Indian Institute of Science

[Addressing the members of the Gymkhana of the Indian Institute of Science on August 21].

I felt quite easy on former occasions when I came here. Now I am called a "Visitor' and I do not really know what to tell you as a visitor. If you will kindly forget that fact, I may be able to talk to you more easily. I want you to realise your responsibilities. You are not here simply studying for a career. That may have been so before. Now everyone of you is studying to help Government which is very anxious to get the help of Science through you. I do not think that we have an Institute of this character and size anywhere else in India.

It was easy to concentrate on getting power transferred from the British. It was easier to fight than to organise. We fought thinking only about fighting. After we had done that, we have constantly found ourselves in very difficult situations. When people develop too much fascination for their leaders, they lose the habit of depending on themselves and rely for everything on the leaders. Those who have taken up the responsibilities of running the country find the position very difficult. I have been saying all this to you to lead up to this: without the help of Science our leaders will not be able to do much for the country. That is why the Prime Minister continually and, I may say so, wistfully looks up to the help of Science so that we may be enabled to do something for the people in spite of all our difficulties. Your studies as a whole are devoted to the service of the country and it must be a joy to you when you succeed in your experiments. I find from your faces that you are more interested in Hyderabad than in the Indian Institute. This is a symptom which the psychological laboratory will have to analyse.

There are some who toil to accumulate money till the very end of their lives without enjoying it. Then they die not knowing what will happen to their hard-earned money. They call a solicitor, draw up a will in a hurry but it goes ail wrong afterwards. The same thing applies to study. It is for you to reason out after a certain stage whether you have studied enough and make up your mind to leave it to others.

It is very amusing for a visitor of the Indian Institute of Science to preach the doctrine of not studying! As long as you find joy in your studies, go on studying, but when you feel inclined to quarrel with your colleagues or find fault with the Director or somebody else, let me as a psychologist tell you that it is no fault of the Director, but it is your joy that is coming to an end and you must find a way out.

Kannada Sahitya Parishad

[Unveiling the portrait of Mahatma Gandhi at the Kannada Sahitya Parishad, Bangalore, on August 21, 1948].

Sisters and Brothers,

It gives me much pleasure to have this opportunity to talk to you. Ever since Mahatmaji's death, I and many others like me have been asked to participate in various functions which serve only to remind us of our grief. Most of you seem to think that it is nice to ask men like me to go and unveil pictures of Mahatmaji. But let me tell you that it makes a difficult task more difficult. If a temple has been demolished by a storm or disaster, a visit to the site where the temple stood makes one only sadder. It is only a compelling sense of duty that makes me accept such functions. If you had asked me to come to the Kannada Sahitya Parishad, I would have come, even if you did not ask me to unveil a picture of Mahatma Gandhi. But to unveil a picture of Mahatmaji and to remind myself of all the disaster and calamity that has happened serves no great purpose. We will not forget his face and these pictures do not look like his face. Whatever the skill of the artist may be, whatever his good intentions may be, pictures cannot look like the original It is unnecessary to remember his appearance It is necessary to remember his speeches. We remembered Sri Ram and Sri Krishna and others better before the introduction of cinemas Our devotion and our piety gave us a true personality of Sri Ram and Sri Krishna Cinemas brought indifferent artists to our mind.

Our duty now is to keep Mahatmaji alive, it is in our power either to keep him alive or to kill him. If you hate anybody, you kill Mahatmaji once again if you do not forgive one who has done you some harm, you put another shot into Mahatmaji's body. A trial is going on in order to decide who killed him But in our hearts the trial is going on whether we will kill Mahatmaji again or keep him alive.

I have said all this in order that we may realise what our work is. It is not filling the house with pictures of Mahatmaji. It is the filling of your hearts with the teachings of Mahatmaji. If there is any virtue in pictures, if there is any love for the picture you put up on the wall, you torture Mahatmaji again whenever you behave badly. That is *Ahimsa*. If you wish to do any wrong, please do it, but do not ask Mahatmaji to look at it. Please do not put up recklessly his pictures about unless you resolve that you will behave better. I want you not to be sad, but I want you to be good Mahatmaji died. He does not want you to be sad about it. Mahatmaji was like the salt or sugar which you must put into your food to spice it. It is unnecessary to grieve over the sugar or salt that has disappeared. Supposing the wife who is cooking sambar, rasam or any article of food begins to weep because the salt has dissolved, would it not look foolish?

We could not have conceived a better death for Mahatmaji Can any of us hope to die when walking to a prayer with Ram Nam on our lips? Can any of us hope to die healthy and strong without pain or suffering. That was how Mahatmaji died. The moment he died men who disbelieved him all of a sudden began to believe him All people throughout the world saw Mahatmaji's virtues and his character and his work. There is no need therefore to grieve for Mahatmaji. There is plenty of need for grieving for our fellowmen when they are not doing what he has asked us to do.

As for Kannada, it will grow whether we work for it or not. If we work for it, we will get credit. If you do not work for it, it can still grow. The mother-tongue is a living language and there is no need to look after it. If you interfere with the growth of a plant, you will be doing it some injury but you will be doing nothing else. We bore holes in ears and nose thinking that we make a girl look more beautiful. All our service to our mother-tongue is like that.

Until recently all mother-tongues in India grew happily like happy children in the forest. Now you catch hold of them, bore holes in ears and noses and send them to useless schoolmasters and ask them to teach your children. We 'weight' with scale pans to find out the weight of the original tongue and how much of other scripts must be mixed into it, like apothecaries. My point is that we must allow our mother-tongue to grow naturally and the less you interfere with it, the better it will be. For God's sake, allow the children to learn the mother-tongue from their mothers Do not make it compulsory in schools. If you compel anything, you make people dislike it. The mother-tongue is too strong to be killed by any schoolmaster.

How to write in Kannada is a great problem to our people now. The best way to learn to write it is not to think about it but to write. Think about the things that you wish to say and not about the words. A horse does not wait to see which of its four legs is to go first and which next. It looks forward, not down at its feet. If you analyse how a language works, you will see that my analogy is not an amusing or a far-fetched one. Let the horse run, it will reach its goal. Keep your ideas clear and the mother-tongue will take care of itself.

Language has its own empire quite different from the empires of Ashoka, Aurangazeb, Great Britain or even Rajagopalachari! Do not mix politics with language. Fill Kannada with good literature and the jurisdiction of Kannada literature will overstep all administrative barriers The culture and the ideas that you fill Kannada with, will govern the people who speak Kannada wherever they may be. Improve your Kannada literature.

Shakespeare had more influence over Germans than he had over the English people because the Germans admired and read Shakespeare The sum total of my advice to you therefore is 'enrich Kannada, do not speak about it'.

At The Parade Grounds

[Speaking at the Parade Grounds, Trivandrum on August 23, 1948].

Friends,

I am asking your General to translate into Malayalam what I say in English. The Army is not the enemy of the people but a useful and faithful unit of the people It is as much the servant of the people as the civil services The people are their own masters now and every individual is the servant of the State It is a noble occupation to give all you have in body and mind to the protection and safety of the land. It should be the noble ambition of every able-bodied young man to serve in the Array if lie can get a place. You need not imagine that you are doing anything which people dislike. You are now doing what people like.

Wherever you may be, whether in battle or in peace, you should look upon the women and children of the land as your own sisters and your own children. Even if you are fighting the enemy, the women and children of the enemy are your own sisters and your own family. This is the Dharma of our land and I hope that the Army of India will serve the Dharma of India. I wish you all good luck and wish you young men good careers and wish the State all prosperity and the Army all fame. The Army in India is now one and you are an integral part of it. Thank you very much for giving me this impressive and unforgettable welcome.

At a Guild of Service Meeting

[Addressing a meeting of the Guild of Service at the Museum Theatre, Madras on August 23, 1948].

Sisters and Brothers,

I am extremely glad to feel that I am again in my own hometown and among friends who will excuse faults, exaggerate virtues and altogether be very friendly. Mrs. Cheriyan told you to prepare yourselves to hear words of wisdom from me, I am afraid I may disappoint you a great deal. I am not yet ready with any wisdom particularly applicable to Madras! I have been moving from place to place so quickly that I can only talk generalities and not much wisdom. We have had a great change in Government. We have raised very high expectations. We have not stinted to say that we are very good and able people. We did not mean to tell lies. But no one can guess what difficulties, will come until they actually arise. With all the help of Science, weather prognosticators do not always accurately tell us what is going to happen. It is much more difficult to guess what is going to happen in the affairs of men before they actually happen There is no body of people in the world more eager to make the people happy than the Government now in charge of India. Whatever discontented people or detractors may say, I can place my hand on my heart and vouch for this.

Our Government has been worried beyond measure by a number of problems. Even the things dearest to their hearts, have had to be put aside for the time being That gives a handle to a number of drawing room politicians who say, "Look at this; it is thoroughly disappointing; we want this thing to be done in this may, but it is done that way". I wish we could play with the fortunes of our people and ask these drawing room politicians to take over charge for a week. We would then have to call in mental doctors to look after them Ordinary people will go mad under the stress which our Government has been through. It is only God's grace and the good luck of our people that has saved these men from going mad.

Now the point is how can we help such people who are so earnest and so eager to make our people happy, instead of just passing judgement on them. It will take some time before alternative governments can be thought of I tell you with all the earnestness I can command that it will take some time for things to stabilise and for wisdom to say "well, let us try another government". It is not mere talent that can command the country. There may be some very talented people outside the Government It is not mere good intentions that can achieve things. There may be very many people outside with very good intentions if not talent But what is required over and above all is influence over the people, and command over the people's affection in the largest measure. You cannot get any body of people who can command the affection of the people to the same extent as the present Government. We must therefore help this Government in the best way we can in order to make the people of India happy.

I hope no one is under the impression that I have suddenly come here at half-past three and taken up the Madras Government as the object of my talk this afternoon. I am referring to the Government of India as a whole, and the Government of India includes in a general way all the Provincial governments in India as well. The authority that has now charge of our country cannot be put aside and an alternative government formed. The present Government must be helped if we are really good and wish to help the people.

That takes me to the present meeting. That which can be done by law, administrative orders or force, may be left to the Government. But a family requires not only a father but also a mother. Just as a family is guided by the authority of the father and by that indescribable force called the mother's affection, which also is necessary for the happiness of the family, in a State, without trying to make the analogy too perfect, all the social service organisations conducted by well-intentioned men and women, specially women, are in the position of the mother. The poor people in the country, the oppressed people and those who are at a disadvantage, all these people require not only laws and regulations, and monetary help, but a mother's affection in the first place to soothe and secondly to relieve distress.

These things cannot be done by government organisations. Even if all the social organisations are clubbed together into an official federation and an expert honorary non-stipendiary officer is appointed to look after it, the ways of government do not suit the problem. It wants something other than mere orders and regulations It demands affection, and for that reason, every government in the world, including that most perfect of all governments in regard to social affairs, namely, the Soviet Republic which depends so much upon official organisations, depends upon non-official voluntary service of a kind, such as the one under whose auspices I have the privilege of speaking today. There may be Government help. The Governor's wife may be the moving spirit in it. There may be grants, there may be inspection and all that, but the moving force must be the urge in the human mind to help people in distress, the urge that I began calling a mother's affection.

No one is more aware than I of the fact that it is not possible to help everybody in distress through voluntary social service. We just touch the fringe of the matter. As our Indian proverb says, it is a drop of asafoetida in the ocean! Still asafoetida is required in our preparations though we put very little of it. I do not, therefore, want you to make light of voluntary effort. It is true that the Secretary of a voluntary organisation may be dressed in beautiful clothes. It does not mean that her heart is not equally dressed in pit or sympathy. I am also aware of the general criticism that is made of fashionable women who come to help poor people. It may happen that a Collector's wife may be very charitable while a poor man's wife is not.

Poverty does not necessarily make people charitable I do not blame poor people. But is it not right that we should encourage sympathy and charity to become the fashion along with dress and other things? Let us make it fashionable really There is no necessary connection between ragged clothes and fondness for social service. The moral is only this. Let us not light-heartedly pass comments and discourage people from doing social service Everyone is entitled to find expression for the urge of affection which God has placed in every human being — sometimes it may be suppressed, sometimes it may find free expression. All these organisations therefore require the encouragement of newspaper men, public men, Government and the people who pass comments on others without doing anything themselves. All these things are necessary and I am very glad that in Free India there will be more and more of these organisations.

Do not think that social service work was a peculiarity of old Government House manners. The new Government House will go on doing the same thing, let me tell you, and every man will hereafter do more in that direction than he ever did before Our new Government in Free India will want the services of these and even more organisations. They will want them to work harder and they are bound to work harder. Look at this organisation. It was doing a lot of work before also After 15th August it has increased its work, widened its scope and taken in more people The Diwan Bahadur (referring to Diwan Bahadur V. Gashyam Iyengar) is not a fashionable young person hovering about Government House. Why has he joined this organisation? Because that is the urge of new India now, 'Almost all people will join this organisation Let all such organisations, whose common aim is to be charitable to people and help them in their difficulties as far as they can, work together. I am here, friends, as the official representative of Free India's new Government to say that all these social service organisations are most welcome to the Government, and everything possible will be done to help them in their work.

Unveiling Mahatmaji's Portrait in Madras

[Unveiling a portrait of Mahatma Gandhi at the Madras Legislative Council Hall on August 23, 1948].

Mr. Speaker, Your Excellency, Ladies and Gentlemen,

It gives me very great pleasure to see so many familiar faces in a familiar hall The Speaker referred to my chair here. I must confess that I do not very much remember this chair. What I remember is the chair in the other hall, the Senate House It was there I felt the thrill of functioning as Premier My impression is I did not sit here very much, I was mainly responsible for not having agreed to have another Parliament House built on a grand scale which my late lamented colleague, Mr. Yaqub Hasan, was eager to build Mere considerations of economy made me stubborn and blasted his ambition to build a suitable ball worthy of a free, democratic Madras. Then I said that we could convert this dark corner into a chamber large enough for members. When a man in authority says it can be made, all the officials say, "Oh, yes". In this case everybody also put his heart into the work and made this just enough to hold the enthusiasm of the members of the Assembly.

Anyway, it brought the Opposition and the Government very close together. In the other Senate House we were scattered and we felt the distance between the Opposition and the Government. Here we sat pretty close. Everyone showered his affection on me as if I was his elder brother or father. There was no difficulty in conducting the affairs of the House or the Government.

When I say all this, I am sure my successor, Mr. Ramaswamy Reddiar thinks, 'was it possible at any time that things were so sweet and nice, how is it I don't see them now?' I shall tell him my answer straightway The world is moving. We cannot remain in the same state; we are moving fast. We cannot help changing the context is all different now. The work of the Government is different now from what it was before I confess that I had a very easy task. Not only had I unqualified cooperation from all, including the Opposition, but the work itself was easier Now the compass of Government work is very much enlarged Everybody is angry with everybody else. That is the atmosphere we are in.

I have been given the very great privilege of unveiling the portrait which my friend, the Rajah of Chettinad, has presented to the Assembly as a token of his regard for the Assembly and for the principles for which Mahatmaji stood pictures we can have. But I must tell you as I told my friends in Bangalore the other day that you do not make it easier for me to toilet the evil that is common to all India You do not enable me to forget my personal grief asking me to unveil this picture where, whatever the talent's of the artist may be, I do not see the man.

It is conventional when you are unveiling a picture to say how very good a likeness it is. It may be a very good likeness in this case also But I do not have the heart to look at the picture, not to speak of judging it. It may not be considered the right thing to talk like this when one is given the honour and privilege of unveiling a portrait of a great man But as it is my habit and conviction to speak out exactly what I feel, I told you what I felt.

It pained me to be asked to unveil a portrait of Mahatma Gandhi. When the Speaker asked me to do this, it pained me also to wrangle with him. I did not wish to tell him 'no' because he would not understand my feelings He would say I was trying to be humble or modest I am not sure whether you all feel like me. Do you find satisfaction in having Mahatma Gandhi's picture painted and kept here? Can you see the man in it? I cannot. I do not see the man because the man was very different from all these pictures. So friends, I do not indulge in the conventional appreciation generally indulged in on such occasions.

It is worthwhile, however, to have a symbol. These pictures are only symbols; they are not likenesses. Mahatma Gandhi asked the people to boycott the Assembly. Later on, he asked people to enter the Assembly But he did not think it was a contradiction of his previous attitude. When the time came for legislative work to be undertaken, he said they should go into the Legislative Assembly He did not believe even then that the world would be made happier by legislative assemblies He himself never thought that he was good enough to be a member of a Legislative Assembly although, I may tell you from my intimate knowledge and detached observation, he would have been good a member as any of us, if not better. Let me add, however, that he had no great attraction for that kind of work.

Why then is his picture here? There is appropriateness because you are law-makers. You make laws from time to time. You make laws reading newspapers every day, gauging public opinion, addressing election meetings and asking people what they desire. Earnest men who serve in the legislature make laws by the sense of right or wrong which they feel in their inner being. Whatever the context, or proposals, they have to go finally through this lost in their own minds, "Does this proposal lit in with the pattern of law in the abstract and not merely law with a capital 'L'?"

Law in the abstract is what you have in your mind. Dharma you may call it in our own phraseology. You must make laws which are consonant with Dharma. Mahatmaji is a symbol which you may keep before you whenever you make laws. If you think that this picture will help you to make laws in that manner, it is worthwhile having it here.

At this distance, even forgetting my personal feeling, it is difficult for me with so many garlands on it to be able to judge the picture. I am told by the Speaker that it is very good. But at this distance, the mike in the picture which Mahatmaji is represented to be speaking through seems to be a symbol of the later half of Gandhiji's life when he invariably used the loudspeaker to enable his feeble voice to be heard so that he might communicate his thoughts to all around.

Let me tell you that Mahatmaji, the exponent of the old spinning wheel, the so-called enemy, as some people believed, of time, machine and advancement, was not really an enemy of advancement or machine. He was the enemy of the machine when the machine became the master and man became its slave. As long as the machine served man, Gandhiji loved the machine as he loved anything that served man. So Gandhiji did not desire to discard the loudspeaker. Indeed, he used the loudspeaker quite often. I wish he lived to use it a little more until all our work was done. When on January 30th, he was about to use the loudspeaker, his life was cut of and he parted company with us.

Let people think that Mahatmaji is not only speaking through the mike to vast audience but putting forward a plea for a continual honest endeavour. He wanted people to work. Work is the only thing by which man can justify his existence. He must work and produce and it is only then he has a right to live. He has to work honestly and without caring for personal advantages. He has to work in a detached way. That was Bapu's doctrine, the doctrine of the Gita and all the other scriptures of the world.

Mahatmaji came in our time to impress that doctrine on us. To work in a detached way and not to remain idle is, in short, Gandhiji's plea. I hope that the members of the Legislative Assembly will draw that lesson from this picture.

In the old days some of my colleagues used to spin with. Take in hand, the Speaker looking on severely at them all the time. Of course, the Speaker might well have said that members were there to debate and not spin yarn. But one thing that we in Free India must remember is that we should not misunderstand one another. We should work hard to overcome prejudice and spread love. That also is Mahatmaji's doctrine. His great desire was that we should understand and work for this country. I can do no better — you can do no better — than to preach this doctrine wherever possible and make it go down to the hearts of the people and not merely remain an empty word without real meaning. Do not misunderstand one another. If you want your villages to be happy and your Province to be happy, get away from the habit of misunderstanding one another and get into the habit of understanding one another. God is in everybody's heart. Everybody will be kind and loving if you will love and be kind.

We do not know the mystery of life or how God works. But I know this that, if you love a man, he returns the love without knowing or without any effort. Try and you will see you succeed, as you all believe that I have succeeded in Bengal. I succeeded, as everybody now claims, because I loved everybody and everybody loved me. If you want to be loved in the world, try hard to overcome prejudice and extend your genuine affection to those around you and make this world happier. If I don't say this on this occasion, I will not be true to the picture. This is all that I have to say and I thank you, Mr. Speaker, for the privilege you gave me to associate myself with this function.

At the Indian Women's Association

[Addressing (in Tamil) members of the Indian Women's Association at Rajaji Hall (Madras) on August 23, 1948].

Sisters,

I am grateful to you all for your sincere welcome. With all the good wishes and goodwill extended to me in your address I am confident I can carry on successfully the great responsibilities entrusted to me I feel very happy to see such a large gathering of women in Madras. The manner in which you have gathered in such large numbers today shows that you are willing and prepared to take your share in public affairs.

Whatever men may say and do, I am sure that women all over the country wholeheartedly support the Government. You have in your address referred to the message I sent to the All India Women's Conference last year. I then said, "May the women of India try to undo what mischief the men have in recent times done to themselves". Thinking over those words again, I am pleased that I sent you such a true message. We must all cooperate, specially the women of India, who can do a great deal.

What is the disease from which this country is suffering today? It is mutual distrust. There is no enmity or ill-feeling in this country. There is only mutual suspicion and fear in the minds of people. That should be got rid of. There is not so much distrust among women of various communities. Women are best fitted to remove that distrust. I feel that this distrust is due more to fear and misunderstanding. We must remove that fear.

We must not make much of small differences between us.

Women may have their own associations, their own meetings and their own activities, but they must all work for one common purpose, namely, the removal of fear and distrust among the communities.

To achieve this purpose, women can arrange to have meetings to which women of all communities might be invited. On festive occasions you can invite the women of other communities. By such gatherings you can promote mutual understanding. South India has earned the admiration of the rest of India by keeping free of communal troubles. Whatever happens, feelings of friendship between Hindus and Muslims must be promoted and maintained. The more women devote their attention to social service the more they will serve the country. God will bless you and guide you in the work that you have set before yourselves.

Civic Address at Madras

[In reply to the Civic Address presented by the Corporation of Madras on August 23, 1948].

Worshipful Mayor, Ladies and Gentlemen,

To the people of the City of Madras I tender my most grateful appreciation for their kindness and unbroken affection. I was trying to see whether there was anybody whom I did not know among the Councillors of the City. Barring one or two all of them are more or less old friends and I have nothing new to tell them and they have nothing new to tell me.

It is a privilege to command so much affection. Words have been generously employed to explain that I have done this or done that; but I know the real reason why we are all so exhilarated. The reason is as I have often observed — we have not understood exactly what we meant when we asked for self-government. Not having understood it, we are surprised when one of our own men is appointed to a high office. If we really meant what we said when we wanted self-government and full responsible government, it must be easy for us to see that nothing else can happen.

We have to bear not only with one Governor General but with many successive heads of state being appointed from our own ranks and from ordinary familiar material. No Englishman will hereafter come to take up the office. One after another, one of ourselves must be appointed and must accept the office. I, having come first, have had the advantage of exciting your feeling of exhilaration so much.

You will get used to such things and you will make no more of it than you would make of a man becoming Prime Minister in Madras or another man losing his Prime Ministership! It will all be in the normal course of things.

We have to bear with another, suffer one another and make the best of one another — that is the most important thing. Men come to serve us in one capacity or other. We must hasten to learn how to make the best use of them.

Important and competent judges from abroad have told me, not to flatter me or our people but to cheer me up when I felt depressed over many things, that our people have produced leaders and administrators, ministers and legislators who can compare with any other officers, leaders, ministers, or legislators in the world. I believe them. Eminent men from abroad have pointed out to me that difficulties, exactly like those we have here, crop up in other places also.

Therefore, when I see things and reflect calmly, I see that our men and our leaders are as good, as sincere, as genuine and as single-minded as anybody else in the world filling a similar position.

Ours is a country of which we can be proud.

We have men and women of whom we can be proud. We suffer from an illusion which makes us regard men and things we know as if there was nothing remarkable about them Let us therefore understand one another. Let us make the best use of those who come to serve us. Let us not make things more difficult than they are. It is difficult for 350 million people to pull together under a democratic form of government. It is easy to govern with troops or through force. It is difficult for a large body like our nation to govern itself through self-restraint which is another name for democracy. It is not possible to run democracy in India as we can run it in a small town or state. Much more understanding is necessary in our country than democracy in smaller countries demands. We have to learn, therefore, how to govern ourselves.

We have excellent material but we must know how to use it. That is why I put it in common language that we must make the best use of those who come to serve us.

Democracy is the process of a number of people coming together to serve the country. It is not a process of mere wrangling. A number of people from the ranks of the ordinary will come to serve and we must know how to harmonise things and make the best use of them.

The Municipal Corporation of Madras has its problems, the one particular problem being how to find money. We go on expanding our activities and we create problems for ourselves. The City is growing, growing so big, that almost everybody in the Province wants to come and live in Madras.

Everyone wants to come and do business in Madras. Everyone wants to come and get healed of some disease or other in Madras. Everyone wants to educate his children in Madras. Everyone wants to be amused in the picture halls of Madras. Everybody from everywhere in the Province is drawn towards Madras as iron filings are drawn to a magnet Now all people come together to Madras and the evil is growing on itself. Our problems go on increasing. What shall we do then? My advice is that we must do something to make the other towns also attract people. It is only then that there is salvation for Madras. Not even an extra quarter anna on the railway ticket as terminal tax will save the City of Madras. The people who come and who pay the quarter anna or half an anna at the railway station, will demand much more from you in the City of Madras than they do now. We must, therefore, do something to make other towns and cities as attractive as Madras.

What is the attraction that draws people to cities? Amenities, facilities for education, facilities for medical help, sanitation, good water, parks, music — these draw people Unless we create similar surroundings and attractions in other places, Madras will go on adding more and more fat round it like a man or woman who gets too stout, and Madras is bound to be unhappy. Neither octroi duties at the roads nor an additional quarter anna, half an anna, or more on railway tickets will save us.

Nothing but commonsense can save us. We must make other towns and cities, if not as beautiful as Madras, at least nearly as good People will go there and our problems in Madras will at least find a limit Let us put a ceiling to our problems; let us not increase these problems.

It is not only Madras that suffers from this. In all Provinces it is the same story. In Madras Province you have at least some other fairly good towns You can, in some other towns also, pull a lever and get a flush to operate. But take Bengal. Outside Calcutta there is no place which can be called a town The whole of Bengal lives in Calcutta. The problem is even more serious there. As all Municipalities are represented here, I say these few things so that you can think about them Municipalities by themselves cannot do much. The financial system on which we are working now is such that other towns cannot be made beautiful or attractive. Hence, we have to discover a way out of it.

There is a great deal of work to do before freedom can bring joy to the people. By itself it is not much. You can ask the Prime Minister of India whether he is more happy today than he was before. He may be compelled for the sake of consistency to say: 'Yes, I am very happy because we are free'. But if you find an apparatus to look into the heart, you will find that he is really less happy than he ever was. Let us be wise Freedom is after all only a means for happiness. Having got it, we must work hard to make one another happy. We cannot make one another happy or be ourselves happy, unless we learn how to understand one another. To understand one another is the first difficulty.

There are many grave dangers before the country of which everyone is conscious. Everyone is afraid of wars and troubles. There is war in the atmosphere all over the world. As you believe in to be somewhat of a successful prognosticator, let me assure you that the world may talk very bitterly and very angrily, but it dares not go to war. You may read of all kinds of terrible language, but you will not see the world so foolishly going to war as we imagine.

Some want war, but they do not want to learn Hindustani. They want everybody to join together and fight, but do not want a common language. We have to learn many truths before we can learn to be happy. I am very sad to see that Madras, famous for intelligence, is, in my humble opinion, still far from real 'intelligence. I am intelligent enough to see that we are very stupid indeed.

We do not know what is good for us. We have to learn a good deal. But of one thing I am sure. We are all good people; but we must understand one another. And we will do so very soon.

I have come to find joy for a few days by staying in your midst. I am trying to see as many people as possible. Unfortunately it is easier to tour in a place I have not previously known than to tour in a place I have known. There are so many friends who get angry because I have not shaken hands with them, or gone to their homes, or looked at them and smiled, or accepted invitations from them. When you visit a place and if you possess some adventitious importance, you leave more enemies behind when you go than when you started. I hope my appeal will be heard and that no one will expect me to do more than I can physically do within the short time I have. I have no hope of gathering the joys of friendship or communion with dear people until I resign from office and come here. Unfortunately we have still so much of the children in us that we believe something has happened to a friend because he has been made Governor General and therefore, he must come while he is Governor General to our houses or sit with us. I really wish it were possible for me to see everyone of you. But it is not possible and you must take it that I have done it. I will come one day and claim the right to meet, visit and talk to everyone of you. I hope you will not then neglect me, because I have laid down my office.

As an old man, I claim the right to offer blessings to you all. May God give you wisdom, much wanted wisdom and may God give you happiness, much wanted happiness which it is only in His power to give.

Muslim Orphanage at Madras

[On the occasion of the laying of the foundation-stone of the new building for the Muslim Orphanage at Thyagaraya Nagar, Madras, on August 24, 1948].

Ladies and Gentlemen,

Just as my old friend, Mr. Hameed Khan said that his joy knew no bounds, I also feel the same and my pleasure may also be described as knowing no bounds on this occasion. It was more than ten years ago, I believe, that as Premier I was associated with the grant that was referred to here. I am very glad that arrangements have been made to secure about two square furlongs of land for this Orphanage.

It was very sweet to hear the children sing the thanks to me and I wish to tell you that I feel that these children are my children just as much as children of any other community are. Since we should always extend more affection to those who feel depressed and afflicted and to those who are afraid, I wish to ask you all, my Hindu friends, to treat Muslim children as your own children and, if possible, with special favour so as to remove their fears and their doubts.

We are, both as a Government and a people unchangeably pledged to treating all people alike. Not only our Government, but the Dharma of our people also commits them to this attitude of perfect equality irrespective of caste or creed. I want you to make this your practical code of thinking and acting. We will not achieve our goal of glory in the world if we in India were to swerve from this path.

We must treat all people alike and if any difference is to be made to remove temporary doubts and fears, the difference must be all in favour of those who suffer from fear or doubt. I am therefore greatly delighted to be associated with this function. It is very pleasing to be told that I was associated with the primary grant in connection with this institution and it is very pleasing again to be here to lay its foundation-stone.

There are many difficulties in all human endeavours and those of you who were present with me when I laid the foundation-stone, saw an example of ii The stone itself was so tied up that I could not lay it quickly and properly.

Our very efforts are sometimes so entangled that we are not able to achieve what we desire quickly. What happened just now is only a small example of the general principle. We should not be impatient. If I had been impatient and cut the ropes that were tied round the stone with a knife, the stone would have landed on somebody's fingers. We must similarly be patient with the delay and difficulties in raising this institution.

Do not lose your patience or your temper with the Government of Madras because owing to many difficulties they are not able to give the money you ask them in the very first year. But they are sure to give.

We shall not progress in this complicated world unless we are patient with one another. This is God's world. You believe in God. He is all-powerful and will look after everything. It is only a question of time. Do not lose patience with your fellow-beings because it would amount to losing patience with God Himself. We shall achieve what we desire in course of time. Any delay, difficulty or opposition will ultimately strengthen the structure. We need not always imagine that every difficulty is the work of Satan. There is no Satan really. It is really the work of God and all our difficulties are God's trials.

I give my best wishes to all friends who are working for a common cause. Your orphanage is not a Muslim orphanage; it is an Indian orphanage. According to the taste and requirements of several groups of people, several different institutions will have to be raised. But they are all Indian orphanages. They are all my children, let me once again tell you. May God bless you all!

Indian Military Academy

[His Excellency the Governor General made the following speech at the Indian Military Academy at Dehra Dun on October 9, 1948].

I am very pleased to have seen your institution. I have spent a very pleasant morning. I am no kind of a soldier. I cannot scale heights, jump a pit or carry a long pole behind my back and manage to walk on a rope But I have understanding enough to appreciate the hard tasks you do and the cheerfulness with which you do them.

I have understanding enough to appreciate how useful you are to the nation as a whole. You get training here for military life — for the first time for a patriotic military life, not merely for a professional military life.

Let me tell you that I never appreciated the phrase "mercenary". It was a common phrase in the newspapers of the previous decade. It was wrong to call it "mercenary". It would have been better to call it a profession. It was professional soldiery; just as a doctor who has the equipment finds joy in practising his profession, incidentally making some money and curing some unhappy and sick people, the soldiers found joy in the professional life of a soldier. Incidentally they made some money for their families and incidentally they protected the country. That was professional soldiery Today you have additional joy. Even if you get a little less money than others before you used to get or less value for the money, you have an additional joy in this that you do not have a mere profession but you are serving your own people.

That new joy I see now in the bright faces of every cadet and every officer in India, a thing we did not see some years ago. In the old days there was loyalty and discipline.

A soldier turned 90 degrees exactly or marched quite correctly with a fixed stare in the face as soldiers are trained to wear. But in the beginning of August last year, senior officers especially were somewhat disturbed. They found that they did not turn exactly 90 degrees but 88 degrees The other two degrees were lost in contemplation of the new freedom that they had got. Senior officers were disturbed by a little slackness in the gestures that made up a salute, a little slackness in the words they used. Some of them said "Jai Hind", some of them said "Namaste", and all of them were confused as to what exactly they should do on each occasion. All that was a little disturbing, but the disturbance was due to the new joy that they all felt.

Things have now settled down and I find that the face of every soldier in India now is more beautiful than it was, because handsomeness comes out of internal joy. There is no disharmony in their mind. There is no conflict in the mind between duty to officers, duty to the army, duty to the profession and duty to the country.

Everyone is more cheerful now. May we not therefore offer thanks to God for all this joy?

You do not know how many people there are who are ready to give money to me or to the Prime Minister, saying

"Distribute this among the soldiers". I can raise any fund for you. That is the state of mind in the country today. If instead of levying a tax and allotting a budget for the army, the Government said today "People are allowed to pay whatever they like for the good of the Army", we would raise a higher revenue than ever we did before in the Legislative Assembly for defence. That is due to the cheerfulness of the people now.

Let me tell you this. Of all the professions in India Today — whether it is a doctor's, a sanitary officer's, a lawyer's, a teacher's, a civil servant's or a barber's — of all the professions, high and low in this country, the Army is the most popular profession among the people — popular not in the sense that they all like to join the army, but popular in the sense that they love the army. There is no greater encouragement or pleasure to people than to be loved by other people. That is the biggest addition to your salary.

Over and above the money you get as salary, you have the current of the living love of the people. The old Commanders-in-Chief and other senior military officials, including the old Subedars, did not get it. But today everybody loves you. Therefore, every rupee that you are now getting from the Government is a golden rupee, not a silver rupee. I wish I were young, if for nothing else, at least for the pleasure of being admitted here and taught as a cadet in this institution.

They seem to teach here everything in the world and so quickly. In other colleges they walk; in this college you run! Find joy in everything. You go through hard physical exercise. You are taught mathematics, science, physics and similar subjects. Many of you are getting practice in the art of talking. In modern times war is conducted not as in the old days by merely killing one another. Now they conduct wars by talking, writing, and by telling the other side how much we can do.

In the old days men were born to obey. There was feudal loyalty-discipline and obedience by birth. Today nobody obeys anyone else blindly. You must explain beforehand why we should obey you. What you learn here by way of talking and explaining is therefore not useless. It is part of the equipment for national defence.

I wish you success in all your tasks. I wish no war should come and overtake us, that we should never have to wage war. It is good to keep your fangs like a cobra in your mouth but not bite anybody.

We have to keep arms, but it is not good to wage war. We have to keep our fangs all right. We have to keep ourselves in form, but we have to keep cool and not lose our temper.

The best pacifists in any country are the soldiers in that country. It is the civil population that often shout war and want battle. But it is the strong that restrain themselves.

It is the weak that do not know how to restrain themselves. I wish you all strength. I wish you all calm.

Doon School

[His Excellency the Governor General made the following speech on Founder's Day at Doon School, Dehra Dun, on October 9, 1948].

This visit has proved most interesting and has helped to create hope in me Education is the most difficult of all tasks. It is one of the most essential things and in a very highly civilized country like ours the aims are always very high. I wish there were other institutions equally good, scattered all over the country and run equally efficiently with swimming pools, workshops, art and music classes and everything in order. But we have not the resources to multiply institutions of the type we have here.

What then shall we do? Can we do with inferior education? Our minds will not accept such a proposition. We want superior education. Therefore, we will have to devise a way to make it cheaper but as good as it is here. You may not have this swimming pool, but you must drive boys to village ponds and make them swim there. You may not have Mr. Martyn, but you must get some local man who has got the instinct for teaching. If anyone tells me that this cannot be made cheaper, then the problem is an impossible one.

We may not all have race horses, but we can all have bicycles. We have beautiful carpets to show what carpets can be, and at the same time we distribute cheap rugs to protect people against the cold.

I went round not as President of the Governing Body, but as one interested in methods of education. I can say the methods are very good here. The boys are bright and happy. If you go to any school and you find the boys looking unhappy, shut that school down. That is my advice. The first essential in all schools is that boys and girls should be cheerful and happy, then they must be made into active and good human beings. If they are not active, then education is not worthwhile. They can remain good in their own homes.

What I like here is that boys are made to do work.

They are made to produce things and to see that there is joy in work. I could see the joy in their faces when they were shaping wood or hammering a piece of iron or painting a picture. The gradual development of this side of a boy's character is the most important part of the system here.

It can be incorporated everywhere without great cost. In all villages, boys can be taken by the local Mr. Martyn to the local workshops and made to see things and take part in them.

Then there is the problem of mixing. You have here an excellent community life. Boys from all parts of India come here Our culture is a synthesis of our own culture plus something which came and has been here for 150 years. 'Quit India' we said to Britain, but the English language remains. 'Quit the English language' some people shout. What language will you use in Doon School? The present synthesis of culture that India has developed can not be undone. This school represents a synthesis with which we have to bear for some time at least and whatever the medium of instruction in other schools in other provinces, I fear the English language will remain here.

It won't suit national self-respect. It may be impossible for you to cope with popular opinion. You will have to introduce the national language as a medium But you will have again to compromise. What I mean is this We will have to give perfect freedom to the efficient teacher to use whatever medium he likes, according to tine class which he is instructing. It depends on the composition of the class and the subject you teach.

That is perhaps the only solution for the immediate problems before us in regard to the medium of teaching. If you try anything else by compulsion, you will have trouble. You will not be able to do anything. If we can sit down, close all schools and think quietly for a year, probably then we might discover a solution, but the schools must run. It is like trying to repair a railway train while it is in motion. All schools will have to be going on, just as all work will have to be going on. Therefore, we will have to make a number of compromises. That is the problem.

This is a very fine school. I was impressed at the amount of science taught in this school. It is wrong to think that science teaches only science. Science brings about a change in the whole attitude of the boys. It brings about correct judgement, alertness and obedience to laws. In fact, science is an excellent culture medium for boys and girls.

I give my blessings to all the boys that are studying in the school. May they have the best careers in life and — if no careers are available — the best of tempers in life. Let them go through life happily and with by which can be got with or without a career.

Id in Delhi

[Following is the gist of His Excellency the Governor General's speech in Hindustani at the congregational prayers offered by the Delhi Muslims at the Idgah on October 14, 1948 in celebration of Id].

This is a day of prayer and sacrifice. All nations in the world have from time immemorial worshipped God through sacrifice. The Hindu scriptures lay down the rule that we should offer food as a sacrifice and consecrate it before we eat. Otherwise, the scriptures say, it is theft.

It is a great thing that Delhi has celebrated Dussehra and Id together and that the joy of human fellowship has not been disturbed. As I have said before, we have turned the corner. Our past griefs may be forgotten and all will be well. Government is determined to treat all alike and India will demonstrate that diversities of language or forms of worship do not matter as long as truth is one and God is one.

Let us learn more and more to see on all occasions the substance behind every form, the reality behind the apparent and diverse exterior of all things. This alone is real knowledge. It is this that will make for peace and happiness in this land.

Swamy Dayanand Saraswati

[His Excellency the Governor General made the following speech at Ram Lila Grounds on the occasion of the 65th Death Anniversary of Swamy Dayanand Saraswati, founder of the Arya Samaj, on October 31, 1948].

Our religion was founded by and added to from time to time by some of the greatest souls that ever walked this earth. Their one passion was the quest of truth. They dug Into the mysteries of mind and matter with a will and an energy and a poise of reason and emotion unsurpassed by any other people in the world. It is our special good fortune to be born to such a rich inheritance. If instead of using and benefiting by an inheritance, we feel it to be a millstone round our neck, no one but ourselves is to blame.

Truth is one and eternal. But by reason of the natural limitations of the human mind, it is discovered by us only in parts. At any given moment there is a sum-total of knowledge which has to be collected and synthetised without prejudice or passion. A continuous readjustment is necessary so that the sum of Truth in our possession at any given time may be combined into a whole. Previous conquests over darkness handed down to us will serve as safe stepping stones and not hinder, if we do not erect impassable barriers between old and newly-found knowledge.

To integrate ancient truth and modern knowledge is the only way to life in the fullness to which we are entitled.

Ancient wisdom should not be treated as a thing apart from modern Truth. Just as the material wealth of our forefathers has merged into our own resources, so also must the moral wealth inherited from them flow into and become one with modern truth and wisdom. Ancient and modern are not like two different valleys divided by an impassable ridge, but one continuous territory, the one imperceptibly passing into the other. If we look back with imagination and clear sight, we can easily see that there was no point of time where the ancient ended and the modern began. It was one continuous flow of time, that is, of human activity.

There is no reason whatever why the religion of the Hindus should in any respect be unsuitable for modern times. Our forefathers could not and did not intend to provide for all time. They gave us more than the forefathers of any other people ever gave to them. They left a tradition of wise conservatism for ensuring continuity of culture. The safeguard is for providing against decay and destruction. They did not prohibit readjustment to modern knowledge. Failure to readjust must lead to decay and destruction. It is our own fault, not that of our forefathers, if we misinterpreted protective conservatism into a deathtrap for truth.

Maharishi Dayanand Saraswati was among our people a hundred years ago. The religion of our forefathers was at that time sore pressed by modern science on the one hand and by Christianity on the other. The chronic attach of Islam was also there. The fault was not in the Rishis who gave us the Vedas and the Upanishads but in us. The Maharishi diagnosed the disease and he treated the cause surgically, by a process of bold excision. In this his method differed from that of some other great men, for example Shri Ramakrishna Paramahansa, who applied an all-embracing tolerance and understanding which dissolved all barriers and made the crudest parts of Hinduism as good as the highest. The goal is the same, but the approaches differ.

Swamy Dayanand's soul rebelled against the idea of Hinduism being relegated to a status of unsuitability to modern times. He strove by a process of merciless chopping off, to make the ancient forest habitable for modern life. Let us not convert the result of his labour into another obstinate sect; but rather, let us understand the purpose and meaning of his noble effort and strive to fulfil it as he wanted it to make Hinduism a habitable tenement for progressive, modern life, a religion whose culture, tradition and tenets make no compromise with evil, and offer no impediment to human progress. If there is one religion that followed the scientific method in the search for spiritual truth, it is the religion of the Upanishad teachers.

If the Rishis were told that out of deference to them, new knowledge would be kept apart and their teachings would be protected in isolation, they would have been shocked. They would have condemned it as the greatest act of heresy in the worship of truth.

The present phase of Hinduism is a period of reabsorption and integration of all reforming sects. It will of course mean a certain amount of self-effacement of denominations. Pride is the enemy of truth as well as of human welfare. Swamy Dayanand's aim can be fulfilled only by reabsorption of his reforms as well as of the Sikh Gurus, the Brahma Samaj and all others into Hinduism as a whole. Truth is automatically self-effacing. This is the very nature of truth. If any reforming school resists this self-effacement and seeks to live apart from that which it is its function to reform, thenceforward it begins to rot and decay. The unreformed may indeed, prove better than the isolated reformer-denomination, for age gives a power all its own. Swamy Dayanand's teachings have permeated wide and a stage has been reached when they can no longer form a denomination apart, but must live in the soul of Hinduism itself, And this has been the trend of thought and of action on the part of all Arya Samajists.

Indian Art Exhibition in Government House

[His Excellency the Governor General made the following speech at the opening of the Indian Art Exhibition in Government House, New Delhi on November 6, 1948].

Maulana Sahib, Ladies and Gentlemen,

It is a great privilege you are giving me today. This collection is the fruit of the labours of many eminent men and women who have spared no pains in assembling together from various parts of the country carefully selected works of art representing various periods of Indian history. It is my duty on this occasion to express, on behalf of the people and the Government of India, our grateful appreciation of the labours of the Committee which was presided over by Her Excellency the Governor of the United Provinces, Shrimati Sarojini Naidu. The experts' work of search and selection has made this exhibition not only interesting, which any art collection is bound to be, but also most instructive.

I am very glad these halls have been temporarily put to some good use, and far from being entitled to any thanks for that reason, I must offer thanks to the Honourable the Education Minister. I should like the Government to consider ways and means of making this Exhibition a permanent collection for educational purposes and to obtain the requisite permission from the various authorities and individuals who kindly lent the exhibits.

Maulana Sahib has explained how these exhibits enable us really to understand the history of our land. We can see in these exhibits the greatness of past efforts in the field of art in India and with imagination we can build up the national life that gave birth and scope to such art. We may thereby find inspiration and hope for the future.

The past is always beautiful and glorious for we see only achievements, and the dreary spaces that intervened unfilled by achievement are necessarily cut out from the picture, In the present on the other hand we are far too conscious of the empty spaces and are prone to underestimate achievement. Still it would not be wrong to say that several causes have contributed to the present times being relatively barren.

For a people to produce works of art there must be very real and sustained emotional power moving people's hearts, faith, love, devotion or the like The men who built or painted or carved, whose art we admire, carved, painted and built as they did because they had an intensity and genuineness of feeling and faith, which we do not possess now. How can men who do not have the feeling do what feeling alone can produce? We can copy, we can measure and reproduce, but creative art requires genuine faith which, alas, we now do not have, however much we may pretend.

We see in figures and paintings, curve, anatomy, colour and all else, but we cannot produce things of art unless there is in us the faith that was in those who in former days produced these things, How can the unbeliever produce a thing like the dance of Nataraja or the Ajanta frescoes? It is impossible. Could any man on earth conceive the dance of Shiva if he did not see God behind all the seeming diversities of good and evil in this world? Could anyone paint the Ajanta frescoes if he did not believe with all the strength of his soul in love and compassion, and that man could be saved through the Lord Buddha? Could anyone build the temples of South India if he did not firmly believe in salvation through the faith of our fathers? We can produce tawdry copies, but we cannot build the original temple or paint the original fresco. Could any have given us the Taj unless he loved as greatly as Shahjahan did? Could anyone plan or build Fatehpur Sikri unless he fervently believed in the unity of all religions and hoped for humanity as Akbar did? To Soordas, Mira and Tyagaraja who sang the songs and composed the music which we enjoy so greatly, Krishna and Earn were utter realities like the things they saw and touched with their eyes and hands in daily life.

Our art has lapsed in the measure of our barrenness of faith and reverence. It is only when love, faith or reverence shines through a picture or a piece of sculpture or architecture that we exclaim, 'How beautiful'! It is not just knowledge of the laws of proportion or of harmony in colour or exactitude of representation. We cannot attain greatness of art for the nation except through greatness of life. We must believe and love and revere truly if we hope and wish to revive art. The utmost we can do otherwise is in landscape painting. Even there we can succeed only to the extent we can approach the sky and the earth, the water and the trees, with the awe and reverence that means religion.

But we have now a new fountain of inspiration in our political emancipation. If we become sincere, we can yet achieve something in art. We can see in this exhibition that we have inherited a very sound foundation of culture and art on which we can build worthily. To achieve anything great, we need a vision that is straightforward and honest. I think we are getting to it There is a tremendous amount of literature on art in various fields, most of which ordinary people like me cannot hope to understand, although I think I do appreciate and enjoy good painting, good sculpture, good architecture and the like. Even the jargon of metaphysics is not so mystic as some analytical art criticism that I have tried to read and have given up as hopeless. I have a notion that art criticism flourishes and grows in the inverse ratio of art itself. It is true as much of art as of literature that genius has often to struggle against learned criticism to get a chance to find expression and present itself. I may take this occasion to put in a public plea for kindliness of approach towards creative effort in art. This Exhibition is a lesson in the history of India. It is also a great lesson in politics and statesmanship. It is a collection that will also help the progress of art itself. I have great pleasure in declaring this Exhibition open.

At the Delhi Rotary Club

[His Excellency the Governor General made the following speech at lunch with the President and Members of the Delhi Rotary Club on November 11, 1948].

Mr. President, Ladies and Gentlemen,

The manner in which the President has introduced me is embarrassing. I am just as good or as bad as any other citizen in India and that is why I am entitled to be the first citizen of India also. If I had been superior to others, I should have been put aside in favour of an easier model.

Having disposed of the claims made on my behalf by the President, I must tell you what I feel about lunches and dinners in general. They are a bit tedious, in my opinion.

I fear you all must be feeling the same, only you think it is not proper to say so. But if the first citizen does not speak out frankly, who else can do it? Although lunches and dinners are tedious, they are necessary. Elementary appetites of eating and drinking are the common denominators for all people and so we meet on that basis so that differences may not be emphasised. The Rotary Club, as I understand its object, shares with some other organisations the aim of promoting harmony and fellowship among the peoples of various lands.

I hope the Rotarians will succeed, where others have not found much fruitful result. I feel like many others the need for this kind of work. Even within the borders of our own country we have many differences to overcome. If we solve our difficulties in India, we set a laboratory example for the whole world.

The world is watching us not only because we are very big, right in the middle of the Indian Ocean, strategically occupying a very important position and have got the largest power element with us, namely, population, but also because we are trying to solve problems in which if we succeed, we might be an example to the rest of the world.

Most difficulties are illusions. If once we make up our minds on the basis of clear truth, most difficulties solve themselves. Here in our country, for instance, we have divided a territory which was governed by Ashoka and Akbar into two political entities. Most people deplore it. I understand even the cricket players deplore it. We have lost some first-class players because of partition. What prevents good players from coming together even though some of them might belong to one territory and some others to another? What prevents people from writing letters to one another even though they might belong to different territories, or from selling and buying? Mutual commerce or friendship is not prevented by the partition of India Humanity is one and we are trying to rediscover this very old truth through many organisations of which the Rotary Club is one.

We have to learn two things. One is to see ourselves as others see us Passion and pride disable us from seeing what other people see in us. We should learn to know ourselves more accurately than our own pride or our wishes make us believe we are. We should also learn another thing — we should understand other people placing ourselves in their position. We apply one yard-stick when we measure ourselves, and we apply another yard-stick when we wish to appraise other people. This makes all the difficulties in life and creates misunderstanding. Take, for instance, common political passions. We wish to apply the strict rule of democracy when we are in the majority. When we are in the minority, we wish to apply quite a different rule and appeal to the sacred rights of individuals. We must understand others placing ourselves in their position and understand ourselves as far as possible as other people see us.

We cannot succeed in anything if we act in fear of other people's opinions. We must be open-minded, we should hear what other people say and give every respect to what they say, but we should stop at respect. Do not get frightened. Do not do anything or abstain from doing anything on account of the fear that other people may not approve of it. Listen with respect to what other people have to say If you like, change your mind, but do not, without changing your mind, act out of fear.

What greater pleasure is there in life than to be bold? In every matter if we try to do what we think is right, everything will go on all right. What I have told you has been said a thousand times before. But it is good to repeat truth so long as we have not reached what we wish to reach.

Thank you very much for giving me the privilege of addressing you.

At the Cosmopolitan Club

[His Excellency the Governor General made the following speech at the Cosmopolitan Club, Madras on August 24, 1948].

Mr. President, Ladies and Gentlemen,

The Cosmopolitan Club is an old institution and one very familiar to me. The decorations which you have very kindly made in the hall to make me feel cheerful have made it look a little less familiar than really the place is to me.

I miss many old faces here, faces of those who were uncrowned Kings of this Club. Death must take away its toll and the Club like other institutions has had to part with a few of its dominant personalities. Still quite a lot remain and I hope you will make the best use of them and not make them feel that there is only room in it for young men. As an old man myself, I wish to warn young men that whatever they do in the outer world, in the Club they must make old men feel comfortable and happy so long as they are there. You will miss them very much when they go away.

Clubs in India should develop good manners and should be places where you can forget all other differences in politics and other controversial matters. In these days everything is controversial—social reforms are controversial and even language has become controversial. All those differences must be put aside. We must have one spot where all men who claim to be enlightened and who have leisure can meet together and overcome various prejudices generated in the course of their daily work. In the days when I was one of the campaigners in politics, there was a prevalent feeling that Clubs were on the whole useless and the members thereof were not doing useful work. When everybody was anxious and busy, these people played bridge, chatted without any serious purpose, wasted time and above all thought they were very important. That was the feeling when I was an active politician; not that it was my feeling, but it was the feeling of the people working in the field I was engaged in.

But as has been found by men's experience recorded in the Old Testament, a stone that is considered less fit may prove to be the corner stone of the structure to be raised. Today institutions like yours and Clubs where there is no politics have become most important for the cultivation of unity, strength and harmony in society, which are the things for which we should campaign now, now that we have attained freedom. The present times are such that we must make it a campaign. It is not enough merely to recognise the value of harmony. We have to work for it very hard. As politics was important before 1947, so is harmony important now and is the one thing for which men like Gandhiji worked. Freedom having been achieved, we have to work hard for harmony without which we cannot find happiness in this country.

Where can harmony be generated? Not in the Legislative Assembly, not in the newspaper offices, not in the bazaars and not even, perhaps, in isolated temples where people isolate themselves from each other, but in clubs where all kinds of persons meet and sit together. Therefore, institutions like your Club are hereafter really Temples of Harmony. There is a great mission for institutions like this and that mission is the cultivation of good understanding, good fellowship and the great art of forgetting differences. I am obliged to say something in a serious manner which I hope will find a response in your minds. Whatever avocation, whatever work you may have outside, when you come to the club for relaxation remember what I have told you. Even in that process of relaxation you are fulfilling a very sacred duty towards the motherland. Try to cultivate friendship where it may appear to be difficult and try to cultivate intimacy where it may appear almost impossible Become friends with one another and do not flock together, according to the proverb, with birds of the same feather, but flock together with birds of different feathers and cultivate harmony that is so necessary for our country.

Madras City has improved in many ways and everything is going on well here and the people are very good people Their heart is full of affection and they have a sense of humour which is the highest philosophy. Do not take anything too seriously. Madras is very good compared to other Provinces. I think a sense of humour is deep-rooted in this Province. Let us never give it up. That is the highest philosophy that Vedanta may discover. Therefore, I have reason to be glad. My impressions of the City are very favourable.

People are depressed all the same on account of many difficulties that present themselves now. We are all responsible to the people of whom we have taken full charge. We are not very confident about ourselves. But as your President has said, there is no reason to be depressed. Very talented people and very good people, universally respected, are in charge of the affairs of the country. Whatever individual feelings may be, on the whole, no country has been so lucky as we at such a critical moment as the one we are passing through. We had for so many years a God on earth, so to say to teach us the way of life. Not many countries have had the advantage of having such personalities in flesh and blood to teach them.

In these days, people of other countries have to look up to old scriptures to fine lessons which we found in that living person who was moving amongst us till the other day Then as soon as the burden of freedom was placed on our shoulders, we had men of ability and character and men commanding public confidence to take over the burden.

Not many countries have been so lucky. Even now in the face of very severe trials, as I am never tired of pointing out, men of the highest ability and character throughout the world have complimented our Government on the way in which they have faced the troubles. Those men have offered to some of us who were depressed by what is going on, great consolation by their appreciation. So on the whole we cannot complain.

All that we now require is that people of all sorts should make up their minds to help one another, rather than compete with one another. Competition is good; but at certain points of time in the history of a people, competition is not of much value. We must help one another, we must pull together, and we must all now work hard together. All of you are engaged in various occupations.

The difference between public servants and Government servants, merchants and citizens — all that is gone now. That kind of illusion has resolved itself. Everyone is the servant of the State now. Everyone is bound by rules of public conduct. We must all work together, each in his own way.

Do not make a distinction between public speeches and private conversations. That distinction must be thrown aside. In private conversation we must observe the same caution and the same sense of discipline that we do in public. These are the secrets of daily conduct which may look very new, but are not really new. That is the lesson I have received from Mahatma Gandhi. What is right is right under all conditions. Let me come to the particular from the general. When you sit round a bridge table, do not talk things which you will not like to say in public. Every little drop of water makes together the waves of the sea.

In the same manner, every whisper, every conversation, every talk in private, all these go together to make national life. Let us purify our national life. Let us all combine to lighten the burdens the leaders are bearing on their shoulders, here or at Delhi. All those who have taken the responsibility of making people a little happier, look to you for every assistance and you should help them.

The Madras University Convocation

[His Excellency the Governor General made the following speech at the Annual Convocation of the Madras University on August 24, 1948].

Mr. Chancellor, Mr. Vice-Chancellor, Graduates of the University, Ladies and Gentlemen,

I am grateful to His Excellency the Chancellor for giving me this privilege of seeing the glad faces of the newly admitted graduates of the University and of giving them my good wishes. Dear young friends, the life-work of men of my generation has been very nearly completed. The lamp which it has pleased Providence to enable us to light will now come under your care. Protect it against the ill winds that blow against it. I value deeply the opportunity offered to me to say a few words to you today. During this initial period of independent national life, many a trite saying gets real and relevant meaning. So if I say some very ordinary and oft-repeated things, please do not think I just fill up time in a conventional way. I am a practical and serious-minded man though I like a joke as much as anyone else, I love you greatly, and what I say is an earnest appeal to you and others like you.

I can claim His Excellency the Chancellor as a friend over and above the bonds that tied us both in official tasks I know that the people and the Government of the Province are sorry that he is leaving Madras But it is a consolation that he as well as Lady Nye will continue to be in India in a different capacity in which too there will be many opportunities for friendly assistance on their, part to those who are engaged in national work, to me and others as well Sir Archibald Nye as well as Lord Mountbatten have, during the past year when they courageously and chivalrously remained with us after the transference of power, shown a devotion to work in the cause of peace and progress in India which we Indians may well emulate. Your Chancellor will be the last Britisher to be dissociated from the conduct of civil affairs in India. His going marks a period of added responsibility on our part for wise self-governance.

The late American Ambassador's wife, Mrs. Grady, while taking the plane to join her husband some days ago, gave a farewell message, in the course of which she complimented Pandit Jawaharlal Nehru and me as men who belonged to the world and not only to India. Mrs. Grady was not referring to our knowledge of world affairs for, whatever may be the case with our Prime Minister, I cannot lay claim to any special or even a passable degree of equipment in that field. Mrs. Grady was referring, I take it, to our obligations at the present juncture in the world. Not only the Prime Minister and I, but every enlightened citizen of India must now rise to the full height not only of national citizenship but of world-citizenship. The world is watching India with goodwill. Our culture, our philosophy and our outlook on life have a new meaning and a new hope for the nations that have suffered and are suffering in the West. Our struggle against British Imperialism is over end, thank God, it has not ended on a note of bitterness but in complete goodwill and mutual understanding. Being citizens of a free country, we should now realise our mission as a nation and our place in world-civilization. We must fulfil the obligations that arise out of our place in Asia and our long and intimate connection with the West. We cannot escape world-citizenship and the particular Dharma which must appertain to India in that regard. By thinking of the world and of man as a whole, we shall purify and strengthen ourselves even in respect of internal problems and anxieties.

Freedom has assuredly given us a new status and new opportunities. But it also implies that we should discard selfishness, laziness and all narrowness of outlook. Our state of freedom implies toil and new values for old ones.

We should so discipline ourselves as to be able to discharge our new responsibilities satisfactorily. If there is any one thing that needs to be stressed more than any other in the new set-up, it is that we should put into action our full capacity, each one of us, in productive effort — each one of us in his own sphere, however humble. Work, unceasing work, should now be our watchward. Work is wealth and service is happiness. Nothing else is. The greatest crime in India today is idleness. If we root out idleness, all our difficulties, including even conflicts, will gradually disappear.

Whether as a constable or as a high official of the State, whether as a businessman or industrialist or artisan or farmer or peasant, all of us are discharging our obligation to the State and making a contribution to the welfare of the country. Honest work is the sheet-anchor to which if we cling we shall be saved in spite of every danger or difficulty. Honest work is the fundamental law of progress.

Next to honest work is the habit of respecting other people's feelings. It takes all sorts to make this world and the highest virtue of every citizen is to try to conduct himself so that a mode of life may be evolved by which people of differing religious faiths, occupations and attainments who constitute our society may live together in peace and amity The law of love is a practical code of life as our dear departed leader so strenuously sought to teach us. My confirmed opinion is that in India there is in fact no communal hatred Greed and fear of defeat in economic competition produce what is mistaken for communal ill-feeling. There is abundant and abiding respect for all kinds of creeds, faiths and ways of life, but selfishness and personal ambitions of a poor variety produce conditions often mistaken for communal ill-will. It is not, therefore, a hopeless task to restore and maintain communal amity and goodwill all round.

Unfortunately certain events have led to the atmosphere being full of alarm and expectation of conflict. We do not desire conflict. But we may not be able to avoid it. All the same, we must do our best to prevent what is admittedly bad for everybody concerned and for the nation. In any case to be calm is the best preparation to face any difficulty.

Excitement is the contrary of preparedness. I am convinced that there is really no hatred between Hindus and Muslims or between any other communities. There is neither hatred nor conflict of interests. There is misunderstanding, pride and consequent stupidity. The long-drawn-out controversies of the recent past cannot be put aside all at once. Hence, all these misunderstandings, this pride and this stupidity. But basically there is, among widely differing creeds and races, far greater understanding of the fundamentals of human fellowship in India than probably anywhere else. This being so, my hope is not ill-founded that India will lead the way in demonstrating harmony in diversity and furnishing a striking example in human cooperation in the midst of seeming heterogeneity.

Whatever may be the immediate troubles, I have no doubt that you who have now graduated will, in your life-time, see a happy India without ill-will, strenuously engaged in reconstruction. There is no need to despair, whatever be the colour of things at present.

To manage the affairs of an independent State, trained leadership is necessary. You have had training in that direction in some measure, for University education is nothing but a training for leadership. Numberless citizens are denied this privilege and it, therefore, becomes your sacred duty to regard your good fortune as a precious debt. In your daily conduct, in whatever walk of life you may be and under all conditions, you should remember your obligation of leadership and set an example to others how to think and speak and how to act. The physical defence of a State is the special responsibility of the members of the Armed Forces. You are the moral and cultural army of India, Her progressive culture and contribution to world-civilization should be your concern. That the youth of today are the citizens of tomorrow is a trite statement. But in a land that has just attained political freedom and whose citizens - have to shoulder new responsibilities in every field of national activity, you young graduates should see in that oft-repeated statement a vital and most significant reality that concerns you intimately.

We have gone through a long and intense political struggle which involved great and unprecedented sacrifices Many of us are engaged now in cashing our cheques on the bank of sacrifice with a feeling of self-righteous anger when delayed at the counter or asked to stand in a queue.

All this is natural and it would be wrong to have expected that anything else could happen. Sacrifice had been sustained unbroken through two generations and it would be idle to expect those who suffered to stand down in self-abnegation when the illusions of power and position tempt. Admitting all this, enlightened men and women should ask themselves the question. "What is patriotism now?"

Graduates, on this great occasion in your life when you must be over-flowing with a sense of achievement and a degree of pride, an older person may offer a few words to you on our immediate future. Independence is a goal for which we worked and struggled for several years. But we must now overcome the habit of mental resistance and opposition which was our pattern of behaviour until now.

We must forget all the disappointments and frustrations we have suffered. We must turn all our experiences now to positive ends.

The years immediately ahead when our freedom has to be consolidated must be years of strenuous work. We cannot take out of life more than we put into it ourselves. The new opportunities that present themselves in our country may seem to be opportunities for individual advancement but they are also, and perhaps more truly, opportunities for service to the country as a whole.

What is wanted is not competitive ambition but intense cooperation. The furtherance of the welfare of the people as a whole in constructive channels is the warp and woof of patriotism now. Melodramatic reiteration of past struggles and dwelling on episodes of suffering may feed our pride in a way but it is wholly irrelevant and is therefore a waste of energy in the present context when what is wanted is speed of realisation of civic duty and energetic positive effort in reconstruction.

A teacher from Kerala wrote to me a few days back suggesting that I should clarify some points in the course of this my address to you He asked in his letter — (1) Should teachers and students be encouraged to take up active politics apart from academic studies? My answer has always been and I repeat it now, NO I Active party politics is inconsistent with fruitful student-life. (2) Should our schools and colleges be scenes of political battles and party squabbles? My answer is an emphatic NO! (3) Should strikes and satyagraha be recognised and encouraged in schools? My answer is again in the negative.

This takes me to my intention to share with the experienced educationists assembled here a few thoughts on education. There is a tendency in progressive political circles as well as among educationists to seek to make anything that is good and useful a compulsory part of youth's educational course, I should like to express all this occasion my doubts in respect of this tendency. The idea that education should cover all useful fields of equipment is futile and erroneous. The limitations of time and immaturity should be kept in mind, and more time should be spent on evolving the capacity to acquire knowledge and to think aright than on substantial equipment straightway. The pressure of too many subjects is not a good thing for the young brain On the other hand, it is only when the brain is young that the capacity to think aright can be developed and correct methods of work can be implanted. To give an example, I would point out that history cannot be understood by boys and girls who have not seen or experienced much of life and its problems. The brain is a machine which should be properly assembled and adjusted during youth. Once this is done, it will take care of itself and there is plenty of time for acquiring information in all branches. The stress during youth should be on training, on creating a habit of correct observation, of scientific curiosity, and of thinking aright and not on cramming the brain with information.

The aim of education is that the pupil should acquire an automatic appreciation of values, moral and other. We do not desire to produce indoctrinated minds. That is not the democratic ideal. Totalitarians might wish to give a twist when the mind is young in a planned direction but our aim should be to produce a free and faithful intellectual and moral apparatus rather than give pre-planned twists.

Again, it should be remembered that what is made compulsory automatically induces a distaste If you wish boys and girls to develop a permanent and unreasonable dislike of anything, make that subject a compulsory subject. If you wish that they may develop a willingness and a capacity to appreciate good literature such as the Ramayana and the Mahabharata, or Shakespeare, or the Bible, for God's sake, I would say to the educationists, do not make the study of the Ramayana and the Mahabharata or of Shakespeare or the Bible compulsory in the school The lessons of both child psychology and human psychology are that mandatory and compulsory direction produces a contrary and rebellious tendency. The conditions for assimilation should be produced, and there should be no compulsion. Youth should be helped to choose good things for themselves rather than be forced and drilled.

Therefore, I would suggest to educationists that less stress should be laid on examinations and more on opportunities for study and assimilation. The examination is the most bitter part of compulsion. It creates an incurable tendency towards superficiality and a paradoxical condition wherein a certain degree of equipment and dislike go together. It leaves in the successful candidate a distaste for further advance, once the examination is over. If in any field the standard of attainment is better in foreign universities than in India, it is not due to stiffer examinations or to superior talents. It is the result of greater voluntary exertion on the part of teachers and pupils born of love of the thing itself, and better facilities for study and research rather than of any stricter or better system of examinations and rejections. It is the result of a condition of things in which aptitude and love of subject rather than irrelevant ambitions and prospects of career and employment guide the students in their choice of studies.

There are two problems which are the cause of great worry to our educationists, the problem of religious and moral instruction in a land of many faiths and the problem arising out of multiplicity of languages. Taking up the education of children, we see that they should be trained to love one another, to be kindly and helpful to all, to be tender to the lower animals and to observe and think aright. The task of teaching them how to read and write and to count and calculate is important, but it should not make us lose sight of the primary aim of moulding personality in the right way. For this it is necessary to call into aid culture, tradition and religion. But in our country we have to look after, in the same school, boys and girls born in different faiths and who belong to families that live diverse ways of life and follow forms of worship associated with different denominations of religion. It will not do to follow the easy path of evading the challenge by attending solely to physical culture and intellectual education. We have to evolve a suitable technique and method for serving the spiritual needs of children through many religions in the same school We would thereby cultivate an atmosphere of mutual respect, a fuller understanding and helpful cooperation among all the different communities in our society. India is not like other smaller countries with a single language and a single faith. We have a multiplicity of languages and faith but are yet one and must remain one people. We have therefore to give basic training in our schools to speak and understand many languages and to understand and respect the different religions prevailing in India. It is not right for us in India to be dissuaded from this on account of considerations as to over-taxing the young mind. What is necessary must be done. And it is not in fact too great a burden.

Any attempt to do away with or steam-roll the differences through governmental coercion and indirect pressure would be as futile as it would be unwise. Any imposition of a single way of life and form of worship on all children, or neglect of a section of the pupils in this respect, or barren secularisation will lead to a conflict between school and home life in the pupils concerned, which is harmful. On the other hand, if we give due recognition to several prevailing faiths in the educational institutions and organise suitable facilities for boys and girls of all faiths, it may itself serve as a broadening influence of great national value.

As for language, it is no good trying to impose a medium of instruction on young pupils which is not their mother-tongue. In the past, parents preferred their children to undergo the disadvantages of the English medium because, as against the drawbacks of a foreign medium, the advantages in life of superficially anglicised culture were great. They deliberately allowed their children to learn language through subjects rather than subjects through language, because facility ha the use of the English language helped one very largely and covered many defects. These advantages must now soon disappear and the drawbacks in using a foreign medium will be more and more obvious as we go on. Nothing is gained by depriving young boys and girls of the advantage of the mother-tongue or some language near to it. In regions where more than one language is spoken I see no other way but one, namely, to form sections in the mixed schools according to language. For certain purposes they may sit together so that the advantages of both mixing and separate attention may be retained. Provided we solve the problems with understanding and patience, the very difficulties which we first deplore often prove in the end to be of the greatest value for progress. What was pain and trouble becomes a source of enlightenment and joy.

I am grateful to the Chancellor and the fellows of the University for conferring on me the highest honour in their gift. I hope I shall ever remain worthy of the degree conferred on me today by being in all matters true to the spirit of law, which is higher than the codes that embody it in various aspects. By accepting this degree, I have, so to say, gone through a ceremony of closer identification with the young friends who have received degrees at this Convocation.

Graduates, I congratulate you on your having taken your degrees. I have told you enough about the sacred duties that fall on you by reason of these degrees. Let your minds be responsible and affectionate. These are the two qualities that best adorn citizenship. Daily and earnest prayer and honest effort will enable one to acquire these two great qualities, a sense of responsibility and an affectionate temperament. If our youth attain these qualities, India will be happy and great external courtesies will help the growth of corresponding internal feeling restraint in behaviour and consideration for the feelings of others are what distinguish a man of culture. Be patient and kind always. Do not give way to jealousy or the desire to boast Be not rude. Do not always insist on your own way. Do not allow yourself to be irritated or be resentful.

Do not rejoice at wrong, rejoice in the right. Try to bear misfortunes bravely. Show trust in others and have faith that love will prevail. This is what Paul said. This is what Gandhi said. May God bless you.

Farewell Message to Tamil Nadu

[His Excellency the Governor General made the following farewell broadcast message to Tamil Nadu from the Madras Station of All India Radio, on August 25, 1948].

Friends,

We have lived to see the day when some of our own people have come to occupy positions of great power and have won the esteem and regard of not only our own countrymen but of the people the world over. The people of Tamil Nadu share the happiness through the position I happen to occupy. Though this is a matter for rejoicing, there is another that should give us far greater happiness.

I must see it in my own life-time. Without allowing differences of caste, creed or religion to breed ill-will amongst us, we must learn to forgive the shortcomings in others, to grow to love and stand by each other, and contribute to mutual happiness.

The purpose of life is attainment of divine bliss. Hatred can do no good. In a free country, though high offices have necessarily to be occupied by a few, really they belong to all. In the years of our servitude, our respect for Government was due to fear. With the attainment of freedom, we must continue to respect the Government and support it out of love for it and out of consideration for public good. We must give no quarter to those who disturb the common weal. Without fear or favour, they should be taken out and reformed.

I have spent three happy days in South India, and I am grateful to you all for the happiness you have given me.

At the Southern India Journalists Federation

[Speaking at the Southern India Journalists Federation on August 26, 1948].

Friends,

I must confess I had expected something very different from what I see now. I had thought I would come and mix freely with old friends who really have been my colleagues and friends for a long time. I thought it would be a friendly gathering but I find it is altogether too formal and has become a repetition of the many functions where I have had to speak during the last few days. But with the hang-over of serious journalism this meeting too suffers as a result. If Mr. Raghunatha Aiyar had decided to put aside all old fashions, I would have been on the same floor with the rest of you, moved about, understood you, breathed the air of affection and gone back with pleasant memories.

Now you have put me very serious questions which, however, I propose to answer, although I have had little time to think about them. I am sorry to say that I cannot accept the compliment or the charge that you make that I am an incipient journalist and take every occasion to End satisfaction in that direction. I thought I was a very poor journalist because I spoke my mind whenever I wrote and did not try to know beforehand what people would like I do not believe that a journalist can flourish if he proceeds in this manner.

You ask me to help you to get the great owners of the Papers — the Press — to deal with those who work under them more sympathetically. I do not believe that either the Government or the Governor General will succeed better in this than in dealing with other employers. I do not know if owners of the Press will listen to Government more than others have done. It is a question of conflict of economic interests to some extent but largely a question of patience and mutual understanding.

I am surprised that you call journalism an industry

Before you came to that part of your address, I was thinking of telling you that the way out of all difficulties is to treat everything as an effort in making the world more beautiful. That is to say, I want you to look upon journalism as an art and not as an industry. If all of you, working journalists, will treat your vocation more as an art than as an industry, then all will be well. Journalists are like painters and poets rather than factory workers. They are really doing works of art. When you, journalists, write an article, when you write a leading article or even when you present an item of news, you are doing a work of art.

Hitherto journalism was too much associated with politics. You thought that you were only an expanded Legislative Assembly, and went on advising, opposing, consulting and debating. I think that is a wrong way to look at journalism now. Now that we have no problem of foreign domination, we must reduce journalism — or rather raise it, to the level of an art. Does a poet ask the Government to intervene between himself and the publishers?

Can a painter ask the Government to help him to get better prices for his pictures? Works of art cannot flourish that way. Although I have refused your kind compliment, I think I know enough of the life of journalists to feel that I am giving good advice. Whatever may be your difficulties, whatever your internal pains and travails, do look upon what you produce as productive, creative art, and then all will be well. Write good books, make good poems, make good pictures and also write good articles and make good newspapers — all will then be well. If you ask me to argue the point, I may not be able to do it within the time given me, or even if you give me more time. But if you take my advice and practise it, I think you will find that all will be well.

We are old friends. There is no reason for me to imagine that I am cleverer than any of you. All of you have dealt with the same subjects as I have All of you have nearly as much experience as I have had, according to the time you have given to them.

As for wrangling and arguing policies, I think our newspapers must throw of the old hangover of imagining that they are just expanded legislative assemblies Launch out on everything in life and bring out things of beauty in order that life may be enriched in our country Journalism is only one of the many arts which enrich life and by continuing in the old style we are not likely to be very useful; I am talking as one of you. You have rightly complained of the hangover of the Government's attitude. I think it will not last very long, even if your accusation is correct. But let us always think of the beam in our own eyes before we speak of the mote in other people's eyes. I am not giving that in the exact proportion perhaps; but that is the old saying and I repeat it. Let us see whether we also do not suffer from old habits. I have just pointed out one.

Do not write about politics and politics alone. One of you, who is a very intimate friend of mine, consulted me once as to what he should do and I told him, "Deal with the administration rather than with the Ministers". He accepted my advice for a couple of days and then reverted to the Ministers. He was not able to stick to the enemy — the administration — but went back to "the Ministers".

Old habits are difficult to throw off, although my old friends seem to think that it is easy to stop drink all over the province straightway! Whether we succeed or not, there is no harm in trying. All good things must be taken up and we must put all our efforts into it. Governments, politicians as well as journalists, all have a way of sticking to old habits. We will have to get over it.

We are now a free country. We have now great opportunities and the Press and the Government should get on together and help one another. The Press must meet the Government more often and the Government must make it easier for the Press to meet it. I do not boast but go to Calcutta and ask the newspapers whether I did not try my best to make them meet me. I found it was very successful. I found no difficulty in understanding them nor they in understanding me. We are all made of the same clay and we only work in different departments. I am sure representatives of the Government of Madras who are here with me will be only very glad to meet you and talk to you. They must only be sure that you will not let them down! I think that nobody will let any other person down in Free India. Those days are gone. We would not gain by letting one another down.

We are all so much together that if we let one another down, the whole boat will sink and none of us will gain.

This is a time when we should realise that we are all co-partners in the business and it is a terrible waste to deceive one another or to be unfair to one another. The most economical way of dealing with our affairs now and hereafter is to be fair to one another.

The problem then arises as to who is to begin. That is the eternal problem in life. When two people quarrel, who is to begin is the eternal problem that prevents the two coming together quickly. I advise you, gentlemen of the Press, you are the cleverer of the two and, therefore, you must begin. The Government is elected on the basis of democracy; journalists are there on the basis of voluntary choice.

I take it, you are the cleverer of the two and the cleverer men must take the first step whenever there is a quarrel. I want you to organise parties and invite members of the Government to discuss problems. Take the initiative yourselves; I have always found it successful. If you extend your hand first, the shake will be the warmer on the other side. If you wait till the other man extends his hand, it is all a question of fear and trembling. I want you therefore to take the first step.

In Free India, we shall get the sort of freedom that, we deserve. All the time we have been wrangling with one another and for some time longer, this will go on. We now have only the flower of Swaraj. We have not yet got the fruit and hence the trouble. If one is anxious to have the flowers and smell their fragrance it would be some time before we can have the fruits. Flowers must become fruit and give joy. When that happens, there will be sweetness in the atmosphere. Till then, you will have troubles. Do not get excited over them. I am very grateful to you all.

At Sewagram

[Addressing a meeting of constructive workers at Mahadev Bhavan, Sewagram, on August 27, 1948].

Friends,

It is usual to say at gatherings such as this that one feels very glad to be with one's friends. But it is difficult for me to say so today. This is the first time I have come here after Mahatmaji's death. According to our custom, we cannot celebrate a wedding along with a funeral. A similar difficulty presents itself to me.

I am very glad to see you all, but I have been over-whelmed by sorrow since my visit to Bapu's cottage this morning. We must try to help one another, whatever may be the difficulties. To those who are young, this place is a place of work. They can forget their sorrow in work using all their energy to learn and to do things. But for one like me who is not young, it is difficult to forget. That is why I am unable to carry on with you now. It is a very good thing that one of us, a common man, has been appointed Head of the State. It is a joy not because I am appointed to it but because an ordinary man has been appointed to it. That is why all ordinary men find great exhilaration in the position that I occupy. Here you have to carry on without the source of energy which helped you all these days. Bapu has left behind him many loyal servants who have survived him and who will help you. You are now in the position of orphans, but you have some good trustees to look after you. If you have faith in God, all will go well.

I do not think that you need depend on men if you depend on God. It is believed by our people that, when a man dies with desires unsatisfied, his spirit will hover over the place where he was living and working. The spirit will have no peace until the desire is fulfilled. Although Bapu had given up most desires and attachments, he did not give up attachment to the people of this country and the desire that we should all be industrious and good. This desire was an imperfection in his complete detachment, and that imperfection will keep his spirit hovering over your charkha, over your hospital, over your beds, and over everything else. All the ten institutions that are gathered here will have his agitated spirit hovering over them until you satisfy his desire. There is no use praying for peace to his soul unless we fulfil this desire.

> Whenever we do our work well, we give him a little peace.
>
> Allow hatred to be lodged there. Keep goodwill afresh.

Work actively to create and increase this goodwill in other people's hearts also. Trifling though it be, our daily behaviour has a great effect on cultivating goodwill. Do not neglect little acts of courtesy. If all of you will exert yourselves for a few months to re-establish goodwill in India, everything else will follow. This is your particular work.

Nothing will come right in the evolution of the world unless you work hard in positive service to the State. Let all women restore goodwill in India by determined work. Equality of rights will come to you like a ripe fruit without your asking for it. Women have served India during the last few years nobly and that is why they have now risen to the extent that they have.

Have not women risen to a level higher than they were, say, in 1920? How did they attain this? During these 25 years, women have served and suffered alongside of men, and put in hard work in equal measure with men. So they have automatically risen to the level to which they have now risen. During the next few months or years, your work will bring you equality whether men pass their codes or not. I do not object to any measure that you want. You may change all the codes.

But our temperament and our national culture will still govern everything. That is the unchangeable law. Therefore, ultimately, what we have to change is not laws but the culture of the country for the better. Men must learn to respect women and not to treat them as born slaves, Man must be taught to have consideration for his wife.

With all due respect to the legislators — and I have been one of them — these things are not changed by laws but by culture and education, and we must attend to that. That is why I ask you to be teachers. Nothing else will save womanhood except having women teachers everywhere.

Fight as strongly as you can that women should become teachers of boys also. There is no reason why you should not monopolise that work, because the mother is the most fitted to teach. I do not believe in the notion that in boys' schools, men must be the teachers and in girls' schools women.

Women should be teachers in all schools — boys' as well as girls'. Then culture will change rapidly and education will progress and all rights will come.

Thank you very much for the beautiful reception you have given me. Maharashtra, it is well-known throughout India, has been taking first place in women's progress. Keep that going.

Bharati Day

[Following is the gist of a speech delivered by His Excellency the Governor General in Tamil on the occasion of the birthday of Poet Subramanya Bharati on September 11, 1948 at the South India Club, New Delhi].

Bharati is an immortal poet; he is one of the chief glories of Tamil poetry. His poems are for all time. They do not satisfy men's emotions only for the moment. Those whc take unchartered excursions into all that he has written will find richness of thought, emotion, imagery, melody and matchless beauty. It is up to the future generations to sing his songs, and realise the glorious pride of our tradition, heritage, cultural attainment and philosophy.

If you begin to translate his poems, the result will be a mutilated copy of the original masterpiece. Much of the charm of Bharati's songs will be lost and no one will derive pleasure from reading them. It will be absolutely impossible to go into the depth of the Poet's feelings.

A poet's genius and immortality will be preserved not by possessing neatly-printed volumes of his works, or by adorning our libraries with well-bound collections of his poems. He must be read and re-read; we must get into the stride of his feelings, his patriotism, his imagination, his emotion and his ideals. Therefore, Bharati will be ever remembered only if every home of Tamil Nadu sings his songs and realises his great contribution to Tamil poetry.

Bharati lived amongst us, talked to us, sang to us and breathed the same air and ate the same food as we. He is not a mythical figure. We are fortunate to have lived in a time which produced such a great poet as Bharati He has depicted in his poems our faults, imperfections and our defects.

At Birla Mandir

[His Excellency the Governor General made the following speech at Birla Mandir on September 26, 1948 in commemoration of the National Thanksgiving Day].

We must humbly and gratefully meditate on the grace of Almighty God which steered us through danger and crisis this month. The way in which Muslims of India belied the fears and evil forebodings expressed about them has inaugurated a new era of mutual trust and national strength. The manner in which all the communities of India stood calm and wise and helped the Government to fulfil its task in Hyderabad undisturbed by any communal incident anywhere in the length and breadth of India is truly a miracle which fills us with confidence in our future.

It is a matter for national joy and pride that our armed forces did their task in such a clean and tidy manner without a spot or a doubt to besmirch honour. May our armed forces in all branches ever keep up this high standard of conduct and efficiency, whether engaged in suppressing disorder within our borders or defending the country against aggression from outside. The best answer to those who charge India with aggressive intentions is the way in which our government will deal with the problems in Hyderabad.

Almighty God, whose grace preserved peace in India during this critical time, will guide us in discharging our duties wisely and without anger God has worked a miracle where almost the whole world thought we would be engulfed by danger. Let us deserve this by preserving our humility and the instincts of love and compassion which alone make for happiness and glory.

First Anniversary of Gandhiji's Death

[Addressing a gathering of Ambassadors, Ministers, Officials and Government House Staff at Government House on January 30, 1949].

Twelve months ago Gandhiji passed away from us.

Like the song which we heard on the violin just now and which has united with Akash now Gandhiji's life ended suddenly and we cannot see him any more. So also Gandhiji has joined akash. We can see the violin made of wood and string. But the song is gone. The musician can play again but we cannot make Gandhiji again. The pictures or busts we have are like broken fiddles which cannot produce the song.

It will not do to continue grieving. Our elders tell us that after the first month is over, there should be no more weeping. We should perform Shradh in order to please the dead spirit. Our daily work and thoughts must be the Shradh for our departed leader. Once a year when we meet and gather like this in memory of our dead leader, we should not weep. We should make it into a festival which will give us inspiration and strength.

We must derive from the memory of our departed leader courage to speak the truth, to be patient and bear with one another If this gathering and the meeting we had at Rajghat this evening and the gatherings all over the country that have been held today, give us more strength to speak the truth and to bear with one another, then there is no doubt about it that Mahatmaji's spirit will be gladdened.

While he lived, everyday Mahatmaji was appealing to God that we may all have the good sense to love one another. We are all men, women and children — born in this world to love one another. It is only fools that hate each other. This was what Gandhiji taught up to the point of his death.

It is not enough if we are proud that we had Gandhiji among us. What we have to do is to do what he desired us to do. Living men may be pleased by flattery, we cannot please Gandhiji's soul by flattery and empty praise We can please him only if we do as he wanted us to do.

Children can understand what Gandhiji wanted us to

Do — love one another. Grown up people find it more difficult to understand it. They think there are difficulties in the way of loving one another. Once upon a time Gandhiji was telling people that they would get Swaraj. Many people did not believe him. In the early days, many people were asking 'How can you get Swaraj without war', whether there was any nation in the world that got free without bloodshed?

India has however achieved the seemingly impossible.

India has gamed freedom and we are now completely independent without having war and without shedding blood. We are not only independent, but without being a great Power, without great armies and navies, India enjoys the highest prestige in counsels of the world. That strength has been obtained by us by reason of the truth contained in Gandhiji's guidance of us.

Just as what Gandhiji told us about achieving Swaraj through non-violence proved true, what Gandhiji has told us about loving one another will prove to be equally true if we try and do as he told us.

Some people doubt whether Hindus can love Muslims or Muslims can love Hindus. Take it from me that what Gandhiji said that we can and must love one another is true. Nothing else is true. If we try, God will help us to succeed. We shall be not only as great as we are today, but we will grow in our greatness before these children here grow up. If we learn how to overcome prejudices in respect of communities, India will be great before the next few years and the world will respect us and follow us.

When on the 1st of this year India and Pakistan said they had stopped fighting, India immediately grew twice as powerful as she was before in the eyes of the world.

Her voice now has influence with the whole of Asia. Asia met recently at Delhi and the voice of that conference has been powerful enough to save and help the people of Indonesia In the path which Gandhiji has shown us lies our greatness and prosperity. If any man hates you, do not bother about it Try to love him and that man will begin to love you If other people tell lies, do not bother about them. Speak the truth and everything will go on well.

Our Government now is very strong and has great prestige in the world, but unless we keep our home affairs in good order, that prestige will topple down. If people in our country in their daily lives speak the truth and do not deceive one another, then our national prestige will be prosper. If we are dishonest and corrupt in our daily lives, everything will go down. Do not think of other people's faults: every man must try himself to be good. No cake can be good if the flour is not good.

Our people are the *atta* and Government the *laddu*. If people are lazy, Government will be poor. When we were not free, we had many people to look after us. Now that we are a free nation each one must look after himself. If I am a gardener and if I am digging, now that our country is free, it should not be necessary to have an overseen above me to supervise my work. I should do the digging properly myself. If you have seen bees collecting honey, you will have noticed that each does its work and the hive becomes full. There are no supervisors over the bees. We must be independent of any supervision. We must be honest and industrious, each by himself. It should be the pride and honour of every workman in free India to do his work properly without anybody goading him or threatening to punish him.

I am very grateful to the boys and girls who sang so well and helped this function.

Civic Address at Shimla

[In reply to the Civic Address presented by the Shimla Municipality on November 17, 1948].

Your Excellency, Mr. President, Ladies and Gentlemen,

It is not a mere conventional phrase when I say that I feel it a great privilege to accept your affectionate welcome.

I was here a few years ago when the affairs of India were being considered in this cool, quiet place. I have come after a great many things have happened — some good, some unfortunate. The faces of the people are as bright today and shine as affectionately when welcoming a stranger who has been privileged to hold high office as when a few years ago we came here to discuss complicated political matters Let us not break our old culture of suppressing our difficulties and expressing our joy when we meet one another. It is not always easy for us to reconcile ourselves to the troubles we have had to face. But when we look back a hundred or two hundred years, we see things differently. All that we have gone through will result positively in honour, prestige and joy to our children and our children's children. Much can be suffered for the sake of posterity.

Let us trust in God and trust one another.

I am very grateful for the kind words of the Municipal President. Many problems have been referred to in the address. You do not get lost in emotion. You have also an eye to business! You have put forward difficult and important problems and suggestions. In the old days my predecessors used to get, and they insisted on having pretty long notice for such proposals and they had plenty of time to deal with them so that they could reply. In the new set-up, not only has the Governor General no authority to speak, but the people also do not give sufficient time to him to consider, concert with others and come with answers.

Allowing for the time necessary for transmission of papers your address reached me only yesterday I So you have to be content with only an explanation. You cannot have an answer to the points you have raised in your address.

I very much sympathise with the difficulties you have set out. Who in India does not know that you have suffered not only greatly but something which was beyond any conception? You have suffered literally an earthquake which rent your nerves beyond description. Man's strength is very great. You have borne all those sufferings very well.

History will record your suffering and your fortitude in a manner which your children will be proud to read. You say very rightly that the Punjab, and I may add Bengal, have both suffered more than any other part of India for the sake of India's freedom. It was not put upon you cruelly by other people. It was the result of the position you-occupied in the unalterable arrangement of nature and the evolution of progress. The composition of population here as in Bengal and the position you occupy in the geography of India, all these resulted in your peculiar sufferings. Please do not attribute it to the callousness of other people or to their cruelty. If in the process of evolution men and women and communities reach a certain position, they have to take it with its joys and glory, its difficulties and catastrophies. For a long time the Punjab had the foremost place in the armies of India. You had the position and the peculiar circumstances which made you a martial people. We must 'take it' as you have put it, not only bravely, but also gladly. You have all read the Ramayan. Did Rama shed tears when he went to the forest? If he had not been the eldest son, he would not have had to go through all that trouble. So also you, in a way as the eldest sons of India, have to bear troubles and misfortunes. You should not shed tears. If tears come on account of physical pain, let them come but you should not let it affect your heart. The problem now is what we must do with the future Do not hark back to what has happened. Let us not try to be as miserable as we can possibly be by reminding one another of the past. God who gives us misfortunes, griefs and troubles, has also given us the capacity to bear them and to remove sad things from the tablets of the mind. Let us use that talent and forget sorrows and look to the future.

I entirely agree with you, Mr. President, that we should have a number of industrial towns rather than develop one very large city as Bengal has done with Calcutta. It is a very great inconvenience that Bengal is trying to overcome on account of the overgrowing size of Calcutta and the absence of attractions in other towns in Bengal.

You are quite right in saying that with the natural urge among the village folk to go to towns where they can have trades, professions, colleges, hospitals and modern amenities, they should find an outlet in a number of towns rather than in a single big metropolis.

I cannot answer your question as to the capital of the East Punjab and the various other problems that you have raised. I am sure that the Government of India will examine all these carefully. They will not act in haste or prejudice.

As regards your complaint that the Government should have done well to levy a Punjab tax on the whole of India, let me remind you that the whole of India is paying taxes for all the needs, of India including rehabilitation of displaced people. By what name it is called is only a matter of sentiment. Supposing the name you suggest were given to a tax, everybody would feel that thereby they were obliging Punjab or repaying Punjab. People always give unwillingly and their children and others who depend on them complain about levies. There is not much point in naming a particular tax by the name of Punjab tax.

Rehabilitation is a necessary charge on the total revenues and it has to be attended to and will be attended to.

Let me say a word generally about the future. I have already said that we should try to forget our sorrows.

During the national struggle when everyone united for a particular goal, they performed well and forgot their private affairs. They all acted like heroes.

These has been some deterioration now but we must bear with it also and carry on. A tree is not quite so beautiful in autumn as it is in spring. Now private affairs are assuming a more real aspect. Many people have suffered so long that perhaps it may be cruelty to ask them to forget their private affairs. Let us not blame one another.

It has now become the fashion to blame everybody else but oneself. Nobody turns his eyes towards himself Even when in those admonitions and rebukes it is possible to include oneself, they do not do so They always look at other people and criticise other people. Let us now try and bear with one another and carry on. We are all citizens of this country. It is no use believing that somebody else will do our work. We have to do the work ourselves. If the character of our people has deteriorated to some extent, we must bear with it. We must carry on somehow and make the best of the human material and the resources that we have. That is what the Government of India and your leaders are doing You must all help them in their task. We are a great people and if we help one another we shall be able to do much more than people think.

There are some who say, "Oh, in the old days everything was good, there was more discipline and greater efficiency. Now everyone is quarrelling and there is more debating than work. The people are poor, the people are hungry. What is the use of this Government?" This is not right or fair. It is one thing to have perfect discipline through mutual agreement, which is the basis of democracy.

Through fear you have silence and absolute obedience, but what use is it? It is only if we have discipline when we are free to be indisciplined that we have order by agreement In the old days we were all disciplined like bullocks yoked to carts. Now we must try to agree with one another. It will take some time. We learn by experience.

Barely we may learn through a great man's precepts and life but mostly we learn from experience. If you see a little indiscipline, be patient. If a father or mother constantly sits near the child and says: 'Don't put your finger in the fire', the child won't know what fire is. Our people will learn efficiency and discipline, by and by, through experience. If you must be impatient, be impatient with yourself. Say to yourself: 'Let me be disciplined'. Don't say to others: 'Be disciplined'. Say to yourself: 'Let me speak the truth', Don't tell others: 'Do not utter lies'. If you speak the truth, other people will follow. If you are disciplined, other people will copy you.

What I have said may appear to be very general, trite and old-fashioned; but please convert what I say into daily concrete action and you will see how practical I have been trying to be. I have talked from the bottom of my heart.

You are people who have suffered greatly and your problems are large and I must talk frankly to you.

Reception by Sheriff of Calcutta

[Replying to the address of welcome by the Sheriff of Calcutta on November 29, 1948].

Mr. Sen, Ladies ad Gentlemen,

I do not think I can accomplished enough to convert this social gathering into a public meeting. I am wondering whether I should concentrate on thanking Mr. Sen for his cordial and affectionate reception or whether I should concentrate on admiring his capacity for organisation. I have seen on more than one occasion how well he organises a welcome reception. This is not merely light-hearted talk.

It is my desire that everyone of us should be efficient in all the things that we take up. It is no use being jealous or trying to find fault with one another. All that is negative and serves no purpose except to increase the total volume of pain in this world. What we have to do is to be good and efficient in our work, cheerful in our outlook, and to love, if not all mankind, at least as many as possible.

Can we not try to do this? It is only if we love people and are affectionate that we look well and succeed in life.

If we do not have that approach, we repel people, and the who repels people cannot succeed in life. I commend to all business and professional men to cultivate mutual affection, it will give good returns in their business and in their professions That is what I have learnt from Mr. Sen's example. He never has anything but a smile. He has shown how to make an occasion like this fine and well-arranged. I am very grateful to him for the beautiful little entertainment that he has provided us I think he will permit me to concentrate on appreciating efficiency in the citizen. I am more grateful to citizens for doing their work well than for the personal pleasure or affection bestowed upon me.

I am very glad Mr. Sen acquires a new member to his family. I take it this party is also a part of his son's wedding. You will join with me in giving our best wishes to the bride and bridegroom on this occasion.

Special Convocation of Calcutta University

[His Excellency the Governor General made the following speech at the Special Convocation of the University of Calcutta for conferring on him the Honorary Degree of Doctor of Law on November 30, 1948].

Mr. Chancellor, Vice-Chancellor, Fellows of the University, Ladies and Gentlemen,

I was overwhelmed when the invitation was sent to me to accept the Degree of Law by this University. I had never expected that my friend, Dr. Bidhan Chandra Roy, the Premier, would launch forth on such a long eulogy of line. I had always thought he was a man of few words and that he would not make any exaggerated statements or deeper cuts than the surgical knife required. I was surprised, although pleasantly, at the very lengthy encomiums which he had chosen to pay.

I am very grateful for all that has been said by him and by the Chancellor. His Excellency the Chancellor and Governor of this Province extorted my admiration when I first met him at Allahabad many years ago on a historic occasion, by his wisdom and patience. I am therefore extremely glad to receive this degree at his hands No one truly is older or younger than any other. We are all eternal and it is only our bodies that differ in age. I have enough humility to understand the meaning of the words I have used. I say sincerely that I receive this degree at his hands with very great satisfaction. The premier University of India has chosen to confer this great honour upon me. I was greatly overjoyed when I received a Degree of Doctor of Laws from the University out of which I was born. But when one receives a benefit from one's own mother, one does not think that anything extraordinary has taken place. But when I receive a degree from the premier University of Calcutta, I ask myself whether I really deserve all this. I shall not weary you with my thoughts in this direction because in the world of affairs such thoughts may pass for conventional humility. I however know how truly I speak.

It is the Degree of Doctor of Law that you have been pleased to confer upon me. "Law" in the singular makes it far greater than "Laws" in the plural.

Am I then receiving a Degree of Doctorate in that Law which is the law of all laws, the basis of all life and the meaning and the purpose of all the laws that men pass from time to time in several countries? In our own great language we have a word exclusively set apart for this connotation — Dharma. Am I considered fit by the premier University of India to receive a Doctorate of Dharma?

I am very grateful, profoundly grateful, to God who has enabled me to have lived a life which you consider a sufficient basis for conferring this degree upon me.

I have often been tempted to laugh at honorary degrees. As I have a sense of humour I am able to laugh at myself, when these honorary degrees are conferred upon people like me without any great academic qualifications But on this occasion I must confess that I am thinking in a different way. Ordinary Degrees are conferred after strict examination and classification.

Now at the age of 70, if all that has done during his life is carefully examined by critical and good men who are members of a University and if they value my performance as good enough for giving me this great Degree of Dharma, surely I may feel proud. But being somewhat religiously inclined, I attribute it all to God who has enabled me to go through difficulties and trials through a fairly long period in the manner I have done and enabled you to appreciate what I have done.

Thank you, Mr. Chancellor, for conferring this Degree upon me. I tender my thanks to the Fellows and Senators of this University. I shall deem it a great honour and I hope in the few years that are left to me I shall be benefited by the encouragement that you have given me by this Degree. I hope that I shall live worthily during the time that yet remains for me and bring this great University no discredit.

Mazharul-ulum Orphanage at Banaras

[His Excellency the Governor General made the following speech on the occasion of the laying of the foundation-stone of the Mazharul-Ulum Orphanage at Banaras on December 1, 1948].

Ladies and Gentlemen,

It gives me very great pleasure to have done something here in the way of helping orphans. Those who have nobody to look after them must be looked after by some institution.

Those who do anything for orphans and who give alms to poor people buy tickets to go to heaven. In all religions this is prescribed and believed, and there is no difference on this point. They may pray in different languages, they may kneel in different ways, but all religions teach that we should help orphans and thereby get nearer to God, I have therefore every reason to be proud of the privilege you have given me of laying this Slab here and thereby promoting the cause of charity and help to orphans.

All orphans to whatever community they may belong are my children and the children of my successor heads of State of India. It does not matter what caps or shoes or trousers they wear. Orphans are the same. In one way orphans are more fortunate. Let not orphans imagine they are miserable. They are looked after by a great State.

Governments teach children to be good citizens. May all the orphans who come under the protection of this orphanage be good citizens of India.

I do not know whose inspiration it was, but it gives me great pleasure that on the same day I have laid the foundation-stone to memorialise Mahatmaji's teachings in Queen's Garden, I am here laying the foundation-stone for an orphanage under a Muslim organisation. I am hot as good a beggar as the illustrious father of my interpreter (Pandit Govind Malaviya). I cannot beg successfully lakhs and crores and build a big University. But may

I be enabled to see that this stone that I have laid will have bricks over it and that an orphanage will be established. At the place where I laid the bricks over Mahatmaji's ashes they sang a song which said that Is war and Allah were the names of God. That song was sung by Mahatmaji thousands of times before he died. He prayed not as we pray, but very sincerely. Most sincerely he sang Ishwar and Allah are the names of God and he prayed that men may be blessed with good sense. He has prayed so often and may we not hope that it may bear fruit, and may we also believe that is why we do not quarrel with one another now? God seems to have turned His face towards us and I think we will not quarrel with one another hereafter. Though I am Governor General, let me tell you this — let Governments quarrel but let us not quarrel. Let all the quarrels be confined to governments, and let men and women, brothers and sisters, love one another.

My best wishes and blessings to the children that are growing in the orphanage and all those who will hereafter come to this orphanage. If I send some orphans when your orphanage is ready, do not refuse admission! I thank all the members of the organisation for giving me this privilege and this opportunity to speak to you. It gives me great pleasure to see you all assembled here without distinction of caste or religion, and helping me to perform this function. May this grace of God continue for all time.

At the Hindu University

[His Excellency the Governor General delivered the following address at the Convocation of the Hindu University, Banaras on December 2, 1948].

Your Excellency, Mr. Vice-Chancellor, Senators of the University, Ladies and Gentlemen,

First of all I must thank the University for the high honour they have bestowed upon me in token of such appreciation as they have been pleased to show of my services. I hope I shall prove not unworthy of the honour bestowed.

As I received the honorary degree, the figure of our beloved Malaviyaji was before my mind's eye with the chandan on his forehead like, the third eye of Sri Mahadev. I hope that with his blessings I shall prove, as I said, not unworthy of the honour bestowed on me.

I have been asked to speak a few words to the graduates.

After the exhortation which the Vice-Chancellor made, uttering the very words of the old Rishis, nothing remains to be said, provided the Rishi's words are understood and assimilated. But it has been customary to invite someone to speak to the graduates on an occasion such as this.

The honour bestowed on me is great, but I do not think I shall trouble you with any long address today.

I do not propose to deal with matters usually dealt with at length in Convocation Addresses. My visit, dear graduates, has come close upon that of Sardar Vallabhbhai Patel He covered very extensive ground in his address when he was here and spoke frankly and impressively.

I do not believe it will benefit anyone if I cover the same ground again. I need not repeat his earnest advice for he spoke out of his heart. He is a great man and is entitled by his service to expect you to pay heed to all that he told you.

If you do so, it will be all for the good of the country.

Our beloved Malaviyaji built with his own hand and left behind him this great University as a solid and useful memorial of which his people may justly be proud. This University may be called by any name, but it will always be associated with the memory of this great man who built it through untiring effort and force of character. Kashi is a great place.

Ganga is a great river brought down from heaven itself, and this place of instruction for youth situated on sacred ground and on the banks of the sacred river should be the subject of special care and concern of all of us but mainly of the boys and girls of India. It belongs to It belongs to all of them. It is a national seat of culture in the truest sense.

From time immemorial people turned to Kashi for enlightenment and to Ganga for purification, and Malaviyaji has helped to maintain unbroken that tradition unbroken, by founding and establishing this great seat of learning here in Kashi. Let us in the years to come, strive to keep the greatness of the Kashi University undiminished in lustre.

Graduates, Kipling wrote some great verses, but a little poem which he wrote with an 'if' before the lines is one of the finest things ever written. It is English Poetry born out of the Song Celestial of India:

If you can trust yourself when all men doubt you

But make allowance for their doubting too.

If being hated you do not give way to hating

And yet, do not look too good nor talk too wise.

If you can meet with triumph and disaster.

And treat those two impostors just the same.

If you can talk to crowds and keep your virtue,

Or walk with Kings, nor lose the common touch.

If all men count with you but none too much.

If you can fill the unforgiving.

Minute with sixty seconds worth of distance run.

Yours is the earth.

And what is more you will be a man, my soul.

I have not given the words exactly, but sons and daughters of Kashi, remember the substance of these lines which is the same as what was said in Sanskrit as the word of God centuries ago by.

We have done well in attaining freedom and in showing a bloodless way of overcoming wrong. Yet, let me touch on some unpleasant things. The processes involved in the attainment of freedom through the method of disobedience have left behind certain less desirable results along with the attainment of the object. These results, like the incidental harm done to the body when you take drugs for curing a serious disease, have to be corrected by convalescent discipline, by effort and determination amounting to religious fervour and faith.

We have to throw of the habit of disregarding law and authority. The movement of non-cooperation involved the disregarding of law and authority that had been imposed by a foreign government and it has left behind an unhealthy habit. We have to take concerted and determined action to get rid of this tendency We must restore the unqualified reverence for the State that our ancients cultivated, reverence for law and discipline equivalent to reverence for Dharma that was insisted upon in the old days In fact we want a revival of feudal manners and chivalry but in terms of modern democracy.

Reverence for the State is different from attachment to a party. It is more akin to worship than to party loyalty.

The State is different from the majority that rules Reverence for the State is essential. Otherwise India, vast and composed of heterogeneous elements, cannot grow strong.

Again, as a result of what was done during the days when we applied every means that was available in order to get rid of foreign domination, some of us have developed, I fear, a very undesirable and wide-spread tendency of sabotage. Free and democratic India cannot function in security and prosper and attain strength unless we totally eradicate this tendency to resort to methods of sabotage for attaining some immediate object.

Short-sighted hurry to attain an objective, however good, may lead to great harm being done to the State and society as a whole. It is absolutely necessary to eradicate the habit of destruction and sabotage that were incidental to the revolution We should revive a reverence — I cannot use a lesser word — a reverence for roads, for bridges, for all means of communication, for the machinery of production, industrial and agricultural. We should automatically and instinctively feel a horror of sabotage as we do when we see any living thing being cruelly killed. Otherwise modern society cannot hope to thrive. Respect for means of communication and means of production must reach the level of religious reverence. We have to rebuild this reverence.

Again, as a result of what happened during the struggle and thereafter, we are in danger of maintaining unless we guard ourselves, a frame of mind and an attitude akin to ill-will against nations other than ourselves and communities other than our own. We have to make a supreme religious effort to maintain and strengthen what Gandhiji taught, namely the doctrine of unilateral effort. In the faith that love will conquer. Being hated, do not give way to hating, as Kipling said. This great doctrine of love arid trust, even where you do not get favourable response at once, is the pivot on which all that Gandhiji taught rested. That was the fixed doctrine round which all his great activities turned. If we have no faith in this doctrine of unilateral effort for love, we forswear all the homage we paid to Gandhiji when he was alive.

Do not be alarmed by delays and failures in our national effort We have not had sufficient time yet. We had to face complicated, unexpected and extraordinary difficulties.

Remember that freedom from British rule does not mean freedom from world-opinion. Equal citizenship in the world is a great status. But it carries with it great obligations. The national government of India today is of a quality of which we can be proud Our Prime Minister's credit among the nations and statesmen of the world is very high. To maintain that high credit and to draw from it we have to be loyal and helpful to him. Our Prime Minister is the beloved of the nation. He and his colleagues have been trying scrupulously to be just and fair to everyone, to governments and to communities, to industrialists and to workers. No people have a clearer conscience than those at the head of the Government of India today. They are just and they have faith in the destiny of India and are working hard. As I have said elsewhere, industrialists should adjust their minds to the necessary uncertainties of democratic government. They must not expect in democracy that certainty of policy which can be got only under an authoritarian government. Policies in democracy depend upon the people's vote which must be taken from time to time and cannot be made the subject of any permanent proposition.

Workers must realise that the State is the real employer whatever be the economic set-up in force. Unless wealth is produced, and continuously produced, no government, no management, no employer can find the resources for distributing the means of securing a good life. Wealth and work form the foundation on which the happiness of the community can be built.

We should trust democracy to ensure just distribution and not look to class struggle for salvation. Class struggle means hatred a fouling of the atmosphere and unhappiness for all and submission to the crudest type of tyranny at the end of it. The delays of democracy are after all better than the violence and hatred of class struggle, better for all concerned There are, no doubt, class struggles going on, whether we like it or not Where there is maladjustment, a fever is a necessary concomitant. But we gain nothing by encouraging or adding to the fever that accompanies a diseased condition We should rather allay the fever even while attending to the root cause. That is the democratic method as distinguished from the method of accelerating class struggle and endangering national life.

Our credit as well as our prestige abroad is high and so is our position in the comity of nations. It is only among ourselves that readjustment is necessary for confidence and cooperation Let us have faith in our destiny under democracy. All will soon be well. Graduates, I give you my best wishes, my own as well as on behalf of the Government of India. May you be enabled to serve the Motherland diligently and with reverence.

Address by the Central Mel-Milap Committee

[In reply to the address presented to him by the Central Mel-Milap Committee, Banaras on December 3, 1948].

This is the last gathering that I shall be meeting before I leave Banaras. It gives me great pleasure to see the stress laid by the people of Banaras on unity. Many things have happened which have to be forgotten. It is no use looking back. We have to look forward. Our people have attained freedom, but freedom is a difficult to perceive unless we have a high degree of education. Just as it is difficult to see God, it is difficult to see freedom.

Just as we pick up some clay from the earth and make an image and see God through it, so I have been picked up from the earth and you have to see freedom through me.

I am as far from the liberty that India has gained as the Mutthi is from God. B is your devotion that can make clay into God. It is your devotion that can give meaning to the office I hold.

It was in India that before anybody else preached it, our forefathers discovered that all denominations and ceremonies and forms of .worship reach God. People from all parts of the world, with all manner of books and scriptures and doctrines, were welcomed in India when they came.

When water is added to milk, milk gets Adulterated Similarly Hinduism has been diluted by the ignorance of those who came In defending the broadmindedness and the large doctrines of our forefathers, we have become narrow-minded and fanatical It is as absurd as saying that in preserving chanty we must adopt stinginess, that m preserving beauty we must make it ugly. In defending and conserving the spirit of tolerance, we have become intolerant. Let us drop this wrong path. Nothing will save our tolerance except tolerance. I wish that men were wise enough to the extent that even if they were Hindus, they could go to mosques and pray. I have no difficulty in thinking of my God while sitting among Christians in a church or among Muslims in a mosque.

It was a great thing that we got rid of British domination and won freedom But it will be a greater thing if we get rid of intolerance and convert religion into really what it is. We will revolutionise religious thought in the world Kashi is a place with particular sacred associations and attractions. All religions are attracted here. If you see a mosque on the banks of the Ganga, do not feel angry. It is but right that Islam also should come and settle down cn the banks of the Ganga. The children of a mother do not look upon the new born as an intruder but as a brother.

Ganga can bear any number of children.

India is a home for all people who believe in God and worship in anyway they like. Free India invites all religions. If you dive into ancient Indian history, you will find that the crudest forms of religious worship and faith have been absorbed in Hinduism. Our forefathers absorbed them in such a way that they made them their own. Why should we stop that process in our time? We must on the other hand continue that process. The object of your association is the object for which I live. My best wishes to you all.

Special Convocation of Aligarh Muslim University

[His Excellency the Governor General made the following speech at the Special Convocation of the Muslim University, Aligarh on December 15, 1948].

I thank you for your words of welcome. I thank you for the great honour you have done me by conferring on me the highest gift in your possession.

You have rightly reminded yourselves and the scholars of the University of the share of responsibility that rests on this University for moulding the ideas and shaping the personalities of the citizens of India.

My Government and I will do everything in our power to enable you to perform your functions in a worthy manner. There is no doubt that this University has a very particular and important role to play in the advancement of culture and education in India.

The Aligarh University was born out of the movement which had as its object the turning of the mind of Islam in India towards modern light and culture. You have quoted the words of the founders wherein the hope was expressed that the sons of Aligarh might go forth throughout the length and breadth of the land to preach the gospel of free enquiry, large-hearted tolerance and of pure morality. There can be no better platform for united endeavour on the part of all citizens in India than the platform of free enquiry and large-hearted, mutual understanding and uprightness of conduct.

The first graduate of the College was a Hindu. From its very start the Aligarh College was open to all classes and creeds. This is a fact which cannot be too often repeated and which should be kept continually before friends as well as detractors.

I welcome your impatience for development. It has become difficult to get money allotted by the Government of India even for the best of causes on account of a number of unavoidable circumstances, but a great deal can be done by men moved by earnestness of purpose — much more than is often imagined. In spite of financial difficulties you I am sure, achieve a great deal in the immediate future.

I am glad to see that in your address you have shown commendable awareness of all difficulties. No one is more conscious than myself that the living sources of culture and enlightenment such as Universities are, form a very important and essential part of the mechanism of democracy. Power from below and inspiration from above are essential for the growing plant of democracy even as good soil and bright sunlight are needed for plants to grow well.

We have seen enough already to warn us of the dangers arising out of a deterioration of man's sense of moral and spiritual values. Nowhere can a sense of values be conserved and promoted in modern times except in universities. I thoroughly agree with you that Islam, which it is your particular privilege to represent, or the Vedanta which it is the privilege of Banaras particularly to represent, will not be a disabling factor but a perennial source of inspiration in maintaining true values in human endeavour as well as in broadening vision. I go so far in my faith as to believe that each faith will help to glorify the other even as the colours of the spectrum glorify the beauty of each tint in the band.

The retirement of my old friend and colleague Nawab Ismail Khan and the undertaking of the responsibility as Vice-Chancellor by Dr. Zakir Hussain should not be understood or interpreted as any kind of political or other challenge. I can never forget how helpful Nawab Ismail Khan was at a Unity Conference that was held in Allahabad fifteen years ago at which I played some part along with him. Dr. Zakir Hussain's arrival at Aligarh is a reunion. In 1920 the Khilafat Movement joined the Swaraj stream as the Jumna joins the Ganga and my dear old colleagues Maulana Mohammed Ali and Big Brother Shaukat Ali, whose memory recalls unforgettable friendship and undying glory of vigorous action, disturbed the calm of Aligarh and raised the old, old issue of conservation versus revolution. "Let us conserve" said the older authorities. "We shall die if we do not move" said resurgent patriotism.

There was a parting of the ways then. Now there is a reunion, and the Jamia Millia has, through Dr. Zakir Hussain's Vice-Chancellorship, rejoined Aligarh.

May the Aligarh University receive the blessings of God along with every assistance from the people and Government of India.

Aligarh Muslim University Students' Union

[His Excellency the Governor General made the following speech at the Aligarh University Students' Union on December 15, 1948].

Mr. President, Your Highness, Friends and Brothers, Members of the Union,

It gave me great pleasure to hear sincere thoughts expressed in such apposite, eloquent language on this occasion. You will forgive me if I confess that I did not expect such beautiful language. The perfection of style in a foreign language shown by your President surprised me. The pledges to which he gave expression are however much more important than the language in which he clothed his thoughts. They will give great satisfaction and joy to all my colleagues in the Government of India. After getting these pledges I have no hesitation in unveiling the picture which he asked me to unveil.

I have always felt great hesitation whenever I have been asked to unveil a picture of Gandhiji. His likeness is close to the original, the greater is the grief that it gives one looking at the picture. If the likeness is bad, the grief is there in equal measure. I do not like a bad picture of a very good man. I do not know what you think of the present picture. I think it is a good piece of work and I congratulate the artist who has done it.

You asked me to sign my name in your book and you showed me Gandhiji's signature on its first page. That was a great joy to me. When I thought of the words you uttered, promising the nation and the Government your loyal and devoted service, I felt it was a truly good thing to have been asked to unveil the picture of Gandhiji as a token of acceptance of the promise. Remember, friends, the solemnity of this gesture on your part as well as on mine. The Union has promised on behalf of the University something serious and far-reaching. I have accepted it as Governor General and Gandhiji has witnessed it in the picture that you have asked me to unveil. It is a completed covenant according to all ideas of jurisprudence, morality and patriotism.

I must congratulate you on having got my old friend Dr. Zakir Hussain as Vice-Chancellor and guide, philosopher and friend of this University. It is not easy to secure one of his stature as Vice-Chancellor for a university. You have in him one who is respected by all in India, irrespective of caste, creed or class. I very much doubted whether he would give up the Jamia Millia which he nursed with so much affection all these years and come here Some people welcome a big and new responsibility But some are so much attached to the work that they have been doing, irrespective of public praise or blame, that they hesitate to give it up and go to what may be considered a more eminent position. Dr. Zakir Hussain belongs to the latter class. I therefore felt doubtful whether he would agree to become your Vice-Chancellor. Then I remembered the connection between Jamia Millia and the Aligarh University It is more like a son-in-law being asked to go and take charge of the mother-in-law's or father-in-law's house. The Jamia Millia was born in pain. But the Jamia Millia does not for that reason cease to be the child of the mother. Therefore, when Dr. Zakir Hussain was asked whether he would go to the mother-in-law's place or father-in-law's place, I could see that he agreed with a whole heart, because he keeps the Jamia Millia in one pocket and Aligarh in another. Do not however go away with the impression that personalities and events like this themselves make for great changes.

His coming is an indication of what has happened in India and therefore it was inevitable he should come here. He could not resist it and it was not possible to make any other proposal. That is why he is here with you.

You, members of this Union, are in a way leaders of the student community in Aligarh and probably of the entire Muslim student body in India. Tour Union in its opinions will give a lead to Muslim students all over India. I want you therefore to make the best of this good luck of yours.

I hope and pray that you, members of the Aligarh University Union, will make the utmost of Dr. Zakir Hussain's presence here. Prom all that I have seen since this morning, I know that you love him and respect him and that you have confidence in him. That emboldens me to make this appeal to you. A man who trusts in God, who is honest, pious and also considerate and not hasty, is eminently fitted to be your guide in the present critical conditions in our country.

This morning the Doctorate of Law was conferred upon me. If I were' asked to answer an examination before qualifying for the degree, the examiners would not have let me off. The University has taken other data to come to the conclusion that I should be the recipient of that degree.

But degrees such as have been conferred upon me are of no great use. The degrees you are working for are of great use. Do not go away with the impression that examinations are of no use and that something else is important.

Whatever may have been the case till now, I want you to think differently henceforth. The patriotism with which you have been familiar up till now is a closed chapter. Hereafter your patriotism is of a new colour It consists in disinterested, joyful service to the State. You must serve faithfully and diligently and you must find joy in service itself. This requires great and careful preparation in the time of youth, and the universities are intended to give that preparation.

The slogan is no longer as in 1920, "Give up Colleges". The slogan now is 'Hold on to the colleges, Go to the colleges and do your college work properly'. I have said this times without number and I want to put it to you in this form. The Government, the Governor General, the leaders of the people who are in charge of the Government — all of them want you to study carefully and diligently without losing time and equip yourselves properly, because we are lacking a great deal in the right type of manpower in this country, and you are preparing yourselves to shoulder the burden of the whole State along with others. You will therefore have to give up all ideas of strikes so far as educational institutions are concerned. Ask any doctor whether in getting something done, like tying up the artery or tying up a vein or a nerve to perform some operation, the heart can be stopped.

Whatever else you may do, you cannot give a holiday to the heart. So is the education of youth. It cannot be suspended in a living organisation. Along with the promises you have made to your President, I want you silently to promise me that you will never be guilty of indiscipiine or of doing anything against the orders of the Vice-Chancellor or any professors or authorities of the University. This is now a free country with a free government to judge things and there is no reason for students to become judges. If you accept the principle of division between the executive and judiciary, you must accept the principle of division between youth engaged in studies and the judiciary. You must not become judges.

The discipline that I have so far seen in the course of the day gives me every confidence that there was no need for me to take up so much of your time over this matter.

We have two great free countries now. We have our own India here and we have Pakistan beyond the wall. The whole world is looking on with great expectations. There is a great future before us. The present troubles which are upsetting people's minds will soon be over. There is no conflict between the two countries. Take it for granted. I am supposed to be a wise man and I tell you with all the earnestness at my command, there is no conflict of interest between Pakistan and India. We are both destined to be great and to help one another.

Whether it be politics, economics, literature, morality, religion or any other matter, we two, helping one another, will give something important and valuable to the rest of the world. You here in this University should make it your sacred duty to keep this in your minds. You are, so to say, crusaders for the cause of unity between the two States, of unity between the two faiths, and unity all round in India.

This responsibility lies on you in a very particular manner I hope you will remember it in all your studies.

We have a record in the Upanishads of a valedictory exhortation given to students after the completion of their studies. The substance of that address holds good for the present times and for students like you as well as it did at the time of the Upanishads. The sonorous Sanskrit words can be rendered thus in simple English:

> "Speak what is true, fulfil your duties; Continue your studies.
>
> Now that you have come to the end of your stay with your teachers and will marry and bring forth progeny,
>
> Do not swerve from truth and Dharma.
>
> Always do something useful in the social economy.
>
> Do not fail to refresh your memory in respect of what you have learnt. Do not give up the desire to achieve.

Remember God, revere your ancestors, revere your mothers and your fathers,

Honour your teachers, honour your guests,

Ever exercise your understanding and distinguish the good from the bad.

Avoid evil and always do what is right.

Follow all that was good in your teacher's life, not any other.

You will meet with better men than the teachers you have lived with,

Show them due respect.

If your mind is troubled with any doubt, follow the example of pious elders who are not ungentle whom you may find in your neighbourhood in regard to those matters.

This is the rule and this is the teaching."

This closes the message I wished to quote for you. This exhortation is repeated in the Banaras University at the time of every Convocation in the original Sanskrit.

Students of Aligarh, I know that in spite of what your President has said with so much fervour, there is a considerable amount of doubt in the minds of many people now. I want you to be brave, and not downhearted for anything that has happened. It is my privilege to claim your confidence and to believe that you will not misunderstand me even if on the surface what I say may seem unpleasant.

You know, without my having to explain it, that many things have happened in the country which were as unexpected as they were unfortunate. They have left results in the psychology of men and women which must be faced.

It is the privilege of cultured Muslims in India to remove this feeling as speedily as possible, but steadily and with patience. We have to bear and forbear. Misunderstandings and suspicion should not make us bitter. I have no doubt that with restraint and patience Muslims in India will see a time arrive when the present difficulties will be recalled with amusement even as differences between the English and Scottish people are now recalled in British social life.

Whether we believe in the Law of Karma as a part of our religion or not, it is absolutely true that we have in this world painfully to work out the results of what has been done by us or by others around us. We cannot get over results by arguments but can do so only by courage and good conduct in the face of every discouragement, I have a right to make an appeal to you. You must believe it of me that enlightened leadership in India will not fail you.

Islam was associated with the highest advancement of Science in Europe. Muslim Universities and Muslim Doctors of Science saved Science when otherwise Europe would have completely lost what had been gained for humanity by the Greeks. The Muslims added a vast amount of new knowledge on the firm basis of investigation and observation. If Islam did not hinder but helped the progress of Science in Europe, may it be a bright token to you for endeavour in India. Indeed no religion, correctly understood, Islam, Christianity, Hinduism or other, ever hindered. Every religion always helped the progress of humanity.

It is the duty of University men to work for and spread a true understanding of all religions. The pious in all religions are one brotherhood. I appeal to you to work for love and brotherhood in India.

Civic Address at Bombay

[In reply to the Address of Welcome presented by the Bombay Municipal Corporation on January 13, 1949].

Your Excellency, Mr. Mayor, Ladies and Gentlemen,

It is difficult for me to go through formal functions, especially before very distinguished select audiences like this. I am a common man and disorderly meetings are more in tune with me than audiences of this type. I am very grateful for the very kind words spoken by the Mayor, which represents the affection of all the people of this great city, I am also very grateful for the beautiful casket and the grand function. Every face here is familiar and it is difficult to pose as a great man before very familiar friends.

I have come in the beginning of a year and I have great pleasure in giving to the people of this city, through the Mayor, my best wishes and prayers for all good luck throughout the coming year.

We have begun well. The year has begun with a remarkable exhibition of statesmanship and wisdom on our part which the whole world has acclaimed unanimously as a great step. Some people even say that we have set a great example to the rest of the world. I am very grateful — and I express it on behalf of the Government — for the promise which the Mayor has been gracious enough to give of complete cooperation in all the endeavours of the Government All finances in our country flow into the towns and into the cities. These are the reservoirs where all the rainfall of wealth in the country flows into and it is from here we have to draw. I am rather surprised the Mayor asks for money from Delhi instead of sending remittances to Delhi. But joking apart, the problems that your Mayor has referred to, I have no doubt, are engaging the attention of the Government at Delhi and the Government at Bombay and I am sure that everything that can be done will be done. Such influence as I have will be exercised with very great caution and if I feel that it would be right for me to press a point, I shall be glad to do so. I do not think there would be any need however for such influence to be exercised. I am informed that a Committee will soon be constituted by the Government of India to look into the question of the finances of local bodies and I am certain that what is right will be done.

At the end of this month we shall have reached the anniversary of the passing away of our great leader and father. According to our own traditional ideas the anniversary of the death should be an occasion not for melodramatic exhibitions of grief but for surveying and for introspection. We have to see whether we have done all that we should do, whether we are going on the right track, and if there is anything to be done or undone, to make up our minds to do so. I am certain that all this will be done by all good men and women on the 30th of January, especially in Bombay which he always felt was his native city. The people of Bombay should regard it as a very sacred day and should review and do a lot of spiritual introspection.

Thank you very much for the affection and the generosity you have shown in giving me this great welcome.

Once more Your Excellency and Mr. Mayor, in thanking you I wish a happy New Year to you all.

Jamiat-ul-Ulema, Bombay

[Replying to the address presented by the Jamiat-ul-Ulema at Kaiser Bagj Dongn, Bombay, on January 9, 1949].

Maulvi Sahib, Friends, Ladies and Gentlemen,

I thank you from the bottom of my heart for your kind welcome. I need hardly tell you how pleased I am to see you all gathered here with goodwill in your hearts If hearts are full of goodwill faces shine like angels' faces.

If we entertain ill-will or distrust we become ugly like the devils painted in pictures for children. I am filled with joy to see faces which indicate confidence, mutual trust and goodwill. Do not believe that I go about in search of addresses and caskets. I go about the country to see people's faces and gauge the state of their mental health.

God has endowed us with faces which immediately shape themselves according to the feelings inside. Every momentary change of heart is shown in the face. If we get into the habit of continually thinking well, continually having goodwill in the heart, the face gets permanent beauty. If you want to look beautiful, Sisters and Brothers, cultivate goodwill Likewise, if you want India to be beautiful, let us cultivate goodwill.

My Muslim brothers and sisters, do not ask for justice. Do not ask for toleration. This is your own country. Treat it as your own home and your own property. When the great poet sang Hindustan Hamara, he did not mean to say that the Muslims should claim it as their special and exclusive property. He wanted Muslims to feel that this was our property, the property of Muslims and Hindus alike. Would you be happy if the children of a family ask for toleration at the hands of the parents? They must ask for the parents' entire love and this is what you owe to and what you can demand of this country.

This hall seems to be the best place in the whole of Bombay to sit together for peace and goodwill. Muslim brothers and sisters, whatever may be your age, so far as the State is concerned you are, to the State, like the youngest children of a family And may the Hindus in Pakistan be similarly treated as the youngest children of that State. To be the younger children of the State does not mean a status of subordination, it is, on the contrary, a status of privilege. The child is the governor of the house.

The wishes of the baby predominate the governance of the house I feel confident that there is peace in India now. The Cease Fire that the Governments of India and Pakistan have declared is a Cease Fire not only for the Kashmir campaign. The Cease Fire is not only the stoppage of the burning of gun-powder. It is a Cease Fire for all ill-will, all distrust.

You have referred to my having been a very faithful follower of our departed Leader. May I tell you — and believe me — that the Government of India is a faithful follower of the departed Leader and not I alone. They know very well that the glory of the Government of India rests on their loyalty to Mahatma Gandhi. His dear colleagues who are now in charge of the Government of India have seen with their own eyes the wisdom of what he taught and have felt in their own hearts the heights to which he rose just before he died. Have confidence, therefore, in your Government.

I thank you once again for the affection you have shown me.

Bombay Union of Journalists

[Replying to the address presented by the Bombay Union of Journalists at the Taj Mahal Hotel, Bombay, on January 9, 1949].

Mr. Gopalaswamy, Your Excellency and Friends,

I am very sorry that my friend, Mr. Brelvi, has not been able to come here this evening I am more sorry to learn the reason for it.

You have not raised very difficult points — not half as difficult as the commercial and industrial people when they meet a person like me. You say you are disappointed that the press is not specifically mentioned in the Constitution that is being framed. Special mention is not legally necessary. Let me confirm the explanation given on the floor of the Assembly that freedom of expression includes the right of the press. It is a correct juridical position There is also the lawyer's theory that if you particularise one or two items in a general proposition you lower the value of the general statement. Judges and lawyers will confirm that if you proceed to particularise, the full meaning of the general statement will be lost; the interpreters of the Constitution would exclude other particular things not mentioned.

You say you will be quite content if you in India had the freedom which the press in England enjoys. But the press in India enjoys the same rights as the press in England does. In England the press is free, just as free as the press here is and no more.

So I do not think that you can justifiably complain in regard to this matter. I claim there is no distinction between the position of the press in England and the position of the press here I claim that if a jury composed of pressmen of the world haphazardly take half a dozen issues of newspapers in India of any date, they will give the verdict that the press here is enjoying thorough-going freedom. I cannot imagine what more freedom you can ask for. I have been reading, both for instruction and for amusement, issues of Bombay journals fairly regularly.

It is astonishing to see how free the press in Bombay is. In our country the courts have not been very rigorous in enforcing the law in libel cases If half the things written in our press appeared in an English newspaper, terrible damages would be awarded by the jury. But I do not envy the state of things in England in this respect It is better not to bother about libel. Our people are not misled by such things Therefore, no harm is done by them.

I saw both in Bombay and Poona that the people felt great joy at seeing an Indian Governor General moving about in flesh and blood among them. The children were the most jubilant It seemed to me that they were delighted that what they saw so vividly, a Governor General of their own going about was not a dream but an actual feet that set me thinking. Perhaps they have an intuitive feeling that in their time things will really improve whatever disappointments you may have now and however impatient you may be now. That is why instinctively they felt jubilant at the sight of the symbol of our newly won Independence. I want you also to think like them and to have confidence that things will improve soon.

The press men are used to my habit of making forecasts and I do not think you believe I am a poor astrologer. I tell you that most of the present political discontent and difficulties which we (the Government) are facing will disappear soon. I do not say all. I only say most of our difficulties. A few must remain, otherwise you cannot enjoy the dynamic condition which life inherently must follow.

You all remember that I told your colleagues in Madras some time ago that they should look upon Journalism not as a profession or occupation but as a fine art. Unfortunately the meaning of my "fine art" appeal was a little blurred by numerous light comments I do not complain. Let us laugh The humour column is a very good thing I like it very much. But it is not easy to make good jokes It is only too easy to make poor jokes.

Now a poor joke can scatter wisdom to pieces but a good joke does no harm. Poor jokes can do a lot of harm. I repeat what I said to your colleagues in Madras. Look upon your work with the eyes of an artist Hereafter in the measure that our country produces beautiful things, in that measure alone will our country be great. Thank you very much for asking me to join you.

At the Indian Chamber of Commerce, Bombay

[His Excellency the Governor General made the following speech at the Indian Chamber of Commerce, Bombay, when unveiling the bust of Mahatma Gandhi on January 10, 1949].

Mr. Kilachand, Your Excellency and Friends,

I have always felt it a painful duty to unveil a picture or statue of our beloved leader, although it is impossible to refuse a request of this kind. It revives pain to look at pictures and statues of one whom we have lost. When you feel grief, how can you judge works of art? The man was different from his form. You cannot get anything out of it by looking at a material likeness of that form. An ancient text in our scriptures says that the person you see in the eye is the Aim an Scholars have given many interpretations of this text. The text itself is the centre piece of a story where the chief of the gods understood it in one way and the chief of the anti-gods understood it in another way. There is something missing in any work of art and that is in your mind all the time when you look at a statue like this The light that shines from inside in the eyes cannot be brought out in any statue So, my friends, Forgive me if I have not been able to give any opinion on the artist's work.

The members of the Chamber here were in one way closely connected with Gandhiji while in other ways they were far apart from him. There are many people who used to look upon Gandhiji as a great bania and you are a Chamber of Banias. The term 'bania' has been used in a very familiar and derogatory sense in modern days. It is used to denote a caste or a miser, a moneylender and so on But really a bania simply means a merchant. To distribute things among the people in a fair manner is the bania's Dharma. You are a Chamber of such people. God has many names in our scriptures and one of them is 'trader', that is to say, He receives and gives. He receives as price the action of men and gives reward in return, weighing it in exact scales just as merchants are expected to do Correct weighment was one of the attributes of God and correct trader is one of His thousand names.

You have erected this bust to be a constant source of inspiration to members of your Chamber. May that inspiration remind you of the correctness of life that you are expected to lead and the manner in which you are expected to fulfil your functions in society Trade and commerce have grown. The community of merchants has come to exist not by a conspiracy of selfish people but as a step in natural evolution All social institutions are as much living organisms as plants and lives that have come into being through evolution and the laws of nature. Your trade and commerce have come into being as part of a natural evolution and therefore merchants have a necessary function in society to perform. As long as they perform the functions that appertain to them, the scriptures of our ancients and the philosophy of our moderns recognise them as having an important place in society.

There are many schools of social organisation. There may be people who dream that we should have a society wherein distribution could be done without the help of profiteering agencies.

But agencies of some kind are required for distribution and whether one agency is better than another is a matter of trial and error. The same smith may get different results working with different tools Whether one method of distribution is better than another depends not only upon the relative merits of the method but also on the men concerned While therefore we try and find out our mistakes, let us not become fanatical opponents of one another. In India, many trials have to be made, many errors have to be committed and rectified If the Government of India brought in controls or if they removed controls or brought controls in again, these are not signs of indecision or instability.

These are symptoms of the spirit of honest endeavour and let us look upon them as such The Government of India have tried and are trying to cope with extraordinary difficulties In a small country, with a relatively small population, experiments are easier and results more satisfactory and decisive. But in a large country such as ours, with a population as vast as it is, where numerous layers are involved, experiments are rather difficult It requires greater courage on the one hand and greater tolerance on the other. Let us therefore be sympathetic and help the Government. The removal of controls had not proved satisfactory and some people could say "Well, did I not tell you?" or "Did I not say you should do something else?" and so on. The Government of India have reimposed regulation to some extent and it has not been very quick in producing results. Every line of work produces new difficulties and we must face them.

When the Government of India said. "We shall try our best to lower prices but we shall begin now at where prices stand", some people were quite happy, others were unhappy. They said, "Do you mean to say that you will go on stabilising prices at their present levels? It would be extraordinarily unfair. We have not been given compensatory arrangements for the high prices now reached", and there is thus great discontent.

When I decided to come to Bombay and knew that I would meet you all, I knew that I would have to say something about this matter. So instead of depending on my own notions of things, I asked my friend and colleague the Finance Minister about this. The Finance Minister of the Government of India informed me definitely that it is not the intention of the Government to stabilize prices at their present levels. It is only a point at which to start. As things ease, prices are bound to come down. It is not their intention to maintain prices at the present levels, They expect all prices to go down as we go on. That is the definite policy of the Government I am in a position to tell you and through you all those who are concerned.

All this has nothing to do with Mahatma Gandhi. But during the last few months of his career in this world, Mahatma Gandhi was very much exercised over the question of prices and showed concern in the consultations people had with him. It was always wrong to go to Mahatma Gandhi with the belief that whatever he said was the word of God. Those that went to him in that spirit returned no doubt very happy, but in my opinion, not very wise. Those who went to him for advice as a great and selfless man and as a friend and patriot and as one inspired by love of humanity and therefore entitled to special regard, came back wiser than when they went to him. It was in that spirit that Ministers of the Government of India consulted him from time to time. All the time Mahatmaji lived, he did not like anybody to go to him with the intention of accepting without examination anything he said. If I may tell you a personal secret, he liked me most because I had the mischievous tendency to argue things out with him and differ from him if necessary. If I had become a cent, per cent, loyalist, so to say, I do not think I would have commanded his love or confidence.

That does not mean that it was an incitement to me to try to differ from him. At no time did I give cent, per cent approval to what he said as during the last few weeks of his life-time He rose, in my opinion to the height of his glory and eminence and usefulness in the world during those few weeks. He was like a rocket which went up and in a blaze disappeared in the sky. It did not come down to die. It died at its highest illumination. He put his whole soul into his passion for communal amity and disappeared in a glory.

Some people think that regulation can make everything. They talk of Government keeping down inflation as if it were simply a matter of physical control The forces that are in operation, act according to the law of nature. A patient gets rheumatism because his heart requires some rest and rheumatism compels him to get that rest. Gandhiji was most concerned not about prices but about the moral condition of our people. It may be that moral condition has something to do with prices also.

But the main thing he was concerned about was a deterioration in the moral fibre of the people, including mutual love and mutual trust. It was towards that he was making his highest endeavour just before he disappeared. Let us try as far as we can to keep his memory not in marble or plaster or bronze, but in the tissue of our hearts. We should try to paint and frame him in our hearts. Other pictures or statues have no life. It is then that every individual member of the Chamber of Commerce will get the inspiration sought from the bust you have unveiled.

At the Hindustani Prachar Sabha

[Addressing the Hindustani Prachar Sabha, Bombay, on January 10, 1949].

It is not possible for one in my position to visit during a brief stay all the places one would like to. There are limitations on my movement. Still I have made time to pay a visit to Perm Captain's organisation. She has been working all her life in the face of many difficulties. She regards her work for this item of Bapu's programme as a kind of sradh, the omission of which would be a sin.

I have come here today to plead with Shrimati Perin Captain for greater patience. The Government of Bombay have their difficulties and if they seem not as quick to respond to your advice as you would like them to be, it is because they know you will understand their difficulties unlike others who are not so good.

I want to tell you this. Please do not take every word of our dear departed leader as scripture and every modification to be heresy. In regard to the question of Hindustani Gandhiji's main point was the spread of Hindustani. We are forgetting the main point but are quarrelling over the question of scripts. Language is sound. Script is only written representation of the sound.

Any language can be written in any script that you like Sanskrit can be written in Roman script or Telugu script.

The question of scripts need present no difficulty whatever It has seized people's minds because grown-up people who have the discussion in their hands cannot learn a new script easily. If, to these same people, Hindustani is presented in their own script, the script that they know, you will see that they proceed to learn the language without objection or difficulty. My advice to you therefore is that you should use for adults the script that they are familiar with.

Otherwise your difficulties will be Himalayan, you will earn merit but not reach Kailash and the difficulty of learning the scripts will be transferred to the language itself.

With children it is different but the child is the ward of the parents who are, however, not wise and think that script is a matter of religion A Hindu parent thinks that only the Nagan script should be used A Muslim lather prefers his children taught through Urdu script. And even when they compromise, there is resentment in the heart.

I would ask that in our work we should not resort to compulsion. It is curious that though we shout freedom all the time, we pledge our faith to coercion. This is all wrong. I feel sad at exhibitions of ignorance and fanaticism.

Those who wish to be workers in the Hindustani movement should in my view know not only the Hindi and Urdu scripts but also Bengali, Telugu and other Indian scripts. Then you will be able to function more effectively and spread Hindustani all over India, presenting it to people in their own scripts.

Let us not spend our energies in quarrels Let us not fight about differences. Bather let us concentrate on the points of agreement and carry on our work with hope, faith and courage. Varieties of *gur* are different, nevertheless they have the common quality of sweetness.

Delhi University Convocation Address

[Addressing the Annual Convocation of the Delhi University on January 15, 1949].

Mr. Vice-Chancellor, Ladies and Gentlemen,

I am grateful to the Vice-Chancellor for having relieved me of the heavier part of today's proceedings. The University is grateful to Sir Maurice Gwyer for having undertaken the responsibility for another term of office as its academic and executive head. It is our good fortune that a man of his eminence has made himself available for such service in this important and growing university It is not everyone of his years who will voluntarily choose to work hard after having already achieved what would have served as quite enough laurels to rest on.

Where, in accordance with democratic ideas, we have adopted the procedure of election for filling positions requiring expert qualifications, to which appointments were made in the old days by authority, it is necessary to create an atmosphere which would attract the offer of such services by the most capable and high minded among us. We have seen bow those who are best qualified to serve in civic administration stand aside, disliking the vexations attendant on election procedure and leaving third and fourth rate men to manage the affairs of local bodies as best as they can The same fate should not be allowed to overtake our universities.

I hope that these remarks of mine, which deal with a matter of very great and growing importance in many of our affairs will be understood in the spirit in which I have uttered them.

I remember what a great and exciting occasion it was to me when as a young man I received my degree as a Bachelor of Arts in 1897. In spite of the many changes that have come about in life in general and in India in particular, I do not believe young men receiving degrees today are less excited about it than young men were in those days over fifty years ago Aspiration and hope and the generous impulses of youth are just the same now, as then. I can guess how your young minds are all charged with noble ambition and hope.

May God bless you and give you every chance. Remember that the battle is the glory and results do not count. I do not repeat empty words. I speak as a man who has gone through many trials, defeats as well as successes, and I assure you results really do not matter and it is the way in which you struggle that matters. God has manifestly given us all in India a chance and we should prove how good we are capable of being We are children of noble ancestors and there is a great deal in heredity India has come into its own at a rather bad time in the history of world morality. Had we eliminated foreign care-taking some 25 years ago, we should have fared much better. But we cannot get everything done just as we would like and so we must make the best of it now. Our freedom has been born when the world has in many respects greatly deteriorated, and this is a great handicap for us who have to start now.

At no time was there in our country such serious heart-searching as at the present moment agitates all circles, high and low, as to the need for reinforcing the sense of values, moral and spiritual. Never was it more acutely realised that no effort to improve conditions through laws or through administrative direction can bear fruit, unless the moral sense of the intelligentsia is quickened.

Precepts lose all meaning if repeated too often. The statements of leaders and their appeals from public platforms are just diagnosis and do not act as remedies for the sickness diagnosed. We have, it is perfectly clear, to make the quickening of the moral sense a definite part of the educational system, even though it may seem to be a slow approach to the problem. And this, not by including in the curricula of schools and colleges, lectures and studies on the subject of morality, but by organising such activities and such discipline as will infuse, in the minds of our young men and women, a reverence for truth and good and an automatic revulsion from falsehood and evil.

An ounce of practice is worth a pound of theory. It follows that in schools and colleges, we should have men and women whose daily lives inspire and infuse enlightened thought and action in the impressionable minds of the boys and girls brought in contact with them. As much care and caution should be taken over the habits of thought and action of the persons recruited for holding teachers' and tutors' posts and other positions of authority in educational institutions, as over their expert qualifications in the realm of knowledge.

The part played by personal contact is great in good as well as in evil. We are imitative by nature. Not only in the early and impressionable years but throughout life, we automatically copy the ways of those we admire. Therefore, a great deal of improvement is possible if responsibility for moulding character and behaviour all round is definitely undertaken by those who are placed in positions of authority and influence. This is the only way and not any set instruction.

In the old days, a sense of values was automatically conserved by widespread beliefs that may be described succinctly by the term Religion. But in modern times, when so much has been irretrievably done rightly or wrongly to undo the work of ages in the matter of religion, we have to find new instruments for shaping the minds of men and women so that they may develop attitudes that enable them to live and act to the greatest benefit of one another. The grand secret of social happiness lies in the cultivation of sympathy and unselfishness as an automatic reaction and attitude on the part of men and women on all occasions. We should all acquire the habit of abhorring unsocial behaviour. Lying, stealing, deceiving, cruelty and indulgence in animal appetites should become as disgusting as filth of unclean food.

The need for cleanliness of mind is as great as, if not greater than, physical sanitation, and we must aim at spreading this habit of cleanliness of mind as a part of enlightened statecraft, as essential as physical public hygiene which is the concern of Health Ministries, Bureaucratic rule under in foreign power having been liquidated, we have now each to find and fulfil our own responsibility in everything The need for dynamic patriotism is not over with the attainment of national freedom. But dynamic patriotism no longer consists in irrelevant adherence to past dislikes and inhibitions but in the crusading spirit of purging out selfishness, and in making men and women constantly keep before their minds the welfare of the State as till recently they kept the elimination of foreign rule.

Citizenship is not merely a right arising out of birth and domicile It is a culture developed by training and right emotional direction Without it, freedom and democracy would be chaos. What I call the culture of citizenship is not to be confounded with nationalism. It is a pattern of individual conduct which alone can help democracy to produce social happiness.

We have eliminated foreign rule but that does not mean we should let the respect for law grow less or the authority of governments and courts to be reduced. It does not mean a reversal of all the good things that have been built up during the period of foreign rule. What has been found useful and built into national life should be conserved.

Nine-tenths of the technique of progress is conservation of what has been found good on trial. More than anything else, patriotism as well as education must most seriously concentrate on restoration of a sense of values and the development of a habitual attitude of sympathy and unselfishness. If this work is steadily and faithfully done for some time, there will be a marvellous change in the face of things and there will be joy instead of anger in the minds of men, and work instead of despair and helpfulness instead of faultfinding. Nowhere in the world does evil continue except for a while. Good sense asserts itself after some time and good replaces evil. This will happen also in our country. So, my young friends, be confident, trust in God and be brave. Work towards the establishment of the culture of citizenship which will operate as an inner law making people think and act rightly without any external sanction.

My best wishes to you all once again. Delhi is a noble and historic place, one of the great places of the world.

Your University has the honour of being housed and looked after in the Metropolis of India where the relics of past greatness are all about you and you live in daily contact with the central springs of future greatness Be worthy of Delhi.

At the Dargah Sharif

[Replying to the aaaress presented by the Khadims of Hazrat Khawaja Sahib at the Dargah Sharif, Ajmer, on February 19, 1949].

It has given me the greatest satisfaction that I have been able to come here. I hope you understand the sincerity of what I say when I tell you that I am glad that I have been with you in this sacred spot. A very great and good man's body lies buried here.

There are many ways which people are following in order to reach what they cannot see with their own eyes, namely, God. God is so great and so omnipresent that all ways lead to him All the ways leading to God are sacred and we should respect them equally.

There are many places in the South where Muslim festivals are participated in by Hindus and Muslims attend Hindu festivals. Scholars may imagine that it is ignorance that makes Muslims join in Hindu festivals and Hindus join in Islamic festivals, but it is not ignorance, it is truly God's wisdom that makes them do so.

The highest wisdom that we can learn from our scripture or any other scripture, is that all ways lead to God and we must respect one another as brothers and sisters. Let each one of us who has some wisdom in him maintain this code of conduct, whatever others might do I give you my own personal assurance that to me every mosque, every church, every temple is equally sacred If in Banaras we see on the banks of the Ganga not only temples but also mosques, we must treat them all as equally sacred whatever may have been their history. Let us forget what has happened in the past, let us behave as brothers and sisters towards one another hereafter.

In free India all of us are free. If India becomes great, all of us become great and derive the advantage of India's greatness Do not have any doubts in your mind about this. This Government and this country is yours as much as it is mine, and I say this not carelessly but in the presence of your great saint. I thank you very much for the affection you have shown me and for the sacred presents you have given me.

The Food Problem

[Broadcasting to the nation from the Delhi Station of the All India Radio on July 6, 1949].

When I was in Shimla last month for a week's holiday, I invited those who expressed a desire to see me to what is called an At-Home. In the old days an At-Home meant alcoholic drinks. But now of course no such thing is possible. We had some soft drinks and what was permissible under the Entertainment Laws by, way of chewing. We had asked everyone who had signed his name without looking into his rank or profession. So that I was able to see the glad faces of nearly fifteen hundred Shimla residents that evening.

The report of this gathering in the newspapers alarmed some good men who thought I had called together fifteen hundred men and women and feasted them tin old Viceregal Lodge and wasted a lot of food when there was so much talk of shortage and appeals for austerity. They did not know that we spent not one ounce of rice or wheat or millet or of pulses over this Shimla At-Home. It was indeed a miserable miser's fraud. But this alarm brings to notice once again the anxiety of people over the food shortage in the country.

I am not an expert but I think you will listen to me all the same. Do we as a nation wish to live and make our mark as an independent and civilized people? I suppose we do Well then we must sit up and think this food shortage out and do what logically follows. Otherwise we break Money can be printed and during short periods of emergency we can use such printed paper to borrow service and labour to meet the emergency appearing to pay for them. Later we should gradually withdraw the excess money and restore normality. Excess money in circulation does nobody good. It just raises prices Money is not wealth. It is just a ratio-tool and a credit-token.

We have to pay for what we import from other countries by producing goods in our own country and exporting them in payment of our dues for imports Our own paper-money is of no use in this connection What we get from abroad must be paid for fully, if not now, next year or the year after, if we can get our foreign friends to wait that long.

If we get machinery for industries or manufactured articles for use or foodgrains to eat, we must pay back either in services rendered or in raw materials or in manufactured articles or in gold or other precious metals All these have to be exported in such shapes and kinds as are wanted abroad and are acceptable.

Now, it is well-known India cannot send much out in these ways. Once upon a time we were growing enough food for our people and were also able to produce certain other raw materials or partially prepared stuff for which there was an eager demand in the foreign countries which supplied us the manufactured articles that we imported.

We were exporting raw materials so much that we had an account in our favour as net result. We are importing of present a great quantity of manufactured articles from abroad as well as a considerable quantity of foodgrains.

For payment we have been depending on our war-time savings banked in England instead of producing extra goods for export This is good enough for the time being.

But this cannot go on for ever, can it? We must stop importing to the extent we cannot export If we do not ourselves stop, it will stop of itself. We must cut our imports down according to what we can now export, and wait for improvement in the latter before we order things from abroad. But whatever we may or may not do, we must eat.

Anything may wait, but not this. We have to produce all the food we require or we invite famine and chaos which will reduce our population. Nature is a relentless accountant and works automatically.

Government programmes to build new dams and reservoirs to bring in new areas under cultivation depend on help from abroad in various ways This again brings us up against problems of foreign exchange, that is, the problem of payment in goods for the expensive machinery and services that we have to import from abroad Government in to get these things on credit and are doing their best.

These and other large problems are being tackled by our eminent who are doing the utmost they can Foreign Governments also have not been ungenerous or unhelpful They are indeed doing all they can to help us because they know India is a great country with plenty of natural resources as well as a very brainy industrious population, and so India is sure one day to be a great and valuable unit in the civilized world Our brains and OUT working capacity, which together form the principal element in wealth, are quite good in quantity and quality.

Every one in the world admits this We cannot however fulfil these high expectations unless we in the meanwhile produce enough food to live and work efficiently Even if we are unable to do much at once in the way of producing manufactured articles in surplus for export, we ought to grow all the food we require.

We are a rice-eating people. We also consume a large quantity of wheat We cannot easily and at once expand the area under rice cultivation. The shortage in one kind of food can be made up by another if we know how to adjust ourselves. We cannot afford to sit still until irrigation schemes for increased rice cultivation are completed We must grow such things as can be immediately grown by way of food, whatever they may be. We can produce more millet and pulses and tubers than we do now. We must raise poultry for eggs and grow fish in our ponds and fruit and vegetables in our house-yards and make up for shortage in calories.

The standard of life among the working classes has gone up It must go up and it is well that it has gone up. The peasants and landless rural labourers who used to eat ragi, maize or millets, and ate rice only on festive and rare occasions, now eat rice generally and are not happy unless they get it. Besides the change-over in habit, population has increased. There is thus on the whole a great increase in consumption of rice. This is as it should be. But it is not altogether good. In the first place a pure rice diet is not so good for health as it may be for taste. But apart from this we have as a result gone short of rite. We cannot easily expand the area of rice cultivation, for it require darns and canals which involve vast expenditure to got ready quickly. We can however use more millet and pulses and tubers without large irrigation projects, it is therefore desirable that the fashion must be set for greater consumption of ragi, cholam, maize and millet Nothing can be done by way of setting a fashion except to the so-called upper classes. What they do is eager copied by others Like jail-going, hobnobbing with out-castes, spinning, wearing Gandhi-caps, millet-food must be made a patriotic high class fashion. This will lighten the present load on rice.

This great mother the ground on which we walk and live, is a wonderful mother, most generous, most forgiving and most skilful Put anything into it, be it the worst rotten stuff, mere offal or what we throw out as excrement, this ever-loving sleepless mother converts it for us by an alchemy of her own into rich food which shoots up, juicy and fragrant. But she requires a little help from us, just a little help and some watchful cooperation You must know what to sow as seed and when, and look after the shoots that come up. The earth returns with interest what you put in receiving offal and excrement, she gives us back pumpkins, cucumbers, bananas, whatever we know how to raise.

Urban authorities should consider it their sacred obligation to collect and conserve town refuse and make good manure out of it and place it at the disposal of gardeners and cultivators of land at a reasonable price. People gather more and more into urban areas and it is the duty of the Civic Authorities to remember then- obligations to the rural areas that feed the towns and return at least in part the nitrogen that flows into the urban areas. This can be done by careful conservation and disposal of the organic refuse of the towns. Apart from animal droppings, what is thrown out by townsfolk is a continuous and considerable drain on the rural areas unless there is an organised movement of manure from towns to villages.

What is required is increased interest in raising something by way of food wherever you can and whatever it may be. Now, who is to go round and tell people all this and not only tell, but make people do it? Who did it for weaving and spinning? Who did it for Hindu-Muslim unity? Who did it for removing untouchablity? Who did it for fighting the drink-evil. Not Government anyway. The people organised themselves under Congress direction Government did not and would not do it in the days that are past Now however Government are not against the people They are with the people But Government cannot do some things They cannot do what individuals and organised groups of individuals can alone do Officials cannot effectively spread themselves over the vast country and even if they could, it would cost so much that it is impossible. An unofficial nation-wide movement alone can do it Government will help, but self-help and patriotism produce more than official patronage or interference.

I am speaking frankly and as a citizen. During these last sixty years, whenever there was a great national movement needed in India, the Congress undertook it and did it. The Congress in constructive work is not a party. It is the aggregate of disinterested energy that belongs to the whole nation In its khadi work, in its Harijan work and in all its other constructive work in the past, every one that was ready and willing to help was welcome to join. While Congress took up responsibility, it did not exclude any one.

Congress can lead a movement for food-growing and save the country from bankruptcy. But it can succeed only if the people cooperate with fanatical zeal in this as they did in other things during the last three decades. It will be a glorious achievement and pave the way for the fulfilment of all our other aspirations.

All India Newspaper Editors' Conference

[Addressing the All India Newspaper Editors' Conference at Bangalore on May 16, 1949].

I accepted the invitation of Mr. C. R. Shrinivasan to have the pleasure of being with you on this occasion because apart from my happening to be in Bangalore at the time of your Conference by a happy coincidence, your new President is a very old and trusted friend of mine and in his elevation I find just satisfaction If my experience of him as a careful and reliable adviser in public affairs has any value for you, you will hail his presidentship as a guarantee for a further year of successful coordinated work. Mr. Shrinivasan is advanced in his views and he is shrewd and conservative in his method and is not ever likely to be led to unreason by reason of emotion He is a staunch friend to friends and a considerate opponent to opponents.

Bear with me if I speak to you, Editors in general, the few words of seeming idealism. I fancy my idealism is never anything but a practical way of life and a guide in the shaping of policy. Even as India has attained greatness in independence, the Press in India has attained great power, but with greatness as with power comes the burden of heavier responsibility. It did not much matter in the old days if in some ways the Press over — did things but — today the great and enhanced power that the Press wields renders every error or lapse very dangerous This is why increased stress is laid by all thinking men on quality and maintenance of standards in journalism. It would be quite wrong for you to feel that this stress laid by public men is due to a desire to interfere with the liberty of the Press or reduce its importance. It is a recognition of its much increased power.

I repeat what I have said once before that the Press in India does enjoy the greatest amount of liberty. It is not the statutes that give us a measure of the rights enjoyed by the Press. There may be terrible-looking laws in the Statute book, but to use a homely expression, the proof of the pudding is in the eating. On any day in the year I can, if challenged, produce a catalogue of things printed that day in the newspapers of India which would prove that there is no sort of restriction over writing or fear in the mind of journalists. The Government as a whole, the individuals composing the Government and even their private lives are subjected to criticism as free and unrestrained as any of the most inquisitorial press in the world.

It is not the law on the statute book but the practice that should be the yardstick of appraisement. The statutes are there to provide for emergencies but hurt and restrain no one in fact. Your Standing Committee when it met in October 1944, adopted a resolution denouncing indecent personal writings bordering on blackmail. At Calcutta in 1945 you condemned the tendency in some papers to indulge in abusive and personal writings. You repeated this warning again in 1948 when you met in Bombay. In your Secretary's preface to the Conference report issued this month, he has rightly stated that the Press has had to move from self-protection to self-restraint and from self-restraint to self-improvement, and he has recorded with satisfaction that despite statutory restrictions there is a larger understanding between the Press and the Government which is based on identity of interests Even as excess of indulgence in pleasure makes it more and more difficult to achieve it, excess of freedom and liberty of expression defeat their own purpose.

The more sensationalism is indulged in, the more difficult it becomes to produce the desired effect, for unreliability grows in the proportion of unrestrained publication. We all know that certain journals that are no doubt read much for entertainment really produce no effect on the readers by way of persuasion. No institution and no newspaper can be said to serve India well unless it promotes in some way or other goodwill and good understanding among the various sections of the people. The master-key to progress in all spheres is mutual friendliness and cooperation and the avoidance of conflicts.

If individual newspapers, and the press as a whole, earnestly work for goodwill and make a determined stand against the growth of any form of ill-will, India will progress in spite of all our difficulties. I wish all our newspapers carried over their title page the motto, "Love and help one another".

Every editorial and every news-item must be written and read on. this background.

I should like to say a few words about the historic conference at London at which our Prime Minister was the central figure. We all know with what universal satisfaction the news of his great achievement was received in India There was distinct political satisfaction in all circles. We know what great joy it gave to all people and all parties in Britain, in Ireland, in America and in all the countries of the world that desire the reign of peace and of democracy But it gave no less satisfaction to thinking people of all classes in India.

There are of course some people who must find some points of difference which, justify their attempt to live a separate and rival existence in politics. I think we may well ignore dissent based on fear and suspicion. India I too big now to suspect and shape her policies in fear.

Every one wants some link with the rest of the world with which we are positively friendly. No one believes in lonely existence. The only alternatives were the one now agreed to and a treaty link. All thinking people were unanimous in discarding the treaty solution as something that would in fact bind more while being morally less valuable. The flexible and nobler link of cultural friendship without any specific obligations and fully recognising the sovereignty of India even up to the point of owing no allegiance to the King of England was therefore the only solution consistent with a desire to cooperate in the task of conservation of world peace and avoidance of war.

India has worked a historic revolution for the whole of the Commonwealth along with the complete confirmation of her own independence. This decision is a posthumous victory for Gandhiji by which he has wrought a sea-change in the character of the Commonwealth. The moral gain for the British is great for which they have expressed unqualified gratitude. But we have gained no less for we have demonstrated that the Indian people can forgive, forget and be great, and give in freedom what they resisted when demanded through force. Civilization itself has taken a big step forward in this historic achievement. I am full of 30 per cent that I have seen such great things in my lifetime.

Thank you for giving me the privilege of opening this your eighth session. In you lies the power to make people good and decent and orderly, and in you also lies the power to help Government to make good laws and govern wisely.

When I spoke to working journalists on a previous occasion recently at Madras I said that I considered journalism a fine art and not a craft or just a profession I still think so and wish journalists would accept my view in spite of difficulties pointed out in the critical comments of some journalists. The difference is not over facts but in the aim and motive of the work. I agree that journalists are mostly poor, so are the greater number of poets, painters, musicians and other artists I agree the newspaper writers have to the leisure required for a fine art. But whether you are forced to work in a hurry or have time, your talents, work and motive are such as are associated with the category of literature, painting, music and sculpture. Bernard Shaw has said in some connection:

> "Daily journalism is beyond mortal strength and endurance. It trains literary men to scamp their work."

Journalism calls for the talents of an artist, the same breadth of vision, the same divine freedom, the same sense of beauty and the same restraints that art requires.

Good journalism requires that its votaries should keep themselves up to the neck busy with other things than journalism, gorging themselves with life and experience and gaining other efficiencies if they are to do their work as good journalists. This is just the same with painters for instance, who have to go round the country and walk in the slums and streets absorbing experience, almost forgetting their particular work if they desire to do justice to their artistic work. I know you are amused at my presuming to advise in a matter wherein I have no experience, but you have asked a man without experience to open your Conference and speak. Whether you find my words of any use or not, I thank you for the honour done to me.

Golden Words of Rajagopalachari

- "If Hindi is made the Union official language, the people of the South will not see identity of language between them and the government, but the domination of a language that is not theirs by birth but which gives to a section of the people of India the position of a ruling race."
- "Swamy Vivekananda saved Hinduism and saved India. But for him, we would have lost our religion and would not have gained our freedom. We therefore owe everything to Swamy Vivekananda."
- "Whatever may be my defects or lapses, let me assure you that I shall never disfigure my life with any deliberate acts of injustice to any community whatsoever."
- "Hindi is as much foreign to non-Hindi speaking people as English to the protagonists of Hindi."
- "My books on the Ramayana and the Mahabharata are my greatest service to my people."
- "On the eve of my laying down office, with the inauguration of the Republic, I should like to tender my greetings and best wishes to the men and women of India who will henceforth be a citizen of a republic. I feel deeply thankful for the affection showered on me by all sections

of the people, which alone enabled me to hear the burden of an office to the duties and conventions of which I had been an utter stranger."

- "As Yama Dharmaraja taught Nachiketas, the vision of the Supreme cannot be attained by the mere study of Shastras; nor could knowledge of the Self come through subtlety of intellect or much learning or argument. The grace of God is the one thing necessary and for that the heart should melt in Bhakti. Bhakti is different from Shastric learning. One may get by heart and recite without cessation the Sanskrit scriptures; one may know and repeat upside down the commentaries of the Acharyas. But righteous conduct and equanimity of mind are different and more necessary gifts. When the heart has not mellowed, study and exposition of Shastras are a mere monkey game. Without wisdom in the heart, all learning is useless. When that which is within and that which is without are one and the same, we have wisdom. When they are not, our learning is no better than the tricks of a trained monkey. The teaching of Sri Ramakrishna gives us, not mere learning, but true wisdom."
- "May the blood that flowed from Gandhiji's wounds and the tears that flowed from the eyes of the women of India everywhere they learnt of his death serve to lay the curse of 1947, and may the grisly tragedy of that year sleep in history and not colour present passions."
- "The spacious imagination, the majestic sweep of thought, and the almost reckless spirit of exploration with which, urged by the compelling thirst for truth, the Upanishad teachers and pupils dig into the "open secret" of the universe, make this most ancient of the world's holy books still the most modern and most satisfying."

Rajagopalachari's Life at a Glance

December 10, 1878: C. Rajagopalachari (Rajaji) was born into a Tamil Brahmin family in a small village called Thorapalli of the then Salem District.

1891: Rajaji passed his matriculation examinations.

1894: Graduated in arts from Central College, Bangalore.

1895: By the second decade of the 20th century, the Brahmins of the presidency were themselves divided into three factions. These were the Mylapore faction comprising Chetpet Iyers and Vembakkam Iyengars, the Egmore faction led by the editor of The Hindu, Kasturi Ranga Iyengar and the Salem nationalists led by C. Rajagopalachari.

1897: C. Rajagopalachari studied law at the Presidency College, Madras, completing his graduation.

Rajaji married Alamelu Mangamma.

1900: C. Rajagopalachari started a prosperous legal practice.

1908: C. Rajagopalachari defended Indian freedom fighter P. Varadarajulu Naidu from the charges of sedition levelled against him.

1916: Rajaji started the Tamil Scientific Terms Society. This society coined new words in Tamil for terms connected to botany, chemistry, physics, astronomy and mathematics.

1917: Rajaji was elected Chairman of the Salem municipality.

1919: He participated in the agitations against the Rowlatt Act.

1921: He was elected to the Congress Working Committee and served as the General Secretary of the party.

1924: The Congress Party split into two factions, one under Chitta Ranjan Das and Motilal Nehru (the father of Jawaharlal Nehru, India's first Prime Minister) favouring the entry of the party into legislatures and the other under C. Rajagopalachari and Vallabhbhai Jhaverbhai Patel opposing it.

1930: C. Rajagopalachari led the Vedaranyam Salt Satyagraha in response to the Dandi March and courted imprisonment.

1932: The issues were negotiated and great nationalists, 'rationalist' pact was signed. The signatories included Pandit Madan Mohan Malaviya, M. R. Jayakar, T. B. Sapru, G. D. Birla, C. Rajagopalachari, Rajendra Prashad, Rao Bahadur Shrinivasan. However, Mahatma Gandhi protested against the communal award (introduced by British Prime Minister Ramsay McDonald), calling it an instrument towards disintegration of Indian society and went on a fast unto death in the Yerwada Jail in Pune. The issues were negotiated and great nationalists, ' rationalist' pact was signed. The signatories included Pandit Madan Mohan Malaviya, M. R. Jayakar, T. B. Sapru, G. D. Birla, C. Rajagopalachari, Rajendra Prashad, Rao Bahadur Shrinivasan and M. C. Raja.

1937: Rajaji was elected Chief Minister or Premier of Madras Presidency and served till 1940, when he resigned due to Britain's declaration of war against Germany. The first anti-Hindi agitation was launched in *1937*, in opposition to the introduction of compulsory teaching of Hindi in the schools of Madras Presidency by the first Indian National Congress government led by C. Rajagopalachari (Rajaji).

1938: Rajaji also issued the Agricultural Debt Relief Act to ease the burden of debt on the peasants of the province.

1938: The Bharatiya Vidya Bhavan, an internationally reputed institution dedicated to the promotion of education and culture, is a charitable public trust founded by Dr. K. M. Munshi. The founding members of the Bhavan include C. Rajagopalachari, the first Indian and last Governor General of India.

1940: Rajaji was arrested in accordance with the Defence of India rules and sentenced to one-year in prison.

1944: The CR Formula: enunciated by C. Rajagopalachari, with which Gandhi was in agreement envisioned, "Muslim contiguous districts in the north-west and east of India, wherein the Muslim population is in absolute majority" holding a plebiscite.

1946: C. Rajagopalachari was appointed Minister of Industry, Supply, Education and Finance in the interim government.

November 21, 1946: The foundation stone of National Metallurgical Laboratory was laid by the first and only Governor General of independent India, C. Rajagopalachari. The objective are to innovate, develop, transfer and standardise and provide specialised services such as Research and Development, Technology Transfer, consultancy and standards and quality to support the scientific and industrial growth and success in the areas of Metals, Minerals and Advanced Materials.

1947-48: C. Rajagopalachari served as the Governor of West Bengal.

1947: To select a flag for independent India, the assembly set up an *ad hoc* committee headed by Rajendra Prashad and including Maulana Abul Kalam Azad, Sarojini Naidu, C. Rajagopalachari, K. M. Munshi and B. R. Ambedkar as its members.

1948-50: C. Rajagopalachari served as the Governor General of India.

1951: Rajaji wrote an abridged retelling of the Mahabharata in English.

1951-52: C. Rajagopalachari served as Union Home Minister.

1952: Rajaji put an end to the rationing of sugar.

1952-54: C. Rajagopalachari served as the Chief Minister of Madras state.

1954: Due to the resignation of C. Rajagopalachari, for his controversial Kula Kalvi Thittam, the leadership of Congress was contested, between K. Kamaraj, and C. Subramaniam (who got the support of M. Bhaktavatsalam).

1955: Rajaji appealed to the Government of India to stop receiving American aid if the country continued with its nuclear tests.

1956: Rajaji signed a resolution along with Annadurai and Periyar endorsing the continuation of English as the official language.

1957: Rajaji tendered his official resignation from the Indian National Congress and along with a few other dissidents, organised the Congress Reform Committee (CRC).

1958: A book under the title *Chakravarthi Thirumagan,* won Rajaji the Sahitya Academy award in Tamil for the year.

1959: The power of euphemism was exempltfied by the most successful of the early conservative parties, the Swatantra party, established in *1959*. Its founding father, the widely revered C. Rajagopalachari (a former freedom fighter, chief minister of Madras). Shortly after the Nagpur session of the Indian National Congress, Rajaji, along with Murari Vaidya of the newly-established Forum of Free Enterprise (FFE) and Minoo Masani, an anti-Communist ideologue and critique of Nehru, announced the formation of a new political party under the name Swatantra Party at a meeting in Madras.

1962: C. Rajagopalachari visited the US and the USSR promoting the importance of nuclear disarmament. President Kennedy listens with rapt attention, later recalling his meeting with Rajagopalachari as "one of the most civilizing influences on me".

June 30, 1964: Former Governor General of India C. Rajagopalachari addresses the Rotary Club in Bombay.

1965: He Rajagopalachari convened the Madras state anti-Hindi conference in Tiruchirapalli. He angrily declared that the Part XVII of the Constitution of India which declared that Hindi was the official language should "be heaved and thrown into the Arabian Sea."

1972: By November 1972, Rajaji's health had begun to decline. On 17 December 1972, a week after his 94th birthday, Rajaji was admitted to General Hospital with uraemia, dehydration and urinary infection. Rajaji's condition deteriorated in the following days as he frequently lost consciousness. Rajaji died at the age of 94.

Appendix

Freedom Movement in South India

The Perception

The British people came to India as traders and then they turned as rulers. The very existence of a foreign rule helped the growth of a national sentiment among the people. There was also a clash between the British interests in India and those of the Indian people. The British had conquered India to promote their own interests. They ruled over her primarily with that object. With the passage of time there was a realisation in India and that realisation brought differences against foreign rule and that was responsible for the growth of the nationalist movement to drive out the foreigners from the country. All classes of people in India joined at one stage or the other the nationalist movement. The intelligentsia in India, the peasants, the artisans and the workers all played their part in the freedom struggle. Tamil Nadu played a significant role in the freedom struggle.

Partition of Bengal

During the time of Lord Dufferin the Indian National Congress was founded by A. O. Hume, W. C. Banerjee and Wedderburn. When the Indian National Congress met in Bombay, Madras opinion was represented there by veteran G. Subramanya Iyer, 'a remarkable Tamil Smartha Brahmin'. Other Tamilians who took an active part in the early activities of the Congress were C. Vijayaraghavachariar of Salem, Kasthuriranga Iyengar and Gopalcharlu.

Congress Split

Gradually the Congress and its principles spread all over India. In 1887, the third annual session of the Congress was held in Madras. Local organisations like Madras Mahajana Sabha carried on mild activity with published speech.

Fiery revolutionaries from north exercised a tremendous influence upon the South. Among them Bepin Chandra Pal was the most important and influential. He was an orator of the type exactly calculated to rouse the patriotic sentiments of the youth. In addition to this Surendranath Banerji greatly attracted the youth during this period. Pal was thundering on the Marina Beach, Madras in 1907 and he soon became the idol of the college students and the white collar employees in urban centres.

Newspapers

Besides, 'The Hindu' and the 'Swadesamitran' were beginning to voice their opinions mildly critical of the British Government. The partition of Bengal by Lord Curzon was severely criticised and condemned by the people of Tamil Nadu.

Moderates-Extremists

In 1907, there was a split in the Congress and the moderates parted company with the extremists. It was due to the question of the loyalty to the English throne and the continuance of British rule in India. The moderates believed in loyalty to the English throne, but the extremists viewed the British rule in India was a curse. Bal Gangadhar Tilak advocated radical and almost terrorist tactics to oust the British from India. Gopal Krishna Gokhale advocated liberal and constitutional methods of agitation. Poona became the centre of activity for these two leaders. Both influenced Tamil Nadu politics profoundly at different stages of its development.

Gokhale chose V. S. Srinivasa Shastri to succeed him as President of the Servants of India Society. Moreover P. S. Sivasamy Iyer, T. R. Venkatarama Shastri and others followed the footsteps of the great leader Gokhale. Indeed they were very great patriots. They had no faith in violence (even in language) which for reasons other than that Gandhiji held valid thought would always be counter productive. They supported the British but at the same time they condemned their repressive measures or actions like the Rowlatt Act. They believed in Council entry and constructive statesmanship.

On the other hand Tilak demanded freedom which he said was his birth right. He wished India to recover her lost image which was truly represented by Shivaji.

Terrorists' Activities

During the short period of 1807 to 1812 all the terrorist activity in Tamil Nadu became very serious. Among the leading terrorist revolutionaries could be mentioned V. V. Subramaniya Iyer, Nilakanda Brahmachan, C. Subramanya Bharathi, Subramanya Shiva and Swadeshi Padmanabha Iyengar.

By 1910, Arovindo Ghosh who had been indicted and imprisoned for terrorist activity in Bengal had arrived at Pondicherry and had turned scholar saint. From there Subramanya Bharathi the Tamil Nationalist poet did wonderful work to induce patriotism in the minds of the people. V. V. Subramanyam Iyer, Subramanyam Shiva and Nilakanda Brahmachari carried on terrorist plans in the French territory. They gave some rifle practice to would be terrorists.

Tinneveli Conspiracy Case

In 1911, District Magistrate Ashe of Tinneveli was shot dead at Maniachi by Vanchinathan. This was the only instance of assassination committed by Tamil Terrorist nationalists. Vanchinathan committed suicide. Fourteen persons were accused. Nilakanda Brahmachari was the first accused and he was sentenced to seven years rigorous imprisonment. Another accused Sankara Krishnan got five years and the rest shorter term. Madasami, one of the accused and the close associate of V. O. Chidambaram Pillai of Tuticorin absconded and could not be discovered. But the master mind in the conspiracy V. V. Subramanya Iyer was not among the accused.

V. O. Chidambaram Pillai

V. O. Chidambaram Pillai an advocate of Tuticorin with the help of Madasami collected money and started a Swadeshi Steam

Navigation Company which would ply steamers between Tuticorin and Ceylon competing with already operating British Companies. The British authorities tried to discourage him. Then V.O.C. was accused for seditious speeches and organising terrorist activities and jailed first in Coimbatore and later in Cannanore from where he was released in December 1912. His later life was pathetic and pitiable.

The Home Rule Movement

The Home Rule Movement was organised by Mrs. Annie Besant in Madras in 1916. She was a theosophist who made Adyar near Madras her spiritual headquarters had known at first hand British methods of repression and governments in Ireland and Britain. Her methods were a combination of agitation and constitutionalism, appeal to the elite and organisation of the masses.

Mrs. Annie Besant was a wonderful orator, brilliant organiser, a great editor of newspapers and an undoubted leader of men and women. She was the editor of *New India*. Sri Subramanya Iyer. C. P. Ramaswamy Iyer and other great men acknowledged her merit. In 1917, she was arrested and imprisoned at Ooty along with her friends George Arundale and B. P. Wadia. She was, however, released soon on instruction from the Secretary of States to the Great Chagrin of the Madras Government. She was then at the height of her popularity. She was elected President of the Congress in 1917.

In the meantime Justice Party was formed in Madras. T. M. Nair and P. Thyagarayachetti attacked her and accused her of supporting the Brahmins. When Gandhiji came to the political scene, her power and popularity began to decline.

Mahatma Gandhi

With the advent of Mahatma Gandhi Indian Nationalist Politics took new and unprecedented turn. The Congress under the leadership of Gandhi refused to enter the Legislative Council or to cooperation with the British in any manner. C. Rajagopalachari was the most important representative of the Congress in Tamil Nadu. The Non-cooperation Movement greatly attracted the middle class intellectuals, lawyers, teachers, doctors, white collar bureaucrats, journalists and writers and a body of professional politicians willing to go to jail and to meet the lathi-charge. Many students came forward to participate the Non-cooperation Movement.

In 1925, the Swarajists in the Congress had decided to enter the Council but they were not in a majority. S. Srinivasa Iyengar, the great lawyer, S. Satyamurthi the exponent of the Congress cause. C. Rajagopalachari the favourite friend of Gandhiji were the important Congress leaders in Madras. In December 1927, the Indian National Congress met there and passed the complete Independence resolution.

Boycott of Simon Commission

In 1928, S. Srinivasa Iyengar the Tamilian Congress leader was presiding over the Gauhati session of the Congress. In the same year, they boycotted the Simon Commission appointed to go into the working of the 1919 Constitution. T. Prakasam and S. Satyamurthi were the heroes of the boycott in Madras.

Salt Satyagraha

From 1928 to 1931, when Gandhiji started his Salt Satyagraha and renewed Civil Disobedience Movement it had its impact all over India. C. Rajagopalachari was incharge of defying the British laws in Madras. He started the Salt Satyagraha campaign at Vedaranyam in Tanjavur District. Thousands of Congress volunteers came to Vedaranyam to defy the laws. The British Government arrested C. Rajagopalachari and many volunteers and imprisoned them. K. Kamaraj also suffered a lot during the freedom struggle.

In the meantime B. Munisamy Naidu and P. Subbarayan were wilting to run the government in Madras.

After 1935

The 1935 Constitution brought about a great change. In 1935 elections, the Justice Party was defeated by the Congress. On the Dravida Kazhagam of E. V. Ramaswamy Naicker the communal mantle of the Justice Party had fallen. C. Rajagopalachari became the Chief Minister of Madras. It lasted from 1937 to 1939. It was the most constructive period of Congress political activity in Madras.

World War II

In 1939, when the Second World War came. India announced that it was one of the allies fighting European dictatorship. In Madras there was a necessary suspension of political activities from 1939 to 1945 — the war period. The leading politicians in Madras were only reacting to all India decisions on the part of the Government of India, the Congress or the Muslim League. The Muslims in Tamil Nadu have always been in a very small minority that they really had no independent aspirations of their own except the understandable one of honourable survival. But Jinnah the leader of the whole Muslims demanded a separate homeland for his co-religionists. The British made many attempts to resolve the tangle. But they failed. Sir Stafford Cripps and the Cabinet Mission could achieve little. C. Rajagopalachari boldly asserted that accommodating Jinnah was a necessary prelude to Indian Independence. The Congress turned angrily against him and he resigned the membership of the Congress.

Quit India Movement

In 1942, Gandhi raised the slogan "Quit India" and it evoked the echo from the Muslim League "Divide and Quit." There was very considerable damage to property by repression by the Government. Many leading Congressmen including Gandhi had been incarcerated.

After War

The war came to an end in 1945. In 1946, the General elections were held. The Congress attained huge majority in Madras. In 1946, they did not want Rajagopalachari back to lead the ministry. After Prakasam, O. P. Ramaswamy Reddiyar became the Chief Minister of Madras. He held office in 1947. It was during his ministry that India became independent After O. P. Ramaswamy Reddiyar, P. S. Kumaraswamy Raja became the Chief Minister of Madras. It was during his ministry that India became a Republic.

Till 1952, the Andhra districts were part of the composite Madras State. The intellectuals, ryots, poets and the youth of the Andhra region actively participated in the freedom struggle and made a mark in the history of modem India.

Vande Mataram Movement: In support of the Swadeshi Movement, the Andhra students of Madras University organised a meeting on the Madras beach in September 1905. Ayyadevara Kaleswara Rao and Gadicherla Hari Sarvothama Rao inspired the people with their speeches, and condemned the partition of Bengal by Lord Curzon.

In April 1907, Bipin Chandra Pal, the famous extremist national leader toured the coastal districts and addressed the people at Rajahmundry, Vijayawada and Masulipatam. At Rajahmundry, his fiery speech was translated by Chilakamarti Lakshmi Narasimham, the renowned poet.

In those days, even openly uttering the slogan of 'Vande Mataram' was treated as sedition. The Principal of Rajahmundry Arts College, an Englishman, rusticated 136 of his students for wearing badges and giving *Vande Mataram* slogans in the College premises.

Home Rule Movement — 1916-17: Mrs. Annie Besant visited a number of places including Rajainundry, Kakinada and exhorted the people to strive for Home Rule. She said: "To live without freedom is to die daily. It is not life but living death." By 1917, she founded branches of the Home Rule League at 52 places in the Andhra region. She established National College at Madanapalli which was later named as the Besant Theosophical College. Gadicherla Hari Sarvothama Rao served as the Secretary of the Andhra Home Rule League.

The Non-cooperation Movement, 1921-22: The Jallianwala Bagh massacre had immensely stirred the minds of the Andhra people. A large number of the Andhras participated in the Non-cooperation Movement launched by Gandhi in 1921. All India Congress Committee held its session at Vijayawada in April 1921. Mahatma Gandhi, Vallabhbhai Patel and other All India leaders attended the Conference. The venue of the session is since then known as 'Gandhi Nagar" in Vijayawada. The tri-colour flag was designed by Pingali Venkaiah and approved as the Congress flag during that session. Duggirala Gopal Krishna, as the General Secretary of the Congress Organisation, made necessary arrangements of the Congress session.

After the session was over, Gandhi visited Kakinada, Eluru, Rajahmundry, Vetapalem and several other places and collected donations for the Tilak Swaraj Fund.

The participation of the Andhras in the Non-cooperation Movement was noteworthy. Konda Venkatappaiah and some others resigned from their membership of the Madras Legislative Assembly, Kala Venkata Rao, Neelam Sanjiva Reddy and many others boycotted their colleges and plunged into the movement. Reputed lawyers like Ayyadevara Kaleswara Rao, Tanguturu Prakasam and Unnava Lakshmi Narayana voluntarily renounced their roaring practice.

No-tax Campaign of Chirala-Perala — 1921-22: The Madras Government decided to convert Chirala and Perala villages into a special Municipality. Consequently the burden of taxation was ten times enhanced on the people. The new Municipal Council was formed despite the people's protest. Duggirala Gopal Krishna took up the challenge and appealed to the people not to pay taxes to the Municipality. He raised a new colony of thatched houses outside the villages known as 'Ramnagar.' He got the entire population migrated into Ramnagar where they lived for 11 months. He maintained an alternative administration run by the people's representatives. At last the movement was withdrawn after the internment of Duggirala Gopal Krishna in 1922.

Pedanandipadu No-tax Campaign — 1922: As part of the Non-cooperation Movement, the No-tax Campaign was successfully organised in Pedanandipadu Firka of Guntur District. All the village Kamams and Munsifs belonging to this Firka submitted their resignations to the District Collector. The ryots of those villages refrained from paying land revenue to the Government. Parvathaneni Veeriah Chowdhari, popularly known as "Andhra Shivaji" was at the forefront of the movement. Rutherford, the District Collector called for military help to suppress the movement. The Congress leaders withdrew the agitation on the advice of Mahatma Gandhi.

Armed Rebellion by Alluri Sita Rama Raju — 1922-24: Alluri Sitarama Raju, was a patriotic young man of Moggallu, in Bhimavaram Taluk. He was very much moved by the atrocities committed by the British officials on the innocent tribals of the East Godavari agency area. He organised the tribals into a revolutionary army with the assistance of Gaum Mallu Dora and others. He followed guerilla tactics and attacked police stations of Chintapalli Krishnadevipet and Raja Vommangi of Rampachodavaram Taluk in August 1922. He took possession of large quantities of arms and ammunition from those places. In 1923, he raided the Annavaram and Paderu police stations. The Government despatched the Malabar and Sikh regiments under the command of well experienced British Generals. Pitched battles took place in the interior forests. Ultimately on May 7th, 1924 Sitarama Raju was captured and shot dead. Thus, ended the famous Rampa Mutiny of the East Godavari forest area.

Anti-Simon Commission Demonstrations — 1928: Simon Commission was greeted with black flags and 'Simon Go Back' slogans at Bezwada, Guntur and Ongole towns. Ayyadevara Kaleswara Rao and N. V. L. Narasimha Rao, Municipal Chairman of Bezwada and Guntur respectively issued notices to Sir John Simon not to enter their Municipal limits.

On 3rd February 1928, the Commission visited Madras where black flag demonstrations were held under the leadership of Satyamurthy, T. Prakasam and Pattabhi Sitaramaiah. Hartal was observed in the city. To disperse the crowds, the police opened fire resulting in one death and several casualties. Tanguturu Prakasam, a reputed member of the bar and a Congress leader daringly faced the Police who threatened to fire at him.

The Civil Disobedience Movement — 1930-31: The Civil Disobedience Movement launched by Mahatma Gandhi received tremendous response in the Andhra region. Konda Venkatappaiah the President of the A.P.C.C. was given the over all responsibility of organising the movement in the Andhra area. The Salt Satyagraha was piloted by T. Prakasam at Madras. Pattabhai Sitaramaiah at Masulipatam, N. G. Ranga at Nidubrolu, T. Vishwanadham at Vizagpatam, B. Gopala Reddi at Nellore and N.V.L. Narasimha Rao at Guntur. Durgabai Deshmukh and Bharati Devi Ranga played prominent roles in organising the women volunteers.

When elections were held to the Madras Legislative Assembly in 1937, Congress swept the polls and formed the ministry with C. Rajagopalachari as the Premier and T. Prakasam as the Revenue Minister.

The Quit India Movement — 1942: The All India Congress Committee passed the Quit India Resolution on 8th August 1942. Immediately all the prominent leaden were put behind the bars. Dr. Pattabhi Sitaramaiah and Kala Venkata Rao were the President and Secretary of A.P.C.C., respectively. A few days before his arrest, Kala Venkata Rao issued a "secret circular" to the Congress workers indicating the guidelines to be followed during the movement. The circular ordained them to cut the telegraph wires, to disrupt the communications and not to pay the taxes. Accordingly, the people raided the police stations, post offices and railway stations. The police resorted to firing at a number of places. The Government took ruthless measures and suppressed the movement with an iron hand.

In 1946, fresh elections were held to the Madras Legislative Assembly and the Congress returned with thumping majority. New Cabinet was formed with T. Prakasam as the Premier.

Bibliography

Ashu Pasricha: *Encyclopaedia of Eminent Thinkers, Vol XV, The Political Thought of C. Rajagopalachari*, Concept Publication, 2008.

Bakshi, S. R. and Lipi Mahajan: *Social Reformers of India*, Deep & Deep, New Delhi, 2000.

Bakshi, S. R.: *C. Rajagopalachari: Role in Freedom Movement*, Anmol Publications, New Delhi, 1991.

Behari, Madhuri, and B. Behari: *Indian Economy since Independence: Chronology of Events*, D.K. Publications, Delhi, 1983.

Bhattacharya, B. K.: *India's Freedom Movement: Legacy of Bipin Chandra Pal*, Deep and Deep, New Delhi, 2007.

Bolton, G.: *The Tragedy of Gandhi*, Allen & Unwin, London, 1934.

Bondurant, Joan V.: *The Conquest of Violence: The Gandhian Philosophy of Conflict*, Princeton University Press, Princeton, 1958.

Brass, Paul R.: *The Politics of India Since Independence*, Cambridge University Press, England, 1995.

Brown, Judith M.: *Gandhi and Civil Disobedience*, Cambridge University Press, London, 1977.

Buddha's Warriors: *The Story of the CIA-Backed Tibetan Freedom Fighters, the Chinese Invasion and the Ultimate Fall of Tibet*, Mikel Dunham, Penguin Books, 2005.

Chandra, Bipan: *India's Struggle For Independence*, Penguin Books India (P) Ltd., New Delhi, 1989.

Chatterjee, Margaret: *Gandhi's Religious Thought*, University of Notre Dame Press, 1983.

Desai, V. G.: *A Gandhi Anthology*, Navjivan, Ahmedabad, 1952.

Dhanki, J. S.: *Lala Lajpat Rai and Indian Nationalism*, ABS Publishers, Jalandhar, 1990.

Diraviam, Leila: *Diraviam -Our Treasure*, Asian Printers, Chennai, 1999.

Erwin Neumayer and Christine Schelberger: *Bharat Mata: India's Freedom Movement in Popular Art*, Oxford University Press, 2008.

Gandhi, Rajmohan: *Rajaji, A Life*, Penguin Books India (P) Ltd., New Delhi, 1997.

Ganjoo, S.: *Muslim Freedom Fighters of India*, Anmol Publication, New Delhi, 2002.

Goldsmith, Raymond W.: *The Financial Development of India, 1860-1977*, Yale University Press, New Haven, 1983.

Goyal, P. K.: *Battle of India's Freedom Movement*, Vista International, 2005.

Hari Hara Das: *The History of Freedom Movement in India (1857-1947)*, National, 1998.

Heimsath, Charles, and Surjit Mansingh: *A Diplomatic History of Modern India*, Allied, New Delhi, 1971.

Hiro, Dilip: *Inside India Today*, Routledge and Kegan Paul, London, 1976.

Hirschman, Edwin: *White Mutiny: The Ilbert Bill Crisis in India and the Genesis of the Indian National Congress*, Heritage, New Delhi, 1980.

Howard Loyd Erdman: *The Swatantra Party and Indian Conservatism*, Harvard University, 2004.

Inden, Ronald: *Imagining India*, Oxford University Press, Oxford, 1990.

Indu Dave: *Indian Personality in Its Developmental Background*, Himanshu, 1991.

Iyengar, A. S.: *Role of Press and Indian Freedom Struggle: All through the Gandhian Era*, APH, 2001.

Kailash Khanna: *History of Indian Freedom Struggle*, Commonwealth Publication, 2004.

Kamat, Jyostna: *The Pioneers: Kamaladevi Chattopadhyaya*, Kamat's, 2003.

Kapoor, A. N. Gupta, V. P. and Mohini Gupta: *An Encyclopaedic Dictionary of Freedom Movement 1757-1947*, Radha, 2004.

Kaushik, A. S.: *Great Freedom Fighters of India*, Indian Publication, 2007.

Kesavan, C. R.: *Unfolding Rajaji*, East West Books, Madras, 2003.

Khairul Anam, Md.: *Indian Freedom Movement and Murshidabad District 1905-1947*, Bagchi, K. P., 2008.

Kishwar, Madhu: *Gandhi and Women*, Manushi Prakashan, Delhi, 1986.

Kothari, Rajni: *Caste in Indian Politics*, Orient Blackswan, 2004.

Krishan Mohan: *Encyclopaedic History of Indian Freedom Movement (4 Vols-Set)*, Book Enclave, 1999.

————: *Indian National Congress and the Freedom Movement*, Book Enclave, 1999.

————: *Political Leadership and Indian Freedom Movement*, Book Enclave, 1999.

————: *Revolt of 1857 and the Indian Freedom Movement*, Book Enclave, 1999.

————: *Revolutionary Politics and Indian Freedom Movement*, Book Enclave, 1999.

Krishna, B.: *Indian Freedom Struggle: The Pathfinders From Surendranath Banerjea to Gandhi*, Manohar Publication, 2002.

Lahiri, Abani: *The Peasant and India's Freedom Movement*, Manak, 2001.

Lion Agrawal, M. G.: *Freedom Fighters of India (4 Vols-Set)*, Isha Books, 2008.

Majumdar, R. C.: *History of the Freedom Movement in India (3 Vols-Set)*, Firma KLM, 1997.

Manju Verma: *The Role of Women in the Freedom Movement in Punjab (1919-1947)*, Abhijeet, 2003.

Maulana Syed Mohammad Mian: *The Prisoners of Malta (Asira'n-E-Malta): The Heart-Rending Tale of Muslim Freedom Fighters in British Period*, Manak, 2005.

Mazhar Kibriya: *Gandhi and Indian Freedom Struggle*, APH, 1999.

Muthaiah, S.: *Women Freedom Fighters*, The Hindu, 2004.

Nanda, S. P.: *Freedom Movement and Constitutional Development in India*, Dominant Publication, New Delhi, 2004.

Om Prakash: *Encyclopaedic History of Indian Freedom Movement (12 to 21 Vols)*, Anmol Publication, New Delhi, 2003.

Panjabi, K. L.: *The Indomitable Sardar*, Bharatiya Vidya Bhavan, 1969.

Parekh, Bhikhu: *Gandhi's Political Philosophy: A Critical Examination*, Macmillan, London, 1996.

Parmanand Parashar: *Kashmir and the Freedom Movement*, Sarup, 2004.

Pradhan, K. B.: *Freedom Movement in India*, Arise Publication, 2007.

Prafulla Kumar Pattanaik: *The First Indian War of Independence: Freedom Movement in Orissa, 1804-1825*, APH, 2005.

Puri, Harish K.: *Ghadar Movement: Ideology, Organisation and Strategy*, Guru Nanak Dev University, Amritsar, 1993.

Rafiya Nisar: *Shaikh-Ul-Hind Maulana Mahmud Hasan and Indian Freedom Movement*, Manak Publication, 2008.

Raghavan Iyer: *Moral and Political Writings of Mahatma Gandhi*, Clarendon Press, Oxford, 1986.

Raj Kumar: *Essays on Indian Freedom Movement*, History and Culture Series, Discovery Publication, New Delhi, 2003.

Ralhan, O. P.: Encyclopaedia of Political Parties, Anmol Publications, New Delhi, 2002.

Ram Sharma, S.: *Education of Women and Freedom Movement*, Discovery Publication, New Delhi, 1996.

Ram, S. and Kumar, R.: *Encyclopaedia of Indian Freedom Struggle (10 Vols-Set)*, Commonwealth Publicaton, 2008.

————: *Quit India Movement: 1942-1945*, Commonwealth Publication, 2008.

Ramanathan, K. V.: *The Satyamurti Letters, Vol. II: The Indian Freedom Struggle Through the Eyes of a Parliamentarian*, Dorling Kindersley for Pearson Longman an Imprint of Pearson Education, 2008.

Ramu, P. S.: *Azad Hind Fauj (I.N.A.) and The Freedom Movement*, Freedom Movement Memorial Comm, 1998.

Ratna Ghosh: *Netaji Subhas Chandra Bose and Indian Freedom Struggle (2 Vols-Set)*, Deep and Deep Publication, New Delhi, 2006.

Ravi Ranjan and Singh, M. K.: *Sardar Vallabhbhai Patel*, K. K. Pub, 2009.

Ravindra Kumar: *Champaran to Quit India Movement*, Mittal, 2002.

Shachi Chakravarty: *Quit India Movement: A Study*, New Century Publication, 2002.

Shailesh Chandra: *90 Years of India's Struggle for Independence: 1857-1947*, Alfa Publication, 2008.

Shantinath Gupta: *Great Freedom Fighters of India*, Anmol Publication, New Delhi, 2006.

Sharma, K. K.: *Encyclopaedia of Great Personalities of India (4 Vols-Set)*, Book Enclave, 2007.

Sirisa Kumar Shadangi: *The Prisons of South Orissa and the Freedom Fighters in Incarceration, 1900 - 1947*, Punthi Pustak, 2005.

Sisson, Richard, and Stanley Wolpert: *Congress and Indian Nationalism: The Pre-Independence Phase*, University of California Press, Berkeley, 1988.

Sumiti Malhotra: *Thoughts of Great Personalities in 20 Century*, Raj Publishing, 2003.

Sundaram, V.: *Great Crusader for Women's Emancipation*, News Today, 2005.

Sundararaja, Saroja: *March to Freedom in Madras Presidency, 1916-1947*, Lalitha Publication, Chennai, 1989.

Surinder Singh: *The Political Memoirs of an Indian Revolutionary: Naina Singh Dhoot (1904-1989)*, Manohar, 2005.

Taneja, Anup: *Gandhi, Women and the National Movement, 1920-47*, Har-Anand Publications, Delhi, 2005.

Thapar-Bjorkert, Suruchi: *Women in the Indian Nationalist Movement*, Sage Publication India (P) Ltd., New Delhi, 2006.

Tope, T. K.: *Dr. B.R. Ambedkar, A Symbol of Social Revolt*, Maharashtra Information Centre, New Delhi, 1964.

Vakil, A. K.: *Gandhi-Ambedkar Dispute*, Ashish Pub. House, New Delhi, 1991.

Vasanthi Srinivasan: *Gandhi's Conscience Keeper: C. Rajagopalachari and Indian Politics*, Permanent Black, 2009.

Verma B. R. and Unnikrishnan K.: *Encyclopaedic Biography of Indian Freedom Fighters*, Commonwealth, 2004.

Vishnoo Bhagwan: *Indian Freedom Movement and Constitutional Acts*, Atma Ram, 1999.

Weiner, Myron: *Party Building in a New Nation: The Indian National Congress*, University of Chicago Press, Chicago, 1967.

Zelliot, E.: *Mahar Movement*, University of Pennsylvania, Unpubl, 1969.

Index

H

I

J

K

L

M

N

P

Q

R

S

❑❑❑